DISCOVERING OZ

A TRAVEL MEMOIR

BY WENDY JAMES

ABOUT THE AUTHOR

Wendy James is an Australian-born journalist and writer, living in the UK since 1966. Since she retired, she is mostly known by her married name Wendy Dear. Her previous book 'A Life in Magazines, a memoir' described her working life on various British publications (*Woman's Own*, *Woman*, *The Complete Cook*, *Choice*) over nearly four decades.

 ISBN 978-1-8383507-5-8

All photographs by the author. The cover picture was taken at Dirk Hartog Island, Western Australia; the map behind the photos on the back cover is a lithograph of Australland by C Flemming 1844

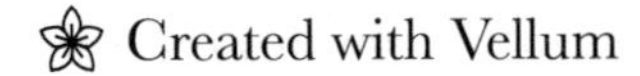

To all my family, in Australia, New Zealand and the UK.
Travelling around the world's largest island made me realise how very lucky I was to be born there

INTRODUCTION

Australia has been in the news a lot in the last few years, particularly in relation to environmental disasters caused by fires and floods. The world was aghast at the plight of the unique wildlife, the horrendous damage to life and property.

Before the coronavirus pandemic changed everything, the country where I was born was one of the world's most favoured destinations, often top of the wish list for people of all ages from many countries. But what is it that makes this southern continent so attractive to holiday makers and those seeking a new life in the sun?

I had been a teenaged bride in the late 1950s and had swapped a career in nursing for journalism. When the marriage failed I went abroad where I started a new life in the UK working on magazines. One of the perks of being in the Press is that I was able to visit many parts of the world and see for myself their attractions and differences. When I retired I thought about what I did and didn't know about Australia. I took a 'filling the gaps' year, to remember what I had forgotten, see all the states, and my travelling companion would be my English husband Ian.

Our first hurdle was the three months' time limit of a tourist visa. At the visa section of the Australian High Commission in London I explained why Ian's had to be for a year. There was sucking of teeth, shaking of head. A spouse's visa requires a health and financial check, a chest x-ray, references – and takes months.

I started gabbling. But our tickets are booked. He has to meet all my family – mother, brother, sisters, nieces, nephews. We want to travel round the whole continent. The young man took our passports (Ian's British, mine Australian and British) and went away to consult. After 10 minutes he returned and without a hint of a smile said that by some miracle Ian had become one of the 3% who manage to get a year's visa without going through all that palaver. If there hadn't been a grille between us I'd have hugged him (this was BC – before coronavirus).

That visa turned out to be part of the red tape that wraps itself around any international journey of any length. On our return to Sydney after a couple of months in New Zealand visiting friends in Auckland and my sister in Christchurch, we arrived at Wellington airport. At passport control, a man handed Ian's back to him and said: 'I'm sorry but you don't have a visa to enter Australia'. When Ian pointed out the visa plainly said it was for multiple entries the man nodded: "I know. That's what it says, but it's not what it means."

He must have seen the utter disbelief on our faces. Don't worry, he said, you can get an email visa (now commonplace as an ETA – electronic Transfer Authorisation). I could have hugged him too, but he was behind a grille. It took time, but we managed to get aboard before the exit gate was closed (and we never did find out what 'multiple entries' does mean). Fortunately it didn't stop us discovering why the land Down Under is the most amazing island in the world.

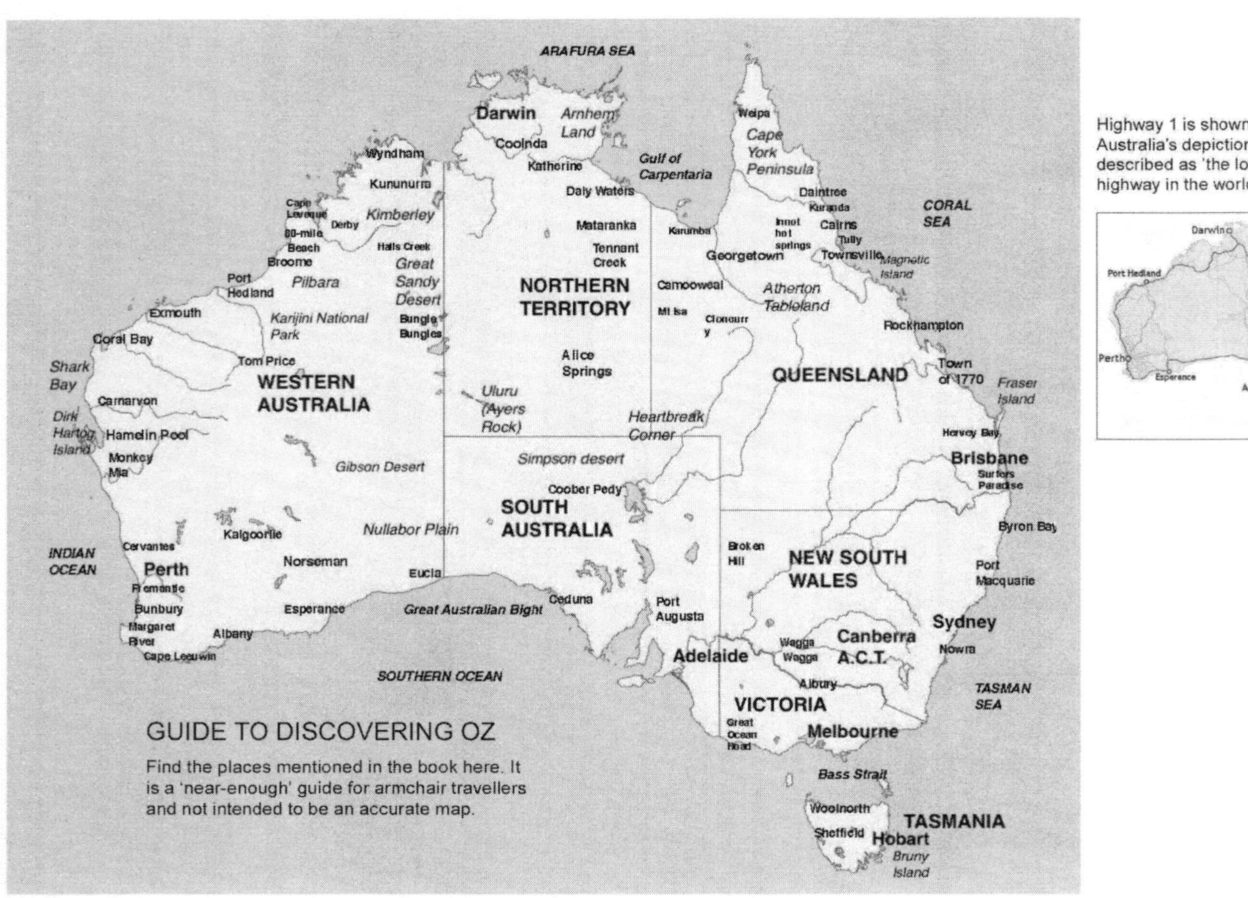

GUIDE TO DISCOVERING OZ

Find the places mentioned in the book here. It is a 'near-enough' guide for armchair travellers and not intended to be an accurate map.

Highway 1 is shown on Explore Australia's depiction below, described as 'the longest national highway in the world'.

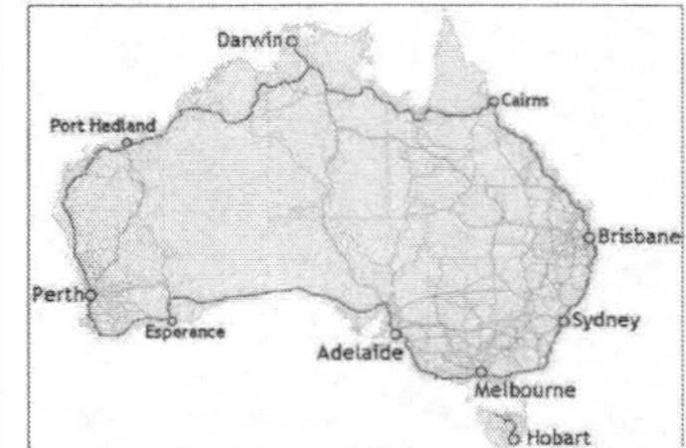

CONTENTS

1

THOSE WHO KNOW THE COUNTRY BEST

STORIES IN EVERY STATE

A CLOSE LOOK AT A map of Australia will show a road that runs the whole way round the continent. It is designated Highway 1 and should be blacktop all the way, although in each state it can change its name and number frequently. When planning our route I decided this was the one to follow but I failed to take into account the significance of weather on the landmass.

I had made the kick-off point the town in coastal New South Wales where I grew up and where my mother celebrated her 100th birthday in the Centenary Year of Federation, 2001, which marked Australia's 100 years of nationhood. Having bought a van – our home on wheels – in Sydney we would drive down the coast then follow the highway right the way round the continent's distinctive shape. But I learnt very early on to be prepared to change my mind.

On our way to Australia we stopped for five days at Bangkok, a 13-hour flight from London, and 13 hours from Sydney. A local 'must do' is a day-trip to the River Kwai on which we met an Australian couple and, over a beer, explained our plans to them.

– You'll be going the wrong way.

John sounded very convincing, the 'I know what I'm talking about' approach.

– Go north. If you go south you'll be travelling in the cold. If you go up the Queensland coast and then inland it will still be winter but it will be warm.

John and his wife May had taken many a trip to different parts from their home in Coffin Bay (it would be some months before we discovered exactly where that ominously-named place was in South Australia). The tropical 'Top End' warmth, between April and November, was most enticing. So we found the right track from the start, thanks to them. Then he added:

– There's just one road all the way round. You can't get lost.

This is a typical Aussie remark. People *have* got lost on this vast continent, probably by straying off Highway 1. You see, the road doesn't follow the shape entirely. It goes inland from Townsville, in Queensland, though a little spur does extend north to Cairns, but not up the finger-like projection at the top of the state called Cape York. And it doesn't go to the Red Centre either, or the Australian Capital Territory, which is the 'home' of the Federal Government in Canberra.

The reality was deciding what we couldn't see, and having to accept the frustrating situation of being relatively close to many temptations and know we had to bypass them. The trouble was people who had done some travelling kept telling us "You mustn't miss..." and, on the JustinCase principle, I kept notes about their suggestions so we could make decisions – change our mind – as we travelled.

The continent was almost an open book to us. We had a rough idea about each of the seven states, but the fine details were what the journey would be about. For Ian much of it was a blank sheet. Before we met in London in the early 1970s, he had lived for four years in Australia, working in Sydney for Angus & Robertson, Australia's oldest publishing house which is no more – though a chain of bookshops retains the name. While he was there, A&R published *The Americans, Baby*, the second 'discontinuous narrative' of Frank Moorhouse, who I had been at school with in Nowra.

Ian had skied at Thredbo in the Snowy Mountains of New South Wales, but hadn't seen much of the rest of the country. I should have been more clued up – especially as I had a keen interest in geography from a very young age, spending hours drawing countries freehand on a white unruled sketch pad using thin-stemmed, tiny-nibbed mapping pens and different coloured inks. I remember being pleased when I managed to draw a passable Australia in red (this indicated it was part of the British Empire).

I read about the countries I drew in my set of Arthur Mee Children's Encyclopedias, and added interesting facts to each of the maps, probably an indication of my future path as a journalist, when I would want to put people and faces to all of these places.

It is too long ago to recall what I wrote about Australia on that freehand map but I had much to learn, starting with Nowra, where my family moved to from

Sydney when I was eight. It was here that, aged 19, I became Mrs Frank Moorhouse Junior – "son of leading Rotarian and Mason marries daughter of local bootmaker and bookmaker", the report in the local paper could have said (being an off-course bookie, as Dad was, was illegal then but he was known for shoes he made and repaired). It was a costly experience for my parents and the marriage was short-lived – which is probably why I've forgotten more than I remember about it. Of more concern was how little I knew of the town itself.

My eyes were opened by an exhibition at the State Library in Sydney called *Private Lives: Families of NSW.* A photograph taken in 2001 showed four women of different generations of one family, members of the Nowra Aboriginal Community. I never knew this group existed. Former school friends with whom I have kept in touch said "Don't you remember Jimmy Little?"

Of course I remembered his voice, his guitar playing. Known as an ambassador for indigenous culture, he became one of Australia's 'Living Treasures' – a delightful way of honouring those who've made an inimitable contribution to the country, and died aged 75 in 2012. He was 16 (a couple of years older than me then) when he appeared on *Australia's Amateur Hour*, a radio show our family tuned into every week. He lived at Brown's Flat, where his father, a Yuin man, was born, on Prince's Highway just south of the town.

This was the area the world discovered in 2019 when the horrendous bushfires surged along the coast and TV cameras focused on the extraordinary and brave rural firefighters, many of them volunteers, doing their best to save lives and homes and the stunning wildlife.

I knew that several Aboriginal families, including a classmate, lived here in makeshift dwellings of corrugated iron – what the Aussies call humpies – among the gum trees. In our last year at primary school we did an exam which decided the high school stream we'd be in for the first year. This boy did well, showing academic promise which would have put him in classes A, B or C (languages, sciences, economics).

This was very unusual. Most Aborigines ended up in class G doing woodwork or gardening, staying only until the accepted leaving age of 14 (if you weren't going to sit the Intermediate Certificate) or 15 (if you were). The boy's father went to see the headmaster and he did not go to high school with us. We were 12 years old.

The significance of his age was revealed when we reached Kakadu in the Northern Territory and took a day trip to Arnhem Land. Here I discovered why going on to secondary education may not have been an option for him. Arnhem Land, right at the Top End, has been an Aboriginal reserve since 1931 and is very remote. You need a special permit to enter the area from its owners, the Arnhem Land Aboriginal Land Trust. Only a designated number of tourist vehicles are allowed in at a time, 16 when we visited, and guides must be indigenous.

Lionel, our driver-guide, was born there to a half Aboriginal mother and half Aboriginal father and had gone to school in Perth where he lived with his white grandmother. That made him quarter Aborigine by our reckonings but that doesn't apparently mean much – to be Aborigine is more a state of mind and attitude than a full blood link. Lionel, in his early 20s, was pale skinned and dedicated to helping people like us know more about his culture. I felt it was my first introduction to it.

His Nana was with us on board the 4WD Mitsubishi bus (specially made for the rough terrain of the outback) as she had come from Perth to return a four-year-old great grandson to his people at Kununurra in the Northern Territory. She'd had him with her almost from birth and now he would live with his mother in their Aboriginal community.

When we stopped to have coffee at the Border Café (which has a wild camping site, where you can stay with ranger permission), she told us it was her first trip to Arnhem Land, the birthplace of her Aborigine husband. When the tide was at its lowest, we crossed the East Alligator River, one of the most croc populated in the world, into a wonderfully deserted world.

Lionel chatted as he drove, explaining how the area was looked after and managed for the clans, the Aboriginal families who have a common link. We went off road to reach several sites of Aboriginal art which he'd learnt about from Joseph, the present elder of the clans who was then in his 70s. They were outstanding. We learnt that the artists often superimpose one drawing on another, that drawings are reworked by other Aborigines – which is why some looked so new. He showed us what he called a typical example of 'x-ray art', in which the inside of an animal is revealed, with cross hatching to indicate flesh.

These early artists only drew what they could see, he said, which is why a foot or a hand is so common. In these outback natural galleries there were surprisingly detailed depictions of a yellowfooted rock wallaby, a hammerhead shark, a recognisable barramundi – a favoured local fish – and a long-legged brolga, a balletic Australian crane.

We saw a woman's gloved hand and forearm, stick figures, and a single masted boat painted blue, so unlike all the rest in ochres, reds and white. This, said Lionel, was Reckitt's Blue, a washing aid of my childhood, to be swished through the rinsing water to make white clothes brighter. The Aborigines took the muslin wrapping off the 'dolly pack' and mixed the blue stuff with water to make paint. We were a long way from the ocean here but the edge of Arnhem Land is the Arafura Sea and Aborigines in this area are nomadic.

Lionel pointed to art that was high up on rocky escarpments. How could such paintings have been done? Had ladders been constructed or had the land altered in some dramatic way since? It wasn't either of these, said our guide. The art was the work of *mimys*, tall spirits who can extend or shrink their bodies at will. (We saw similar work later at Katherine Gorge, described as being done 'in the beginning of time...by Nayuyungi, the First People'.)

We left the coach and walked through scrubby and completely silent land – not one bird sound – to an initiation place. This is where boys about the age of 12 are introduced to 'men's business': hunting, art, body decoration, corroboree, didgeridoos. Those being initiated have to throw their very light bamboo spears, using a *bandock* or *woomera* to launch them, to land high in the surrounding rocks – not just once but 28 times, each from a different place at the base of the rocks.

It seemed to me an impossible task, yet it meant

much to each boy. How he fared at this challenge designated his future path. Is this what happened to the boy from my class in Nowra? What initiation did he take part in?

Lionel skilfully demonstrated the use of bandock and spear to us, though he had missed his initiation having been well into his teens when he returned from Perth and therefore too old. He trained instead to be a guide, to learn about his people, with Joseph as his mentor. He said he was fortunate to be accepted for this responsibility. In the Northern Territory and Western Australia more and more Aborigines are being trained as guides, and, with the blessing of their people, can take visitors to places not normally accessible to the public.

We visited one of the oldest Aboriginal settlements, the Arts and Crafts Centre at Gumbalanyah, not far from Oenpelli, where a group of women sat in a circle on the grass with their children around them; this was 'women's business', into which girls are initiated. As they talked they plaited and wove dried rushes into mats and other goods which were sold in the shop at the centre. Women's business, in fact, encompasses quite a range of activities, from child rearing to foraging for food.

Around and inside the building about 250 craftsmen were at work. They were painting on sheets of bark, silk screen printing, and making didgeridoos. These musical instruments are hollow branches which produce a range of dirge-like sounds and feature in a lot of Australian music, including pop. Each didge is different, depending on how much effort the arboreal termites have put into the hollowing and how much resonance the blower can create. The local Aborigines know exactly when the branch – from stringy bark and woolybutt eucalyptus trees – is ready, that it has been sufficiently excavated. Didges are made in other places now, but this is where they originated.

A long length of fabric being screen printed was a special commission for the community. The design, in a mix of greens and blues, would eventually adorn windows in a city home a long way from where the work was done. We watched freshly-baked screen-printed tea towels being removed from the heat-setting oven and were able to buy them from the shop for $10 each. Of the price paid, 80 % goes to the artist, 10 % to the community organiser and 10 % to the Northern Territory government.

Lionel was obviously lucky to have had a grandmother who would bring him up and see him through his schooling. While writing my book I found out about the Aboriginal Protection Act of 1909 – one of several called a 'Half-Caste Act' – which allowed a state to remove Aboriginal children with white blood from their families. Why was this not taught to me as part of Australian history? What worried me more was that I didn't remember that one of the first institutions established in New South Wales for those children was at Nowra's 'twin town' Bomaderry, on the other side of the Shoalhaven River and the terminus for the railway line from Sydney.

The Bomaderry Children's Home, run by Methodists and Baptists for the United Aborigines Mission, is no more. The New South Wales Aboriginal Land Council bought it and there is a memorial garden on the site. In 2001 a ceremony recognised and honoured the Stolen Generation, as the children who were taken from their families were known. It was a day of reconciliation – a term that implies awareness of many past mistakes – and an effort at healing the hurt these appalling policies caused. I will never understand why anyone thought anything good would come of it.

In my late teens I went through a stage of reading the novels of Arthur W Upfield whose improbable lead character is a half-caste detective called Napoleon Bonaparte who had his white father's blue eyes but inherited his sense of country from his maternal forebears. This made him vulnerable to the power the land has over the Aborigine but also gave him insights into people and their motives. This amazing mixture made him a good solver of murders, a determined pursuer of justice, which often put him in danger.

I thought that Upfield might have been buried in the mists of time, but from the web I discovered that he has many fan clubs around the world and is particularly popular in America, Germany and France. His works fall into the genre of crime fiction but what he wrote was unique to the homeland he'd adopted when, aged 19, he migrated to Australia from Gosport in England. His descriptions of the landscape, which even if you have never seen it, bring alive the look, colours, the incredible brightness of the light, the distinctive smells and the dramatic confrontations with nature.

He cleverly makes great use of the outback's extraordinary weather in his plots, and builds well the tension in Bonaparte when his white and black sides are in conflict. In reading the 'Bony' books you accept they couldn't be anything but fiction – that such a person existed or could be an Aussie copper was highly unlikely, particularly in the Queensland of the time that Upfield was writing. Then Aborigines might be police trackers or stockmen on the vast cattle stations, but were not generally highly regarded. They were the *blacks*, nothing more.

Upfield wrote 29 Bony novels between 1929 and 1962, 15 of them before he was published in 1951. After this he enjoyed success, probably because what he created was so different from anything else being written at the time. He knew the land he set the murders in, having had several jobs as a stockman in the outback. His accounts of life on the stations, the furnishings and traditions established by the new owners in relation to the Aborigines on whose land they were now living are fascinating. His plots are many layered, punctuated by Bony's determination to find the murderer, but each book introduces an element of this amazing country.

On the back of the 1963 paperback of *Madman's Bend*, a publisher's note says: Upfield "used to wax bitter about Australians who would read any tripe from abroad, but would not touch an Australian book". He died in 1964, aged 76. A&R published him until the 1980s.

I wish Upfield had been part of my reading for the Intermediate Certificate, but very few Australian writers were included on the list – perhaps Frank Moorhouse is on it today, having won the coveted Miles Franklin prize for *Dark Palace*, the second of his trilogy about the ill-fated League of Nations formed after World War 1 to maintain world peace.

That my class even read any was thanks to our

teacher Clive Hamer, who felt it was a shame that we studied only English, not Australian, literature for the purposes of the exam. It was he who chose Patrick White's *The Tree of Man* for the Apex prize I received in 1956 for senior study, leadership and sport; White, an Englishman like Upfield, was awarded the Nobel prize for literature in 1973.

Upfield helps you to get a 'feel' of the place. On rereading just a couple of brown-leaved paperbacks from my bookshelf, part of my luggage all these years, some of it seems quaintly old fashioned. Even so, having travelled around the country and seen the enigma that the Aborigines present in modern-day Australia, I would like to reread them all.

He seems realistic about the indigenous people and makes no effort to romanticise them or their relationships with the whites who employed them. He obviously admires their talents and abilities and sees how at odds they are with trying to live in the whites' ways. But did he reveal just how badly so many of them were being treated, how young children were stolen from their mothers' arms?

THE POIGNANT FILM *RABBIT-PROOF FENCE* OPENED THE eyes of the world to the appalling mistreatment of Aborigines. It tells the story of two young half-white Aboriginal girls, Molly and Daisy, who run away from the Moore River Native Settlement near Perth to find the families from whom they had been taken in 1931 'for their own good'. They don't know exactly where their mothers are but decide to use as their guide this constructional feat crossing a huge part of Western Australia. Following this would lead them back to their people.

The building of the fence began in 1907 to stop the rabbit plagues that inflict horrendous damage on the land. The girls' journey covered an incredible 2,000 km to Jigalong, an outback community set up to service the fence, where they found their mothers. It is a story that brings everyone to tears.

Every single state has a history of maltreating Aborigines, as I was to discover, but this film struck a chord because of its honesty and chilling dramatisation of a true story. The original book *Follow the Rabbit-Proof Fence* was written by Doris Pilkington Garimara, Molly's daughter, who, by a terrible turn of fate, was also taken from her mother under the same Government Act, as was her sister Annabelle. When Doris and Molly were reunited after 21 years, she learnt the extraordinary story and wrote it down. It was her book that inspired Australian film director Philip Noyce.

The film has won international acclaim. You couldn't do better than to see it and read at least one Upfield if you want some insight into the Australia that's beyond cities and fences, and the people who called it their home, their nation, long before the whites – among them my ancestors – arrived.

2

SOUNDS OF AUSTRALIA

WHY AUSSIES ARE NEVER LOST FOR WORDS

NO ONE SHOULD GO TO Oz expecting it to be like Britain. But you'll be familiar with the accents because of the Australians in the entertainment industry. In the 1960s, the radical of the feminist movement Germaine Greer was possibly first, then came affably humorous Clive James followed by Barry Humphries with his co-conspirators Dame Edna and Sir Les Patterson. But it was *Neighbours* with Jason and Kylie, and the other favoured soap *Home and Away* that popularised the Aussie sounds.

I still have the first record Barry Humphries made of Edna and husband Norm in the 1950s – a 45 rpm in the old measure. Could anyone have guessed then that this odd couple would be a hit around the world, and that the purple-rinse dame with her sandpaper and treacle greeting "Hello possums", and stories of life at Moonee Ponds (a suburb of Melbourne) would still be entertaining in the 21st century?

Television certainly helped to spread Aussi-ness. The now discredited entertainer Rolf Harris, who lived far more years out of his home country than in (just as I have), became a household name with his song *Tie Me Kangaroo Down Sport* (*sport* is similar to *mate*, but mostly used by the older generation today).

On the global scale the accent is probably familiar through sport, at which the country excels. Perhaps it was Pat Rafter's endearing "Sorry, mate" that rang out over Wimbledon's centre court. It could, conceivably, have been through cricket. Australia gave the game the googly (an exceedingly tricky ball to bowl and play, let alone describe), as well as the smooth TV commentating of Richie Benaud, former Australian cricket captain and inheritor of the famous Don Bradman's mantle.

There's no doubt Aussie is an original language. It came into its own through the mouth of the sadly deceased Steven Irwin, an unconventional conservationist and snake-lover who, in talking about his "Austraya", knocked "l" out of his homeland.

You'll hear the country called *Austraya* in many places, yet when the anthem *I am Australian* is sung every syllable is pronounced! The world heard the rousing "I am, you are, we are Australian" during the 2000 Olympics, and it remains a chorus of commitment to nationality, indeed nationalism – although *Advance Australia Fair,* which replaced *God Save the Queen* as the national anthem, is always sung before important events (especially international sporting confrontations).

Television revealed 'bush tucker', foods to survive on in inhospitable places (also, in fact, in hospitable places as lemon myrtle, one of the Oz flavourings, does very well in modern recipes). Funny man Paul Hogan and his *Crocodile Dundee* films did wonders for the land Down Under in opening the country up to worldwide interest. Superstar Mel Gibson is not a 'sound' Aussie like the others (he was born in the US), but he's claimed to be a true blue as this is where he began his career and brought up his large family.

They are a truly mixed bunch, and the message that comes across from all of them is that Aussies are cheerful, quite disarming, and their language is filled with great expressions. I grew up with words like *bonzer* and *corker* (both describe anything that appeals, such as a good meal, the weather, a woman's looks – not so politically-correct today), *tray*, *deaner* and *quid* (names for a three-penny bit, shilling and pound in the old currency), *fair dinkum* (honestly) and *dinky di* (as in: is that real?). Bed linen and towels, called manchester, goes back to the time when these items were manufactured at that city in the "old country" – near where my mother was born – and exported to Australia.

Aussies have a keen sense of privacy and have a saying for anyone who is over inquisitive. *Sticky beak* could come from the very unusual Australian mammal, the echidna (spiny anteater), which sticks its long snout into ant hills and termite mounds to collect its food. It's equivalent to the British *nosey parker* which means placing your nose where it isn't welcome. There's nothing set in cement about the Aussie language; it's impressively adaptable, particularly when an insult may be needed. *Ratbag* and *larrikin* can be used fondly to describe a person who's out of the ordinary or, equally, can be words of abuse for someone who is wayward or disruptive.

My mother always used *dumb-cluck* to mean *stupid,* and I suspect that came from her English background. The Aussies call someone who's not very bright a *dill*, while a *drongo* implies that he or she isn't the full quid (or to put it in today's currency, not a full dollar). You only have to witness the aerobatic performances of the spangled drongo, one of the more interesting Australian crows, and its odd range of sounds (shrieks and whistles, chittering and scolding) to get the connection.

If you call a fella a *galah* – an Aboriginal word – you're calling him a show-off; if the word is used for a female, you're saying she's a chatterbox. Galahs are wondrous birds, unique to the continent, and certainly can be noisy *en masse* but out in the wide open spaces, as we were at the Auski Roadhouse in northwest Western Australia, they were a pleasure to see. A huge flock swarmed among the trees at the campsite, chattering and squawking so loudly it sounded like parliamentary pandemonium. (Tune into a broadcast of the Canberra parliament in session and you'll hear what I mean, as insults are hurled across the floor.)

At Dampier, further north, we watched the birds waddling around beside our van in groups, heads nodding, softly twittering, seemingly gossiping. They live to a very good age and mate for life it seems – but, as they are identical, and appear to be exceedingly numerous how can anyone be sure?

When visiting the Pinnacles, a must-see desert in Western Australia, our guide pointed out a pair: "They've been coming back to the same old hole in the limestone for years." I photographed the two nuzzling up to each other, looking so sweet, their grey and pink plumage standing out against the yellow-gold desert. Then I thought: how could she know it was the same pair? Galahs aren't as silly as their reputation makes out. When they find a nesting place they mark it in some way so that others coming across it will know it is occupied. On this basis, only one needs to remember the address for the future...

There has been a move to call this Aussie bird a rose-breasted cockatoo which sounds pretty feeble. Its indigenous name is great. No, Down Under a galah will always be a galah, particularly if he's a member of a Victorian Australian Rules team. Who would dare tamper with the sacrosanct Aussie Rules, one of the country's top sports?

In our family, one word, 'crook' was all purpose, as it is today. '*I'm crook*' means you feel sick. '*It's crook*' means something is in a bad way. '*Buggered*' is an alternative, often referring to an inanimate object such as a car that's broken down, frequently used with a 'she' – that is, *she's buggered* (a constant expression of my brother-in-law Les, to my emerging-feminist fury). If you're *crooked* on someone (pronounced as in the nursery rhyme "*there was a crooked man lived in a crooked house*"), it is because he or she has done you wrong (a commonplace denunciation of my oldest sister Mildred, implying a situation beyond repair).

There were other words, too, I remember. A *whinger* moans far too much and a *wowser* doesn't like to see people enjoying themselves. A *perv* ogles females, particularly on the beach, and a *letch* (in pre-politically-correct days, this was) would today be guilty of sexual harassment. Today I doubt you'll hear anyone use the words *dago* and *itie*, but in my teens this is what Greeks and Italians were called. They were the New Australians who wanted to find a new life in the southern hemisphere after World War II.

In 1957 a book called *They're a Weird Mob* was published, the first wholeheartedly funny, and affectionate, attempt to highlight some of the problems incomers had trying to live with and work with Australians and their language – *mob* is used by Aborigines to describe their people and clans. John O'Grady, writing as Nino Culotta, did a great job in pinpointing the way misunderstandings come about, and even many years later it makes me laugh.

After this, in the 1960s, came *Strine*, the first attempt to create a dictionary of Aussie sound and slang, written under the pseudonym Afferbeck Lauder (if you run the words together fast enough you'll have your first example of Strine – alphabetical order). Another common phrase you'll hear is "*Emma chiset*?" ("How much is it?") – after a while your ear does attune itself! What started off as a bit of a joke has helped visitors to realise that English as spoken here may not be the same as in other English-speaking countries.

Reading up on Strine is good preparation. Knowing that you'll be expected to pay for a round of drinks when someone says "*Your shout*" saves embarrassment in a *rubbity* (meaning rubbity-dub, pub – the Aussies copied the rhyming slang of London's Cockneys). You'll also be aware that '*See you later*' doesn't mean anything more than goodbye, and '*howyagoing*' is a greeting that requires only 'fine' as a reply and is not an open invitation to explain any ills you might have.

You get used to sentences ending with 'but' – as in "gee, I like that but" – and generally on a rising note so that a statement could be taken as a question (which it isn't!). As anyone who watches British-made 'soaps' will know, Northern Englanders often finish their sentences with 'but' – though not quizzically, and it's pronounced like 'put' – which indicates a link to the early incomers to the country.

In Oz-speak drivers talk about doing a *uee* (a u-turn), wine and beer's bought at a *bottle shop* (off licence) which may or may not be in a hotel (pub), and if you've got any *nouse* (brains) you'll wear your *sunnies* (sunglasses) to protect your eyes all year round. Chicken is mostly called *chook* and if you hear something described as *grouse* it means 'very good' and doesn't refer to game pursued by people toting guns.

Poms were and still are the English (from *pommies*, relating to the French word for the apple-eating enemy), who paid £10 a head to migrate to Australia (as my husband Ian did, in 1967). I remember my father calling a tenner a '*brick*' but I can't recall anyone talking about the British, the Scots or the Welsh. People from 'the old country' were always the English. Dad used to call Britain 'the Old Dart', an expression I've heard in the southwest of England, referring to Dartmouth and the River Dart. As quite a few of the early convicts came from this part of the world, or sailed in the prison ships from there, perhaps that's how it took root.

On my father's side we were convict stock, not that this was talked about in my younger years. Now genealogy is much more fashionable and, in ancestry terms, my family might well be considered 'aristocrats' as Irish-born William Halloway who was convicted at Warwick, England, in 1790, to seven years' transportation, is thought to be my great, great, great, great grandfather. It was a lesser sentence (the real baddies got 14 years, or life), but length of time meant nothing compared to the penalty of being sent across the oceans to an unknown land – another prison – on the other side of the world.

With the help of my cousin Warren Halloway's research I found William in the Convict Indents (1788-1804). He made the 'free trip' from the old country on *Britannia* – Robert Hughes in *The Fatal Shore* described it as an "early hell ship" – and that he survived the journey can be considered a miracle. He must have been in gaol until embarking on that dreadful voyage of 1791, when 11 ships of the Third Fleet carried over 2,000 convicts to Botany Bay, and many died.

William Halloway and his fellow convicts would all have had some input into the development of the Australian language and its unique sound. Their dialects (from the many regions that made up the United Kingdom) must have mingled and coalesced with those of their gaolers, the administrators, the free settlers from quite a few countries who came for land as well as gold, and the indigenous Aborigines, who were there long before anyone else. French, Chinese and Afghans were part of the mix too.

However it evolved, Aussie English was not appreciated by William Churchill, a member of the American Philological Association, who in 1911 described it as "the most brutal maltreatment which has ever been inflicted on the mother tongue of the great English speaking nations".

It probably was a shock if you were used to speaking or hearing pukka Oxford English (which was likely at that time), but at least Aussie English is consistent and the same wherever you go. Though there may be small differences in accent in the different states, you'd have to have a good ear to distinguish them. It is nothing like the US, for instance, where each area of the country has its own accent. In Oz, where you might get caught out, is the pronunciation of local names.

When we were heading up the east coast it was suggested we go via 'Lake Cateye'. We couldn't find it on the map. Not too far away was Lake Cattai, and we might have taken that route, except that, after careful scrutiny, we found a Lake Cathie. It was a guess, and only later, when we checked the local website, was it confirmed that *cat-eye* is, indeed, how it is pronounced. And why not! Many places in England are written one way and pronunciation makes nonsense of the spelling.

One pronunciation I became particularly aware of is that of the British home of tennis, the area of London where I lived for more than 50 years, one of the world's leading sporting venues and therefore, for Australia, a place of reverence.

At the Lawn Tennis Association museum the Aussie greats are all there: Sedgeman, Hoad, Rosewall, Fraser, Laver, Emerson, Stolle, Trabert, Newcombe, Roach, Margaret Smith Court, Evonne Goolagong Cawley, the Woodies (Woodbridge and Woodford) – winners all on an outstanding roll of honour. Yet why is it that so many Aussies, who eagerly watch those two weeks every year, call it *Wimpleton*?

While Aussie English is the accepted language of the

country the indigenous people continue to use the tongues of their ancestors. Driving through the arid Top End, home to many nation groups, it seemed apt that we should hear on Radio National the multi-talented Rachel Perkins, speaking what she hoped would become a common language for all Aborigines. I was captivated by the sound, yet it was as foreign as any I have encountered.

Rachel is an Arrernte and Kalkadoon woman, born in Canberra and daughter of Charles Perkins, the first Aborigine to be a recognised leader and probably the first real spokesperson for the indigenous people. As a film and TV director, producer and screenwriter, Rachel has a nationwide platform.

She would like there to be a common language and dictionary, no mean achievement when not one of the languages – and it is thought there were literally hundreds in all the states – was written. This has been slowly changing as tape recordings have been made to prevent the traditional knowledge preserved in the ancient languages being forgotten, and transcriptions have been written down.

The land the Aborigines know had different names from those given by the white explorers, administrators or settlers. The naming was haphazard from the start of the continent's takeover, and generally boiled down to who needed to be paid, or would expect, a tribute. It's a funny old mix: in all the states you find English and French names as well as Aboriginal (as heard, and translated, by the early arrivals). Aussies have put their own accent on French place names (Cape Leveque, in north Western Australia, is pronounced *leveek*) and food (*crossance* are commonly filled with ham and cheese and served hot).

The best known Aboriginal words are probably *cooee* (a greeting), *corroboree* (ceremony) and *didgeridoo*, an instrument used in ceremonies and often called a didge. Aborigines also use the graphic expression '*three-dog night*' which means a night so cold you need to curl up with three dogs to keep warm. We understood the meaning when we reached Central Australia and at Tennant Creek learnt that the overnight temperatures at Alice Springs had dropped below freezing. Aborigines here wear beanies to keep their heads warm!

Aborigines tend to be lumped together but they are not 'one people'; they come from many different clans and tribes, and this in itself prevents them being a cohesive mob. Though there is no tradition of reading and writing, they share the custom of orally passing on basic values, laws and sacred myths, using narratives or song/poetry. Rachel, who inherited her late father's hope of finding a way of bringing Aborigines together, believes language is the key.

Ideally, if all children, in the earliest years of school, learnt Aussie English alongside an acceptable Aussie Aboriginal – as Maori (indigenous) and pakeha (white incomers) do in New Zealand – there might be greater understanding of each other's needs and wants. It is not straightforward. In Aboriginal lore the passing on of information is complicated by criteria such as who has the right to tell or sing or hear or interpret matters, particularly if secret or sacred. This becomes more of a problem when, by tradition, a younger person cannot ask an elder a direct question – something we learnt from Lionel, our guide on our trip to Arnhem Land.

Imagine how much skill it must take to find out the facts. From Rachel's point of view a dictionary, of an acceptable language, similarly conceived to the universal language Esperanto, would be a worthwhile starting point (though, it must be said, Esperanto has not achieved the hoped-for success). The objective is to close the gulf between indigenous Australians and those whose ancestry may lie in other countries and cultures.

It is interesting that today's situation regarding who owns what began with the legal fiction expressed in the Latin words *terra nullius*, meaning uninhabited wasteland. This is what the British thought Australia was when they made it a colony of its empire in 1788, and the men and women of age-old cultures they found there were not regarded as having any claim to the land on which they lived.

It was not until the 1990s that *terra nullius* was proved to be a nonsense, and it was decided that, in law, Aboriginal people do have land rights. Each claim has to go before a Native Title tribunal and much consideration is given to how the Aboriginal group will make use of the land.

Success has been seen at Uluru and Kata Tjuta, the name of Australia's most visited national park. These stunning rocky places, which used to be Ayers Rock and the Olgas, were returned to Aboriginal ownership, and the park is managed jointly with the Australian Nature Conservation Agency. It is the same at Kakadu where, after years of hectoring, the Aboriginal people have stopped any mining on their sacred lands. Nearby

Arnhem Land, measuring about 97,000 sq km, is entirely Aborigine owned.

Tasmania is one place where nothing can make up for the past, as the Aboriginal people here were systematically wiped out by the white settlers. In the five weeks we travelled around the state in the van we became very aware of the island's link with the past, including the horrendous treatment of convicts at places such as Sarah Island.

Much later I came across a book called *Citizen Labilladière* (by Edward Duyker), and was struck by its poignancy. Labilladière, a French naturalist, went to Van Diemen's Land – the earlier name for Tasmania – in 1792 and again in 1793, as part of an expedition to find the missing French explorer La Pérouse (after whom a suburb of Sydney, where he landed at Botany Bay, is named).

Thanks to Labilladière and French artist M. Peron sketches were made of the Aborigines they saw; these became engravings and were included in Labilladière's Atlas of the voyage, published in 1817. The naturalist's other achievement – which would be dear to Rachel Perkins' heart – was his *Vocabulaire de la langue des sauvages du Cap de Diemen*, comprising 84 words used by the Aborigines he met while travelling around the island collecting his specimens. Sadly, they were the words of the native people – the French word *sauvage* does not mean savage – who largely did not survive.

I became aware of how languages differed from a young age, probably from going to the pictures (*fillums* and movies are used mostly now) three times a week and hearing an abundance of English English and American

English. While American has hardly altered, the more excruciating accents featured in 1950s English films have almost gone from the Britain of today. What concerned me as a child was why my English-born mother didn't speak like those actors did and why Australians sounded so different.

My first understanding came in high school when it was suggested that the way you spoke, your accent, could have a political bearing. How was it that the revered right-wing Prime Minister Robert Menzies spoke 'cultured Aussie English' while Opposition Labor leader Doc Evatt, as he was known, did not – though he was far more cultured, learned and erudite than Menzies? As one was in power and the other never made it, this was a lesson in Making a Good Impression. It could also be interpreted as upper class Aussie and lower class Aussie – though most Australians fiercely believe there isn't a class system there. Money may divide, yes, but not class.

The early 1950s, when Menzies – a favourite of the British royal family – led the country, was a tempestuous time. Many of the seeds of Australia's political move to the right were laid down with the Menzies Government's attempt to ban the Communist Party in 1951 and, after this, the religious split in the Australian Labor Party over its attitude to communists. The Roman Catholics left the ALP to found the Democratic Labor Party and the 'left' was never the same again.

After living so long in Britain I enjoyed being back with Aussie English, a colourful language whether spoken or written. There were changes. No longer did I hear *ta-ta* or *hooroo* for goodbye; now it was '*Take it easy*'. '*She'll be apples*' (it will be OK) has become the universal '*no worries*'. The most noticeable of the innovations I found, especially in the newspapers, is the contraction of words so that they become words in their own right. *Pollies*, for politicians. *Pokies*, for poker machines. *Rego* for car registration.

When I started out as a junior reporter – working on the 'free' local weeklies in Sydney owned by the Packer family, publishers of *The Daily Telegraph* – the dailies were much more straitlaced though the *Sun* and the *Daily Mirror* were beginning to show the signs of irreverence commonplace now. The only national paper *The Australian* tries to present all sides, as did *The Sydney Morning Herald.* But perhaps it isn't irreverence with the others. Perhaps it is just because Aussies are born sceptics and don't like to take things too seriously – unless it is pollies getting up to no good, and then everyone has a field day.

A favourite Aussie word is *rort*, and a good rort is worth reporting. By law, citizens over the age of 18 have to vote in all elections or be fined, which may (or may not) be the reason why politicians are the least trusted members of Australian society, according to the pollsters. Money is always part of a rort – through backhanders, kickbacks or fraud including tax avoidance – and revealing every little detail of the latest scandals sells papers.

The Aussies also know how to take the piss out of other people's accents. In the months preceding the war on Iraq, when United Nations' involvement was somehow bypassed, the outspoken papers summed up the UK-US alliance as the *Blah-Dubya show.*

They like to call a shovel a shovel, hence roadsigns like 'horse poo for sale, $1 a bag' – manure would sound rude. Goods vehicles are trucks or utes (occasionally they may be called lorries), you suck lollies not sweets. Australians like nicknames. Being a redhead I was either Bluey, Ginger Meggs (a comic strip character with red hair) or Copper Nob.

They have backhanders too, like *wog*, an acronym for 'worthy oriental gentleman'. When used as a description it is not a word of praise. It has had an upsurge in recent years with the ongoing concern over asylum seekers, from Asia and other countries. Before they took up this chief place of pillory, verbal venom was aimed at the *Abos*, *Whingeing Poms* and *Kiwis*.

With the reverence paid to Anzac Day (April 25, a national holiday) you would think Aussies and Kiwis would be the best of mates, both having lived with the horrors of Gallipoli since 1915. Perhaps it's the only day of the year when there's a moratorium on the natural enmity. It is an urban myth in Australia that New Zealanders are *bludgers* and flock over the Tasman Sea to live off the state. What is a fact is that more New Zealanders live in Australia than in their own country though this may change under the leadership of Jacinda Ardern. And the pandemic may affect movements of people between countries for years to come.

The idea of mateship has evolved hugely. It has always been a strong theme Down Under, going back to the early days after 1788 when people had to rely on each other in extremely difficult conditions to survive. The two world wars developed it further, when the experiences the men shared brought them closer together. Not in a sissy way (which wasn't acceptable), but in the shoulder-to-lean-on way (which was).

The generations before mine (I was born in 1939, as was Germaine Greer but earlier in the year) were vehemently opposed to any form of sexual relationship between men. *Poofters* and *queers* got a bad time of it from 'real men' like my brother-in-law Les who was outrageously damning of anything outside the 'Me Tarzan, You Jane' way of life.

He was so hostile, says a family tale, because once when he was *perving* at Bondi Beach (a common pastime as he never worked for an employer in the 84 years he lived) he realised a woman he was putting the hard word on had a penis. A *mongrel* he'd have called him, one of his favoured words of denigration.

Les was a joker with a quick wit and he enjoyed making light of things that made people laugh. He was 'macho' before that expression was popular, and a dinosaur. To him, anyone who drank wine and ate salad – which he called rabbit food – was a *poofter*; he was very wary of my hard-drinking journalist friends. Once he tried to get into bed with me when I was staying at his house, which severed my relationship with him for the rest of his life.

He was faithful to the 'man's man' notion, spending his days in the company of his mates (while my sister went out to work), doing deals, drinking endless cups of tea (he never drank alcohol) and spinning yarns. At Aussie parties it was usual for the *blokes* to be at one end of the room – around the keg – and the *sheilas* at the other with the food (which they had prepared).

My father, who was one of nature's gentlemen (albeit with a fiery temper), considered *sheila* to be disrespectful and never allowed it to be used in our house. I don't remember asking him why he felt that way. New light has been shed on the word which first appeared as shelah in Australian English in 1832, referring to a woman of Irish origin, but from the late 19th century it became a general term for a woman or girl. In Ireland 'Sheela na gigs' are ancient carvings of naked women with enlarged labia which were thought to portray the evil of lust – and today are being reclaimed as symbols of fertility and feminine power. So it's ok to be a sheila whichever way it's spelled.

I'm sure my father would somersault in his grave if he heard a couple of the words used today to describe women. A Catholic to his dying day, he couldn't abide swearing, and his anger erupted if we used *strewth* or *bloody*, both being corruptions of religious expressions – 'god's truth' and 'by our Lady'.

Times have changed. Swearing is now commonplace, Sydney has a world-renowned gay Mardi Gras and Pride parade, same sex partners have rights in law, and bisexuality is not considered unusual. In my time in Australia, which was very male dominated, women didn't call each other *mate*, but today they do. The American '*guys*' is universal, and can be applied to anyone – as we found on the day we arrived, when we had a sharp lesson in the use of language.

Flying in to Sydney's Kingsford Smith airport from Bangkok at 5.30 in the morning we were bleary-eyed as we joined the queues to go through Customs. We were surprised to see dogs sniffing around our feet, led by their handlers through the snakelike assemblage, but all we were thinking about was that we were in Australia after months of planning and we wanted to be out in the June sunshine. Then we were directed to a separate desk where the forms we'd filled in before disembarking lay in front of our interrogator.

I'd been to Australia many times on short visits and never before declared that I was carrying food supplements – I thought omega 3 oil, co-enzyme Q10 and selenium, were universally accepted health aids. To cover him for the year Ian had brought prescribed medicines, obtained from his GP in London, so he presumed there was no need to declare them. In fact, when we read the Customs form, neither his nor my tablets seemed applicable to any question. How wrong we were.

All our bags were opened and the contents examined. The female interrogator gave way to a more aggressive male and a well-built sidekick. We had a very uncomfortable 15 minutes, with three people asking questions while I tried to explain why I'd thought anything we had in the UK would be the same in Australia.

— Why would you think that? I was asked.

I was completely confused but took my cue from Ian, who was calm and apologetic. Suddenly the young woman put on a big smile and said:

— You guys have broken the law and coulda been fined. But hey, we're gonna let ya go, havagood visit. Take it easy.

Both of us noticed the American-style 'guys' but were so relieved the ordeal had come to an end that we quickly closed up the suitcases and wheeled our trolley out to freedom.

Months later I obtained from Qantas a booklet offering advice to incoming visitors which everyone should be given when tickets to Australia are booked. Called

Know Before You Go: a must read for travellers, it should be carefully studied. It explains about quarantine and why everything that enters the country is assessed very seriously. What it basically says is declare everything you are bringing in, and not on the JustinCase basis. It is up to those who check the forms to decide whether they need to investigate further.

The booklet puts goods into categories: 'prohibited', 'must be treated', and 'needs inspection'. The rules are made to protect Australia's agriculture and environment, so, for instance, you mustn't bring in any food including anything you might have obtained on the plane as part of a meal (bins are supplied at the airport where you can discard them). Gifty things such as corn dollies, wreaths, dried arrangements that include pine cones or grains, fall into the 'must be treated' group (and you may have to pay for the cost of treatment, fumigation or whatever, so they are not even worth taking as presents).

The food supplements I'd brought with me – and which the sniffer dogs must have detected – are available in all the states, though permissible strengths can vary, and Ian's prescribed drugs would have been acceptable. What we omitted to do was say we had them, and that was the offence that could have brought us a huge fine. We were bloody lucky (sorry, Dad).

According to the booklet, all herbal medicines/remedies, therapeutic medicines, vitamin/mineral/nutritional/dietary supplements, have to be inspected. Australia is very drug conscious and the message they are giving out loud and clear is 'we won't let you bring dangerous or illicit drugs into our country'. (There have been very serious drug problems in recent years, so someone's found a way of getting them in!)

No worries mate. I hear what you're saying. Getting roused on did the trick, and I'm not going to be picked on again. Shocked by the experience, my Aussie English came back in a rush!

3

FINDING JOY IN SMALL SPACES

COMFORT IS AN ATTITUDE OF MIND

WHEN WE CHOSE the Toyota Hiace for our travels we knew it was compact and for a short time after buying it, when it was empty, it even seemed spacious. Then we showed it to my brother Don who looked sceptical but laughed.

– Better you than me. I wonder if you'll be talking to each other when you get back.

I think he was surprised that we had bought something so small when anyone wanting to take to the road in Australia can choose from a wide variety of vehicles. If money's no object, you can have a mini-house-size Winnebago which is luxury on wheels. As soon as I saw one in Sydney I remembered the very funny Lucille Ball film – *The Long, Long Trailer*, made by Vincente Minnelli in 1954. It involved spine-chilling manoeuvrings by Desi Arnez to get the home on wheels round tortuous mountain bends, the rear projecting over a deep chasm. Truly a cliff hanger, but a laugh a minute.

Of course, Winnebagos were unknown in Australia in the 1950s, but three quarters of a century later, when the country is being explored by the same sort of Third Ager, or Grey Panther, or Golden Oldie who have been roaming the US for years, it is understandable that they would want to travel in style.

There is a part of Australia where you might find the sort of conditions that gave Lucille and husband Desi Arnez pause for thought: the road from Cairns to the Atherton Tableland which goes across the Gillies Range. Opened in 1926, the Gillies Highway is black top now, which is an achievement, but its twists and turns as it climbs higher and higher are a challenge for any driver. The road, often described as undulating or serpentine-like, is always thrilling, particularly as you go through spectacular rainforest. It is understandably designated a UNESCO Wet Tropics World Heritage area.

We couldn't afford a Winnebago on our budget. We were interested in the ute plus trailer option, which we'd never seen before. The 'ute' (Aussie for utility) is like the front half of a van or truck, on to which, at the back, a trailer with wheels can be joined. At the campsite, the trailer opens sideways and vertically to reveal fully furnished sleeping and living quarters. As each part had to be bought separately, this combo was beyond us financially as well. But the principle we liked.

Conversions, changing a vehicle from its original use to another, are popular, and coach built – ie, done by a contractor – is generally preferable to DIY. We saw one poptop, of 1980s vintage, which was the pride and joy of a Scotsman who'd lived in Australia for 46 years and who'd travelled the country many times with his wife. He was a handyman who did his own servicing and oil changes, and pointed out many of the additions that made life easier when they were travelling: better lights to read by, stacking racks for cans and food, so they didn't roll about, and a microwave oven.

Single deck buses are often lovingly converted. We came across one with two bedrooms, bathroom, kitchen/diner, that a couple with three children had spent a year travelling in, but they were selling as they had run out of money and the kids needed to go to school. The price included a small car, which was towed along behind, and a *tinnie* – the Ozword for a lightweight, aluminium boat used for fishing – on top. It was much too big for us, but a great set-up for several people.

For a while we considered a caravan/car combo, for we had experience of living in this way for three months in France in 1997. Ian made it a personal challenge to walk from the Atlantic to the Mediterranean, roughly in parallel with the Pyrénées, the rugged mountain range that divides France and Spain, a distance of between 640 and 800 km (400-500 miles). My job was to get him to the start of each day's walk, pick him up at the end, and to keep him well fed. No problem at all in one of my favourite parts of the world where I could spend my days discovering local specialities.

We learnt a very important fact on this trip: you have to be of a certain temperament to be able to live with another person for a long time in a small space, particularly when the weather is not as the time of the year says it should be (interminable rain rather than sun, if you're wondering). And, our experience in France stood us in good stead when, now in our Hiace – smaller than the

Elddis caravan we lived in during Ian's walk – and hoping only for all-encompassing warmth Down Under, we struck foul conditions.

The small-space dweller lives by the Pollyanna Principle: it could be worse, so do the best you can. It didn't take us long, for example, to find out that there wasn't room for both of us in the morning to dress in the space available. Getting up one at a time solved the problem. The weather aspect took a little longer. It may be the world's smallest continent, but Australia is still enormous and there is every type of climate to be experienced. Humidity is a very trying factor in many parts of New South Wales, for instance; Sydney and the southern coast are renowned for daily temperatures and humidity ratings being remarkably similar. Summers can be very hot indeed.

People will often tell you that Australia doesn't really have a winter, and, as we were heading north, we didn't think it would be cold. It never occurred to either of us that we would need heating in the van. In fact, we thought that the machine we'd inherited with the Hiace would mostly be used for its secondary function – as a fan in hot weather. It wasn't long before we found out we were wrong and were glad of the warmth it gave out. It only had to run for a few minutes to heat the space, so it was certainly economical. Not that we had to worry about the cost of electricity – it's all in the price you pay for a camping site with hook-up facility.

Sleeping was never a problem. Once all the curtains inside were closed, the van was snug and dark. We had a doona (Aussie English for duvet) and a large wool blanket which my sister had thoughtfully suggested we take with us. And were we glad we had it! Even though we hardly lingered in New South Wales in our determination to reach warmer weather we covered a fair few ks before we could take it off the bed. Only when we got to Rockhampton and crossed the Tropic of Capricorn did we begin to feel a change in the air. It was bliss. At last, we thought, summer has begun.

We continued north and having enjoyed a couple of hot sunny days in Townsville I suggested we take a ferry across to Magnetic Island. Many years ago, when I was working for *TV Times* in the Brisbane office, I was sent there to talk to people living in this tropical paradise about how much they were looking forward to receiving the same television programmes as the mainland, thanks to the erection of new booster stations. I remember wondering then why anyone would want to take their eyes off the natural beauty and focus it on the man-made (in the old nonPC jargon).

I wanted Ian to see this place where I first discovered that the flowers of the glorious frangipani were not just classical cream touched with vibrant yellow at the centre, but were other colours as well. It was where I saw how brilliant bougainvillea could be, cascading not just in a profusion of fuchsia but also in orange and yellow. Here the air was scented day and night and the seawater was as warm as a bath. I'd never been anywhere like it.

On the day we took the ferry across to the island we woke to the sound of rain and set off clutching our trusty brolly. Eccentric though it might seem, we'd brought a blue and white striped golf umbrella with us from London and it proved to be very useful. It was big enough to shelter us both as we wandered around the island – there is a bus, but walking is easy – and it was soon obvious that it was the wrong time of year for the glorious blossom that lived in my memory. In unpromising weather there was no point in sitting around on a golden-sand beach but we could imagine how lovely that would be.

Back at the campsite, after the rain stopped, we decided to enlarge our living quarters by setting up the annexe, a canvas awning that slid along a channel on the side of the Hiace and was kept up by poles and guy ropes. Once this was in place we could cook and eat outside. As we had camped with a tent in the long-distant past, we both thought it would be easy to do.

Should anyone ever wish to devise a test for compatibility, simply provide an awning, a van, and instructions that defy understanding. (Of course, we should have tried it out before we started our journey.) We found ourselves becoming more and more short tempered, unable to control a large piece of canvas that was droopy in the extreme. We couldn't get the hang of which poles to put up first – there were five along the front and two on each side.After a while a man from a neighbouring campervan, having watched our dismal efforts, inquired politely if he could be of assistance.

Under his guidance, we very soon discovered the knack: corners first, then the middle, then the sides. And he showed me how to hammer in the pegs at an angle to ensure they gripped – a trick we were glad we knew when at one West Australian campsite our base was sand. He was a kind soul and I bet he and his wife had a good chuckle at our expense. But so did we, and what's more celebrated the occasion sitting in the open air with a nicely chilled bottle of Jacob's Creek Chablis.

THE ANNEXE CERTAINLY GAVE US A FEELING OF EXTRA space but it was useless if there were a lot of flying insects about. The winged ants we struck in the Northern Territory were everywhere and we retreated into the van to escape them. There wasn't any point putting it up in the rain either which, unseasonably, we found even on the Nullarbor Plain which *The Great Australian Gazetteer* says is the largest single slab of limestone in the world, covering around 250,000 sq km mostly in South Australia. (The Gazetteer is a fascinating compendium about the whole country and includes recipes from people in all the states.)

On the days we drove across the no-trees desert, from west to east, everything was khaki coloured from ground to sky. Even the miserable looking dingoes blended in with the gloomy surroundings.

As soon as we reached Ceduna, on the edge of the Eyre Peninsula, we decided to turn the annexe into a room by adding walls, and we found just what we wanted at a big DIY/camping store. Australia has an amazing material called shade cloth which, as its name implies, shields out the sun but also has a wide weave that allows circulation of air. It comes in a sandy colour, black or green and is sold by the metre in different widths, one of which was near enough to the drop we needed (from the edge of the canvas to the ground). We chose the sandy colour and bought grommets and a grommet press so that we could make holes in the cloth where it fitted over the poles.

Back at the camp we hammered in the grommets and slipped the walls into place so they rested on the ground. Almost by magic, the moment we finished, there was an almighty thunderstorm with lightning coming from everywhere – it was forked as well as sheet, not an uncommon phenomenon on the edge of the desert. We sat inside our walled annexe as everything rumbled and splashed around us and felt only the lightest spray which came in through the weave. I hope someone won an award for inventing the stuff. We certainly tested it well.

There was a complete blackout at about 5 o'clock which affected the whole area, but we could cook on the van's two gas rings, so having a meal wasn't a problem. We sat in the annexe, reading by torchlight, as the heavy rain continued to fall. Above our heads it began to pool on the canvas roof, causing it to sag, but we solved that by pushing the canvas bulge up with our hands so the water spilled down at the sides. The electricity came back on at nine o'clock, but we went to sleep that night to the sound of unceasing precipitation and, next morning, found the canvas collapsed in the centre with a virtual paddling pool on top.

We quickly emptied it and wiped it as dry as possible – leftover moisture can all too quickly turn into mould – before packing it and the new walls away before the rain started again. Fortunately, both fitted under the bed. This type of action became routine in this year in which the weather broke all records for the most rain here, the lowest temperature there, etc. As a summer it was 'up to putty', as my Dad would say of anything that didn't go right.

In Tasmania, we were really looking forward to thoroughly investigating Cradle Mountain, about which endless prose has been written – and justifiably, as it is a rare and wonderful World Heritage area in the centre of the island. From all accounts you are supposed to be able to see the mountain across the delightfully named Dove Lake which, when we were there in early January, was completely shrouded in mist – of a dove grey colour (possibly the inspiration for its name).

The first month of the year in Australia is allegedly one of the hottest of their summer, yet inside the van we were wearing sweaters as well as padded jackets to keep warm. Outdoors we needed to put on thick socks and our walking boots. But we didn't have to venture out to see the wildlife.

Late one afternoon when the fogginess was heavy around us, I was lying on the bed reading, keeping warm under the doona, when I looked out of the window. There was a big black currawong with our plastic bag of rubbish in its beak (I'd left it by the slightly opened door ready to take it to the garbage tin later). The bird dropped it when I pushed open the door and it flew off with a disgruntled squawk.

A light drizzle was falling as I settled back to my book. I heard just a faint sound outside and when I looked there was a mother pademelon and her baby foraging in the grass beside the van. Pademelons are also called rufous wallabies of Tasmania and are abundant on the island. They used to be on the mainland, but they have disappeared now, wiped out by foxes. They are quite stocky in look and, according to a website about Australian animals, are solitary and territorial. We meant nothing to them. They posed for pictures without taking the slightest notice of us, then softly hopped off. I couldn't have asked for a better front seat for watching wildlife.

We did venture out to the lake. The car park was packed. Despite signs all round about being prepared for bad and changeable weather and not taking risks, adults and children wearing shorts and sandals – some were draped with plastic see-through ponchos – disappeared into the mist to follow the 2 km circular walk around the water. Hardy lot the Aussies; I just hoped they weren't also foolhardy.

The campsite at Cradle Mountain is very attractive. It doesn't cater just for people who carry their accommodation with them and need a site for a van or tent. Many people drive there and stay in a cabin, which is not unlike staying in a motel – in Australasia these frequently have self-catering facilities, and are usually excellent value for money. The sites, divided off by greenery, are a tad snug – fortunately we had a sliding door at the side of the van and could get out despite being close pressed by the hedge. The careful divisions probably do make the best use of the available space – this is one of the most visited parts of the island, after all.

The communal buildings are made of timber, and are octagonal-shaped with high coned ceilings. This gives an airy spaciousness inside but, in the weather we were having, the air that swirled through the ablution block felt as though it had come straight from the snow. The campers' kitchen is excellent, with modern cooking facilities, and large tables with benches. Most importantly, right in the middle of the octagon is a double chimney with a big fireplace on each side and as much wood as you need to keep one or both fuelled. That night, on the second day of the new year, about twenty of us sat around a blazing fire and thawed out.

The most undaunted among us were Swiss, a young couple who'd bought a tandem pushbike in Launceston and were cycling around the Apple Isle, pitching their tiny tent at the end of the day. Obviously they were at home in the mountains – perhaps the area does have something in common with Switzerland – but I was very glad it wasn't me who had to sleep out in such weather. They must have been constantly wet but they weren't put off by this at all. They were very cheerful.

We were, too. When we were looking for the vehicle that would take us around Australia we had seen a Landcruiser, a hefty 4WD, which I had been quite tempted by. The price was good, and the young Dutch couple selling it were brown as berries and full of the joys of driving mostly off road for three months, but the drawback was that we would have had to carry a tent and sleep in that on a blow-up mattress. Ian put the case against such a buy succinctly. "No", was his exact response.

Here in the Tasmanian rain I delighted in the all-in-oneness of the Hiace. We'd spent Christmas at a tiny place called Port Sorell, on the north of the island, where we'd sheltered in our shady room drinking an excellent Ozbubbly (Brown Brothers Pinot Noir Chardonnay), a gift arranged by our daughters in the UK. The elements raged around us but what the hell, Josephine, what the hell! That was one sweet Christmas where space or the lack of it didn't matter a jot.

4

SHE'LL BE RIGHT, MATE

HELPING OTHERS IS AN AUSSIE TRAIT

AUSTRALIA ALMOST FIZZES with optimism and it is easy to get the impression that people Down Under don't have much to worry about. Apart from *goodonya* and *g'day*, "she'll be right, mate" is one of the most common expressions you hear wherever you go. And so is "No worries" or "no probs", either of which is the usual response when you thank someone for even the smallest thing they've done for you. If Australians have problems I think they do what they can to find solutions rather than relying on others to solve them.

The world recognised how different Australia was with the Sydney Olympics in 2000, when the pure enthusiasm and energy of it all surged out of TV sets to the four corners of the globe. The showmanship and efficiency set a standard that modern Olympics aim to meet, even try to surpass.

One of the unique aspects of the Sydney Olympics was the involvement of volunteers, men and women who formed a veritable army of goodwill. Aged between 18 and 80, quite a number were retired – known as seniors, not pensioners, in Australia – and all had put their names forward a couple of years before, not knowing exactly what was planned but willing to be part of it. Australia didn't invent volunteering, but the Olympics organisers struck gold when they realised that those who no longer have to work for a living enjoy being involved in their community.

My brother Don and his wife Maureen had a great time. They were designated jobs, either in their own area of Bankstown or at the Homebush site itself, and their reward was tickets to attend a heat or final of the sport of their choice. In sports-mad Australia, what could be better!

The tradition continues ever since, with volunteers turning out whenever there's a reason, for example on Australia Day – January 26, the date when Captain Arthur Phillip and the First Fleet landed at Botany Bay. It's a public holiday in all states, and there is usually a range of local events (which may include protests by those who prefer it to be called Invasion Day, marking the takeover of Aboriginal lands by the British).

Volunteering on the Olympic scale was a brilliant idea; people from the whole country, not just New South Wales, were invited to participate. It established a pattern for other occasions where the presence of volunteers can make all the difference. One of the best examples was the Paralympic Games which are traditionally held immediately after the Olympics and also attract thousands of visitors from many countries, both able and physically challenged.

Now it was the turn of the youngsters, as schools everywhere hosted teams from competing countries. The children helped on the field, at the swimming events, took part in awarding medals, and became enthusiastic cheer squads for every type of competition. The last place-getters received the loudest cheering of all. It was an outpouring of impartial support that brought tears to everyone's eyes, said my cousin Warren Halloway who, with his wife Maureen, were among the teachers and volunteers who escorted the children to the games every day.

Volunteers set a fine standard, too, in welcoming visitors, being on hand at railway stations to give advice on travelling around the city or handing out event schedules or whatever, while the paid officials can get on with making sure everything else runs smoothly.

For the time that they give, the volunteers get back perhaps a T-shirt, sweatshirt, a cap or a scarf – emblazoned with the event's name and place. But collecting souvenirs is not the reason they want to be part of what's going on. I would guess it is because they get the chance to meet people and chat. And having a yarn is a popular pastime in Australia.

THE VOLUNTEER SYSTEM WORKS WELL IN THE HOSPITALS where former patients and retired staff take on activities that can make life more bearable for those in pain. The roster system is not demanding; most people give perhaps a day a month, but their presence in the wards means a lot. At St George's Hospital in Sydney, where my oldest sister learnt that she had terminal ovarian cancer, the women volunteers were there as adjuncts to the nursing staff.

They wandered around quietly, putting flowers into vases, changing the water, bringing fresh drinking water for patients, offering to do the patients' fingernails, cut their toenails or wash their hair – all of which people who are ill can't do for themselves.

A smile, a hug, holding someone's hand, helping someone to eat or drink, even fluffing up the pillows – such little things make a difference when life is under threat. The big ward windows were kept clean by the male volunteers so that the expanse of blue sky was always bright. To my eyes the men seemed to risk life and limb shinning up the big ladders, but they smiled and waved cheerfully as they balanced on the rungs.

In the canteen, a refuge for sad or bewildered relatives awaiting news or taking a break from watching a loved one in distress, volunteers were ready to nourish visitors with freshly-made coffee and tea, home made cakes and sandwiches. The canteen's not designed to make a profit, and is self-funded – there was an array of crafty things to buy which the volunteers had knitted or sewn, mostly for babies or toddlers.

Over seven emotionally painful days the volunteers didn't intrude on my privacy, never asked who I was visiting, but somehow they made me feel they understood and sympathised. The women made their volunteering day special by having a hairdo and putting on makeup, looking their best for those they gave their time to care for.

Australians feel strongly about giving something back to their community. In Tasmania, at a tiny place called Latrobe, we took an evening 'platypus' walk with Phillip Hedditch, a volunteer who knew all about these extraordinary monotremes – egg laying mammals that suckle their young – and he enjoyed introducing them to visitors. In fact, no visit to Australia would be complete if you didn't see them. No country in the world has anything like them.

An Aboriginal tale explains the animal's odd shape – at the time of creation it just couldn't make up its mind what it wanted and, as a result, it has what looks like a duck's flattened bill, short webbed feet, a truncated body covered in fur and a big thick tail like a paddle. When, in the early days of white settlement, a stuffed specimen was taken back to London it was rejected as being a prank, an animal made up from bits of others. When it was found to be authentic people then worried about the sort of country that would have such an oddity.

As the darkness fell around us in the Latrobe park we stood in the bush by the river watching the very shy animals diving, then surfacing, in the blackish water, looking around, then diving again. You really have to concentrate as they move extremely fast and you need the right sort of camera to catch them in action in the fading light. That's when a silent digital camcorder or iPhone comes into its own.

Walking through the woods back to where we'd parked our van, Phillip told us how he and his two brothers, plus a fourth man, were fifth generation Latrobians. His ancestors must have been among the earliest of the settlers as the state came into being in the early 1800s when the British established the brutal penal colony on what was then called Van Diemen's Land. When Phillip retired, the park where the platypuses frolic was in a terrible state. The four men opted to take over management of the land, building ponds and keeping down the ever-spreading noxious weeds such as blackberry and lantana.

One of the biggest jobs was to clear the willows from the river – no ecologically-minded Australian thanks the British for bringing the weeping and basket willow trees to the southern hemisphere because of the damage they have done to river water and the fish.

Each night a volunteer makes sure that there's no one left in the park before the gates are locked, and that's how the evening walks came about. It's a task that's much more interesting with company. Phillip's made himself knowledgeable about other wildlife in the park too – bandicoots, rufous wallabies, white faced herons, black cockatoos – and feels he's in his own bit of heaven. As the light faded and we watched the rare monotremes' activities in the water, we understood what he meant.

We'd come across other eco-volunteers earlier. From Cairns we took a Trek North day trip to the Atherton Tableland, a plateau of the Great Dividing Range, and then travelled on the Skyrail – the longest cable-car ride in the world. The gondolas carry you up high above the rainforest to Kuranda, a place designed for tourists – and it is very successful indeed. To return to Cairns we were going to take the train: built in 1891 and described as antique, it is one of the most unusual lengths of track in the world, with 15 tunnels and 100 curves through dramatically beautiful surroundings.

As the train didn't leave for an hour we wandered around the town. We watched Aborigines busking, their bodies decked in their painted symbols and dancing to the 'beat' and drone of a didgeridoo, then took a side street away from the main area. It led us to Bat Reach, a rescue station for injured flying creatures.

Now this was volunteering with a difference. There can't be many people who will happily let a bat cling to their fingers or don't mind if one curls up inside their jacket for a sleep. Pam Tully was one of those volunteers. She cheerfully unhooked a couple of spectacle bats from the wall on which they were hanging and introduced them as Bruce and Darren, popular names in Oz. After this came Puddles, a baby bat, found in a puddle near a town called Mareeba. All the bats brought to the sanctuary will have been found in similar situations and in need of help. The work is ongoing: when they've been restored to health they will be released, then a new lot will come in – to which Pam usually passes on the names of the ones before. She laughed.

– You lose your originality after a while. And they do look the same, anyway.

A charming, attractive woman, she put her hand into an inner pocket of her fleece and brought out Emily, a tiny red flying fox about 5 cm long, which she offered to me to hold. I had no difficulty resisting. Bats are not among my favourite wildlife. As small as a sparrow, Emily didn't, however, look as though she could do much harm. Pam smiled.

– You wouldn't think anyone would even notice such

a little thing flying about, would you? Unfortunately, they leave their mark.

Emily, bright black peppercorn eyes watching us from her wizened face, was now in good fettle and was about to be released. But she's nomadic and plant eating, and that's where the controversy begins. Bats present a problem for Australian farmers. They are protected, multiply like mad, and cause terrible damage to the tropical fruit trees which are a multi-million-dollar industry in Queensland and northern New South Wales.

By day the large fruit bats (so called flying foxes) hang around the towns on the huge eucalypts and other trees, supposedly asleep but never entirely still or even silent as they move by their hooked thumbs and clawed feet along the branches, shitting as they go.

We saw this on Hamilton Island, a classy resort off the Queensland coast, where from a distance the trees look as though they are draped all over with the shards of exploded tyres. At dusk the trees seem bare as the bats fly off to find food, covering long distances if necessary and being guided to the fruit by its scent. By next morning they'll be back in the trees again. The mess they create on the ground below is not a pretty sight. They call it guano, though that's usually reserved for seabirds' droppings, but it sounds better than shit.

Pam and the other volunteers at Bat Reach are not in best odour with the fruit farmers but they feel the bats are worthy of rescue. One thing many bats do is eat insects, mosquitoes in particular, and having been inflicted with their venom, I put a few dollars in the collection box in the hope that little Emily and others given a second chance will not hesitate to feast on them.

At Townsville we met more ecological educationalists at Reef HQ, a magnificent living museum where you see displays of growing coral, and the fish, snakes and sharks that inhabit the famous Great Barrier Reef, a World Heritage site lying off the coast. Volunteers are the secret of the museum's success.

We met Florence, the turtle lady, who had notched up over 2,000 hours explaining her subject to visitors. Her husband Max (they had been married 55 years) had given 3,000 hours on his specialist subject, the wonderful seahorse. Because he had motor neuropathy (which affected his hands) he could no longer help out in the tanks housing the live displays – the volunteers will take on anything – but he could still spin a yarn. And the seahorse gives him a lot to spout about: they are something special.

There are about 50 species in the world but the most unusual ones are in Australia. *Hippocampus hippocampus*, the short-snouted seahorse, can be white, yellow, brown, red, black, grey, spotted or striped, and Reef HQ makes a feature of them. It is hard to believe a seahorse is a fish. It has the head of a horse, the snout of an aardvark, spines like a puffer fish, a brood pouch like a kangaroo, 'lizard' eyes that look in two different directions at the same time, a tail like a monkey and armour-plating like a Stegosaurus. It's magical in that it can change colour like a chameleon and uses its tail to hook on to a bit of reef or seagrass to prevent being swept away by a sea current.

They just don't look real the way they glide and bob along in their tubular tank, movement achieved it seems by a transparent dorsal fin that beats so fast it can't be seen. They go up and down by controlling the volume of gas in their bodies, just as sharks do. But seahorses are only tiny, 15 to 18 cm long.

Apart from all this, Max was impressed because these animals mate for life and, round the time of the full moon, have several days of courtship rituals before the female places up to 200 eggs in the male's pouch where he fertilises them and leaves them to grow. Between 40 and 50 days later those eggs will be seahorses, about 1 cm long. Max found this very amusing.

– The seahorse is the only male animal to carry the babies. Isn't that something?

The parents take no part in their offsprings' survival; they have to fend for themselves on a diet of shrimp and other crustaceans. Seahorses live for about four years unless they are caught for the lucrative Chinese, Indonesian and Filipino medical market. These unusual creatures are much favoured as aphrodisiacs as well as cures for a range of illnesses from asthma to impotence.

Reef HQ entertains as well as educates, and you need time to see everything, including the aquarium which you walk through as sharks and rays and superbly decorated fish glide above and beside you. The tour starts in the 'theatre' – the stage is a huge tank in which a diver is feeding the fish while at the same time replying through a microphone to questions from the audience.

– Do the big fish eat the little fish?

– Of course they do!

On the far side of Australia, off the coast, near Rockingham, south of Perth, we met an English woman, formerly from Bournemouth, who was one of the volunteers working with the state-run conservation and land management group CALM on Penguin Island. This sanctuary has no human residents but has a population of birds (a breeding ground for gulls, cormorants, pelicans), dozy sea lions and penguins. These small animals spend their days at sea feeding and come ashore to stay overnight on the island among the limestone rocks, scrubby trees and under the boardwalks which have been put up to keep visitors on the straight and narrow.

It must be a wonderful sight when the penguins swarm out of the sea onto the beach at the end of the day, but it is isn't something visitors witness. The last ferry leaves for Rockingham at four o'clock in the afternoon, and no human is allowed to stay there overnight (though, it seems, drifters used to).

The volunteers, mostly retired people, are happy to give so many hours of their time each week to keep the island spick and span and organise the meals for the penguins that have been rescued and will never be able to survive on their own. These unusual and fascinating little animals are of course the major attraction.

In the visitors' centre they are fed three times a day by the CALM ranger, and actually line up to take the fish from her hand. The way they waddle makes everyone smile (between taking photos, of course, but no flash allowed as this can damage the penguins' eyes). Two of the penguins were fed in the pool where they swooped and dived after the whitebait (not as substantial as the northern hemisphere species). They are truly charming to watch and seemed to like showing off.

All the volunteers, Australia wide, are worth a fortune to the country. The Australian Bureau of Statistics collects information about contributions by non-profit institutions to the economy (millions of dollars a year) and surveys volunteers on their views. For the men and women involved, it doesn't seem to be the money that counts so much as being involved in the way of life of where they live.

Local radio is a perfect example of this – anyone who wants to be part of it can, and listeners tune in to find out what's going on in their town and be entertained at the same time. That it can sound amateurish is beside the point. We enjoyed it in many places, hearing people chiding or deriding, praising some noteworthy event or playing their favourite music, probably their own personal CDs or tapes.

The biggest volunteering group we came across was at the Auski Roadhouse, on the Great Northern Highway in Western Australia and central to the vast Hamersley mining region. We had to go off Highway 1 in order to see Karijini National Park and we booked into the campsite at Auski so that we could take a guided tour. There was a pub, but apart from that the site looked altogether unprepossessing. It was very warm and gusty winds were whipping up the red dust around us when suddenly, with a great deal of whistle blowing and hooting, a charity cavalcade rolled in.

We would be sharing the place with The Bash, an annual jamboree of volunteers who get together to raise money for disadvantaged children. Sponsored by friends, workmates and family, people join in from all over the country, in all sorts of vehicles and weird gear. Nothing was too garish for the 100 or so participants and clowning around was the order of the day. It was obviously much fun as well as hard work but everyone seemed to be in good form and high on the experience.

The campers carried their fold-up chairs to the central area to enjoy the country and western concert put on by the volunteers that night. Naturally the hat went round to swell the collection for the kids who benefit from this week-long trip. As we left the camp next morning, the cavalcade was forming for the next leg to Port Hedland. What a great way to have a holiday, I thought, as we waved goodbye.

We were impressed too, by the kindness of strangers. When we took over the van the former owner gave us an impeccable file about the Hiace so we knew about its service history and its contents. But there were things we didn't know about, starting with the solar panel on the top. In reading the pamphlet in the file we learnt that a battery was fitted under one of the seats and charged itself in daylight so that we could rely on that for electricity, instead of hooking up to the mains at a campsite. This meant that we could free or wild camp, as it is called, staying out in the open if we wanted to.

What we couldn't find written down anywhere was how we could tell it was charging, and how many hours of sun-driven electricity we could reckon on. There was a contact number on the pamphlet but this proved dead when we rang it. At Port Macquarie on the north coast of New South Wales, once a convict settlement and now a bustling, prosperous city, the yellow pages revealed a solar panel specialist to whom we took our queries.

Our panel was only a few years old but solar power technology had obviously moved on a lot. Our specialist – a big man with a massive beard – explained how useful solar heating could be to a traveller. We accepted that, but decided it wouldn't be economical to upgrade the one on the van, and so he cheerfully looked at the battery, checked that it was charging, told us that we had to keep it topped up with demineralised (distilled) water and explained how to read the visual display in the cabin. When we asked how much he wanted for the time he had given us, he said: "She'll be right mate. Glad I could help." Lovely man.

Much later on we were to see quite big vans with several panels. These are popular with people who go on fishing trips and whose lives revolve around the tides, getting up before the crack of dawn if necessary for the chance of a good catch. These travellers, mostly men taking trips together, don't really need electricity, as they go to bed as soon as it is dark, are up before it is light, and cook on an open fire (if allowed – in many places there are restrictions) or a barbecue. The panels are the JustinCase factor, insisted on by the wives who sometimes accompany their husbands and don't necessarily want to follow the spartan life of their mates. Sometimes there is a television set, too.

On the morning we left Port Macquarie, we went through what would become a regular procedure, ensuring everything was shut tight and didn't rattle before driving off. The door of the small built-in fridge closed in a fiddly way – it had a dinky little bit that was held by a chain which slipped into a slot. On this occasion the dinky little bit came off in my hand. We shut the door with strips of gaffer tape – everyone on the road should carry this sturdy adhesive – and headed for a local caravan group to see if they could help. Though friendly, they said they carried no spares for Engel fridges, but we were going in the right direction as the maker's HQ was in Queensland.

At Surfer's Paradise, where most people stop because of the renowned razzmatazz and holiday atmosphere, all we wanted was a phone book. We found Engel Australia and Engel Brisbane, and rang both. We could either keep the fridge taped till we got further north where we would find a service operator or we could call in at Brisbane and see what could be done. Following directions, we bypassed the city – now much modernised and more spread out than when I lived there in the early 1960s – and easily found the Engel address, which wasn't a service centre but a sales office.

Alan and Peter were fascinated by the age of the fridge (it was just a few years old but things obviously change fast in this business) and the problem. Alan found a spare of the fastening used on the newer fridges but then we couldn't work out how to get the fridge out of its insulated casing to fit it. Peter, a do-it-yourselfer if ever there was one, considered a minute, then gave it a hefty pull. Out it came and on went the new catch; in just a matter of seconds, it was pushed back in place. The price? $15 should do it, said Alan. That really was a lucky day.

It is the fiddly bits that confound you. The front of the van was fitted with a large metal grid which did an excellent job in collecting flying wildlife – such as the locust swarm we struck when crossing the Nullarbor – and preventing millions of these pests smattering against the windscreen. After many months of travelling, including some excursions on corrugated clay and gravel roads – which 2WD vehicles do not like at all – one side of the grid sprang off. We were in Tasmania and it was the Friday before a three-day holiday weekend. In Australia they take such breaks seriously and few shops are open on a Saturday. Would we be able to find someone to fix it?

We went to two auto repair shops, what Brits call garages, but both said they didn't have a riveter on the premises. Then one man suggested we try a double glazing company and gave us an address. We were only there for a few minutes. The man heard what our problem was, took out his heavyweight riveter and bang! It was all done. And the cost? Not a brass razoo.

– The world would be a fine place if I couldn't spare a bloody rivet. Have a good trip.

Another hero.

5

AN ISLAND OF TWO HALVES

ABOVE AND BELOW THE 26TH PARALLEL

AUSTRALIA IS a vast continent with two parts, the top and the bottom, the dividing line being the 26th parallel, the boundary between South Australia and the Northern Territory. I presume this particular line was chosen to distinguish one state from the other simply because, once reached, you are in the north, and South Australia, by its very name, had to stop somewhere. It has its own logic.

Just above the 26th parallel, at 23 degrees latitude south, is the Tropic of Capricorn, which could have been the dividing line – but early geographers obviously didn't think so. On the east coast it goes through the city of Rockhampton, which for some people is renowned for its production of excellent beef, but for others (tennis players, for instance, or vegetarians or pub quiz devotees) it was the birthplace of the great Rod Laver, the Wimbledon wizard known as the Rockhampton Rocket.

Travellers arriving here, on the main road in from the south, Highway 1, can't miss a huge object called the

Tropic Marker. It stands in front of the Visitors' Information Centre and is a popular place for photographs as everyone wants to record the fact that they've reached the blissfully warm tropics. Now they can 'go troppo' – bare the body, forget their troubles and just get happy (to paraphrase the old song).

In the Northern Territory, the Tropic of Capricorn crosses the continent just north of Alice Springs; is just above the mining town of Newman on the edge of Western Australia's Little Sandy Desert; and emerges on the west coast at Coral Bay, south of the Ningaloo Marine Park and its outstanding coral reef. Here, by the side of the road, in pretty dismal looking land that has earned it the description 'marine desert', is a simple sign saying 'Tropic of Capricorn'. No razzmatazz. If you are going north it will bring a smile to your face. If you are going south, it will be a farewell to the warmth of the top end.

ONE OF THE THINGS WE LEARNT TO DO WHEN TRAVELLING above this dividing line was to watch the sky very carefully. At night, during the winter months (June to August), the southern sky is a vast, velvety-black space, glittering with distinctive patterns of stars. You can see the Southern Cross, the four big stars and one small one that make up the Aussie flag, and the multi-star collection called the Milky Way. There are many others as well, all of which reveal themselves even more clearly with good binoculars.

The night sky is one of the pleasures of being in remote areas; in the cities, an excess of lights – called light pollution – lessens the opportunity for appreciation. If you are in the area around Tully in Queensland (it is Australia's wettest town, with a rainfall of 4252 mm a year) you may even chance upon UFOs – it boasts of hundreds of sightings a year of aerial objects no one can identify!

By day, above the 26th Parallel, the clouds catch your attention. The huge size of the winter sky, the way it just stretches away to forever, was with us for much of the time – and, when it is cloudless and blue, that is the true sign of the Dry season. But as we moved into what might loosely be called 'Spring' – September, October and November – the tiny changes in the atmosphere attuned us to what might be coming.

Hair-like streaks or filaments, much like white fairy floss forming inside the drum as the sugar is whisked at speed, were *cirrus* clouds, which showed strong winds high above. When we saw the puffy *cumulus* appearing in the bright blue sky, they indicated that the countdown to the monsoon season – the Big Wet of the tropical Top End – was perhaps beginning. Sometimes these cumulus clouds gathered together, and, with the sun's rays on them, glistened brilliantly, looking like very well beaten egg white (essential for the favoured Oz dessert Pavlova).

If the blue were patterned with *cumulonimbus*, which are much puffier, because of the rain they are carrying, and joined together, we'd know that the Big Wet was about to start – but we were headed south by the time they made their appearance.The cloud builds up during October and November and leads to daily downpours which, along with excruciatingly high temperatures and humidity, are known to cause tropical madness in some people – the 'real' going troppo. While the Wet might have its own dynamic, the physical discomfort it can cause is the main reason why people are generally not encouraged to visit the north at this time.

The indigenous Australians understand their environment; they know what they are looking for in the sky and, when the clouds signal imminent change, they moved to more congenial weather conditions. RoundOz travellers today would give that as a very good reason for being nomadic. Many Aborigines object to the use of this word as it has come to sound pejorative, an accusation of shiftlessness. But, as they know (and we found out), being on the move is really the only true way of knowing this great country.

There is an interesting insurance angle to driving in northern Australia, and it concerns the line known as the 26th parallel. For instance, you have to inform your insurance company that you intend crossing it and are going north, or any claim you might make later will not be accepted. In the Australian summer, heavy tropical rain and floods can change the landscape dramatically in minutes, so travelling in tropical Australia is best done in any months except November, December, January and February. Stories of what happens in torrential rain are legion – rivers can rise by 10 metres in minutes, roads simply disappear.

Travelling as we did in Oz's benign northern winter and protected by the Dry, we could only marvel at the aftermath of the annual climatic violence in the wide, muddy bed of the Fitzroy River. This massive artery in the Kimberley region, draining 100,000 sq km of land, was named after Vice-Admiral Robert FitzRoy, the commander of *HMS Beagle*, the ship that is synonymous with the evolution revolution. John Lort Stokes was mate and assistant surveyor on the ship and shared a cabin with the 21-year-old naturalist Charles Darwin on the groundbreaking expedition, from 1831 to 1836, and later became its captain.

Stokes ensured that the names of Fitzroy and Darwin endure in this part of the world. He also named Beagle Bay, on the northwest coast of Western Australia, where Trappist monks founded a Roman Catholic Mission for Aborigines in 1890 – it is still there today, its mother-of-pearl shell-bedecked altar a sight to behold. That it has survived the cyclones that batter this area is a miracle in itself.

Both Darwin and Stokes wrote extensively about their visits to Australia. In *The Voyage of the Beagle*, chapter 19, Darwin covers the early months of 1836, still a time of privation for the settlers, and hell for the convicts and "black aborigines" whose numbers were rapidly decreasing "owing to the introduction of spirits, European diseases and to the gradual extinction of the wild animals". He makes many observations of the land and its people, at a crucial time in Australia's history, but it really was a new country then compared to what would happen in the future and it is difficult to know what he expected to find.

Darwin was in his mid-20s, the age now when many can't wait to explore the Southern continent, and was not unhappy to leave. "Farewell, Australia!" he wrote. "You're a rising child, and doubtless some day will reign a great princess in the South: but you are too ambitious for affection, yet not great enough for respect. I leave your shores without sorrow or regret."

Stokes, on the other hand, had much longer to investigate. He came back to chart the continent from 1837 to 1841 (when he took over command of the ship) and his report, on the *Beagle*'s third voyage (*Discoveries in Australia*. 2 vols. London: T. & W. Boone, 1846), is clear and thoughtful, and he shows much interest in the Aborigines and their knowledge.

Hoping they would help him find an inland lake in Western Australia, he wrote: "Their notions of distance are, to say the least, exceedingly rude; with them everything is 'far away, far away'. The size of this water the natives describe by saying that if a boy commenced walking around it, by the time he finished his task, he would have become an old man." [The lake, in fact, was discovered in 1843 by Messrs Landor and Lefroy, 100 miles south south east from Beverly. Called Dambeling, it was 15 miles long and seven and a half broad, and quite salt.]

He also observed: "The natives have a superstitious horror of approaching the graves of the dead, of whom they never like to speak, and when induced to do so, always whisper. The most curious superstition, however...is that the white people are their former fellow countrymen, who in such altered guise revisit the world after death." Much later, on the east coast, he wrote: "The natives of Australia vary as strangely as its soil; the members of the tribes that dwell about Shoalhaven and the small southern ports, and come up in coasting vessels, are good looking, useful fellows, and may hereafter be made much of." [This was the area where I grew up and lamentably knew nothing of these people.]

Stokes and his men traced the Fitzroy for 22 miles before returning to the ship. When we saw the river it had a few pools of water, but mostly was a mess of uprooted and smashed trees lying every whichway on the brown silt – all probably from the forest on the banks. Paperbark and river gums, freshwater mangroves, native figs and pandanus grow along its length. I took photographs from a bridge which seemed very high above the riverbed, but a sign nearby warned that the road was subject to flooding.

There are many road signs like this in the north, but in the warm and wonderful sunshine, with no sign of rain whatsoever, you don't take them seriously. It helps to know, however, that in the 'normal' Wet, if you can call any of this normal, the Fitzroy rises about 16.5 metres, and that every so often it knows no bounds. In 2002, for instance, there were record floods, with the water rising an estimated 13 metres over the old concrete crossing.

What is pretty impressive about the Fitzroy River is how, over time, its floodwaters carved out the 30-metre deep Geikie Gorge through the limestone at the junction of the Oscar and Geikie Ranges, where there is an ancient coral reef formed 350 million years ago in the Devonian Period. That's the sort of geological talk that's commonplace out here, because the continent is just so old. What it actually means is that the gorge is an ecological treasure, and explains why the area is sacred to the traditional owners, the Banuba people – and why a plan to dam the river and flood the heart of the Kimberley caused much distress. It doesn't seem possible that any modern-minded person would want to jeopardise heritage in this way.

In Arnhem Land in the Northern Territory, we had

seen how the East Alligator River rises daily. When we crossed the concrete ford in the morning there was hardly any water, by mid-afternoon the river was flowing strongly, well above the road, and our vehicle had to wait in a queue with others for the right time to get moving. A marker by the roadside, which indicated that daily tides could reach 2 metres, was taller than Ian. No wonder exhausts on 4WD vehicles are snorkels.

A sign at the crossing warns drivers and pedestrians to:

PROCEED WITH CAUTION – this causeway is subject to flood and tidal inundation, causing deceptively dangerous and slippery conditions."

Lionel, our Aboriginal guide, kept us occupied watching out for the local birds – he was still learning about the 286 known species in the area, he said, including Australia's tiniest one, a mistletoe bird, which to my delight I saw – while, at the same time, keeping one eye on the river. We saw a big croc, a 'freshie', idling on the other bank, but it oozed itself into the water, which, by now, was fast-flowing and oddly coloured, like a whipped-up milkshake into which some liquorice had been added.

As you will have guessed, the river was given its name because of its major residents – the discoverer must have thought of them as alligators, though, in Australia, these reptiles are crocodiles. The difference is all to do with snout length and rows of teeth, the sort of details the non-specialist in a difficult situation is not likely to be interested in.

In this river, most are 'freshies', which eat frogs, fish and birds, but the more dangerous 'salties' can also find their way here. One may be smaller than the other, but I have no doubt about whether I would ever want to be in the same stretch of water with either type.

As the tide went out the waiting vehicles took turns to cross. Rental agreements are strict here. Anyone in a rented campervan, motor home or a car, should not be in the queue. Such vehicles are limited to sealed roads, and those renting would not be insured if they ignored the contract. Arnhem Land has few roads and permission to enter is given by the Aboriginal owners only to 4WD vehicles, which is why we took the day trip with an authorised tour guide.

Knowing the difficulties that can face drivers in the tropical north, motoring organisations recommend that anyone, including those in 4WD vehicles, if towing a trailer or caravan, should stick to black-top roads. I imagine that clay roads awash with terracotta-coloured mud would be even more daunting than the baked-hard, corrugated surfaces – often described as 'gravel' – that we encountered on the few off-roads that we just couldn't resist.

Though we knew it would be impossible to follow it in the Hiace, we both felt a sense of regret when we had to ignore the sign to the famous Gibb River in Western Australia. This road, which crosses the Kimberley region and was built as a cattle route between Wyndham and Derby, is regarded as one of the great Australian challenges. Signs warn drivers of its notorious surface, but in the right vehicle for the conditions, packed with all you need to be self sufficient (fuel, water, food, spares, including tyres, two-way radio, good humour), you can go off road to see the fantastic gorges and pools and national parks which, like the vast cattle stations, are a feature of this mountainous area. That is serious motoring.

There are big powerful buses in which you can take a tour of this road; they go from Kununurra in the north-east, or from Broome in the west. I had really wanted to go to the East Kimberley to see one of its jewels, El Questro, still a working cattle station but is now more like an American dude ranch offering a range of activities and different types of accommodation – from safari cabins, bungalows, camping, to luxury rooms and suites.

It was the pet project of Eton-educated William Burrell and his Melbourne-born wife Celia, who bought the station in 1991 and made it a world-famous resort – a 'million acre wilderness park'. It has changed owners a couple of times, in 2005 and 2010, and was closed entirely during the Covid 19 pandemic.

At one point we were quite close to it, when the plane we took to see the Bungle Bungles landed in the middle of nowhere to drop off some of the passengers who were to spend a couple of nights at El Questro. It was surreal. Around us seemed endless ks of odd-shaped escarpments and scrubby desert, then, suddenly, a white 6WD bus arrived in a cloud of dust and pulled up at the end of the clay landing strip. Right on time, said the pilot. Top marks for efficiency.

Back in Broome, where we were staying at the peaceful (and very popular, so needs to be booked ahead) Roebuck Bay campsite, I inquired at the agent's office in the town about the cost of visiting El Questro – and put it on a wish list for the future. I was pleased to find an attractively illustrated children's book, *Colour the Kimberley*, created by artist Celia Shelmerdene (the maiden name of

Mrs Burrell), which I bought for our grandson Max. It might be a place he would want to visit one day.

IN WESTERN AUSTRALIA, THE 26TH PARALLEL AND TROPIC of Capricorn are regarded as synonymous. Employees living north of it are entitled to an annual leave travel concession as going anywhere in this state involves huge distances. Pensioners – in Oz called seniors, with state pension cards – who've lived above the 26th parallel for two years or more, continuously, are entitled to one return journey by air or coach a year to Perth or elsewhere in the south west (provided the fare is not greater than that to Perth, though they could pay the difference). Unused trips do not accumulate, and holiday-makers have to return within three months.

These are thoughtful ways of helping people get away from the effects of the Wet season, if they so choose. In the south, pensioners holding state cards are entitled to one free return trip on government bus and train services a year – these operate south of the 26th parallel.

If you look at a map of Australia and pretend that this line continues across the continent, the vast area above it – parts of Western Australia, the Northern Territory and Queensland – is designated Northern Australia. It is not a political division, more a mutual promotion society with its own representatives who believe it is essential to draw attention to the different needs of more than 50 nationalities who live and work here. In tourist terms this is usually what brochures call the Top End or The

Outback – and common features are the ginormous cattle stations, which you drive through, and Aboriginal settlements, which you don't enter unless you have permission.

This vast area is very sparsely populated, and distance is always a challenge. Two major train links have opened up the continent: the one between Adelaide and Darwin has closed the gap between south and north; the one from Cairns to Perth crosses the continent from east to west. Both are leisurely journeys, very attractive to tourists. Most long-distance travel is done by air, which is expensive. The cost of goods and services increases, simply because of the expense incurred in providing them in outlying places. Networking Australia, bringing everyone closer together through the internet, is at least making it easier to keep in touch, and the will appears to be there to make more changes.

An increasing number of enterprises have grown up to meet the demands of the tourist influx. But these businesses and the areas they service just don't have enough workers and there is a particular need for those in skilled professions. The people shortage has encouraged the state governments to find ways of expediting immigration applications of doctors, dentists, builders, engineers and mechanics prepared to live in out-of-the-way shires, and people from the UK are especially being targeted. It's certainly worked in the case of doctors: one in ten of the medical practitioners who've taken up the challenge to live in northern Western Australia is British-trained.

There is certainly much more than desert in Northern Australia and there is a notable symmetry of bays and islands on the east and west coasts at 26 degrees latitude south. On the right, in Queensland, is Hervey Bay Marine Park and Fraser Island, and on the left, in Western Australia, is Shark Bay Marine Park and Dirk Hartog Island, and Hamelin Pool Marine Park. All are World Heritage Sites.

Four essential criteria must be met for this designation to be made. An area must have outstanding examples of the major stages of the world's evolution (all of which these certainly do); have significant ongoing ecological and biological processes; have unique, rare or superlative natural phenomena or features of natural beauty; and have significant natural habitats where threatened animal or plant species still survive. It is extraordinary that Australia should have equally precious places on both sides of the landmass. Another reason why it is the world's most amazing island.

I MIGHT NEVER HAVE KNOWN OF THE EXISTENCE OF either if we hadn't done this trip, or even of the 26th parallel if I hadn't seen a sign by the roadside near Monkey Mia in Western Australia announcing its position. I collected photos of many weird and wonderful signs in all the states, and their messages are usually immediately understood. But what was the reason for this one, displayed rather forlornly in this windy and desert-like area of the coast? In looking for its meaning, I discovered more about constitutional geography and constitutional history than I'm sure I was ever taught. Or, to err on the side of caution, perhaps I'd just forgotten...

At least it answered for me one question: how the

states came to be the shape they are. They are all odd, following no discernible natural divisions – except, perhaps, in the case of New South Wales and Victoria where the boundary, at least in most part, is the Murray, one of Australia's greatest rivers. I was interested to come across an Aboriginal story *Kubbitha and the Tuckonies* (one of a charming collection by AW Reed), set in the Riverina area of New South Wales, which began: "In the days when there was no Murray River..."

It's a revolutionary tale, in a way, about determined women at a time of drought searching for the life-giving water their husbands kept secret from them. Kubbitha, the most stubborn of the wives, is nearly dying of thirst when lo and behold she is rescued by the 'Tuckonies', which, to my mind, the Irish would call leprechauns, the little men. They show her how to drive her digging stick – *gunni* or *wanna* – deep into the mountain, which creates the free-flowing Murrumbidgee, a river that cuts the women off from the husbands who were so unkind to them. On their side are trees and green bushes, on the men's it is hot and dusty. And so it was that the women, the Black Ducks, found the green, well-watered land, while the men, the Goannas, were relegated to the dry, sandy places.

As the Murrumbidgee flows through what non-Aboriginal Australians call New South Wales, and eventually joins the Murray River, this tale must be set somewhere west of Wagga Wagga which is indeed not too far from a desert. I'm guessing, of course, but having lived in Lockhart, to the west of Wagga – which I remember as a parched town on reddish-sand plains where, when the wind blew, the cobwebs turned red – I know that going east towards Canberra and the Australian Capital Territory is distinctly greener. It's certainly more mountainous. It is also, today, one of the extremely prosperous wine-growing areas of Australia.

HAVING CHOSEN THIS LINE, 26 DEGREES LATITUDE SOUTH, as the division between the Northern Territory and South Australia in 1836, why wasn't it continued right across to the east, dividing Queensland from New South Wales? The states just didn't develop like that, as I found out from a section of *The Australasian School Atlas* (physical, political, economic and historical) published by Oxford University Press in 1939, which my cousin Warren Halloway, geography professor, sent me.

The southern continent, known variously as Van Diemen's Land, Terra Australis and New Holland, after 1788 had two parts: New South Wales on the east, and the rest was marked 'unattached'. It was this part that became Western Australia in 1829, after which South Australia, a settlement of free colonists, was inset into New South Wales; to the north was the 26th parallel and its eastern boundary was 141degrees longitude.

Between its western boundary and Western Australia was a narrow 'No Man's Land', though why this should be so I have no idea – I suspect it had something to do with the new settlers thinking there was nothing to be gained from this bit of desert. South Australia did claim it as part of the state 25 years later, and it is still as arid.

Everyone lived in hope in these early days. The determined explorer Edward John Eyre, accompanied by an Aboriginal man called Wylie, in 1840 followed the coast of the Great Australian Bight – from Adelaide to Albany – hoping to find a stock route, but instead proved how valueless that 1,600 km length of land was. At one of the windswept lookouts on the Nullarbor, there's a rusty piece of machinery, used by the Eyre expedition, on which a plaque says the explorer had "survived thirst, hunger and death to reach Albany". Under this someone had written: "How do you survive death?"; the answer, scratched below, was "Ask Lazarus".

New South Wales shrank further in 1859 when Queensland became a separate colony, its southern boundary at 29degrees latitude and its western a continuation of the eastern border of South Australia. This created another 'no-man's-land' on the Northern Territory side, which Queensland drew to itself in1863 when the Northern Territory was added on to South Australia – and the 26th parallel disappeared entirely! It was, however, restored in 1911 when South Australia handed over control of the Northern Territory to the Federal government which had come into being on the first day of January, 1901.

Australia calls itself a commonwealth and includes the former British New Guinea, the southern half of eastern New Guinea which was annexed by Queensland. It is today called Papua and became part of the Commonwealth of Australia in 1906. [More confusingly, the former German New Guinea, which was the northern half, is now called New Guinea; the combined territory is known as Papua-New Guinea. The western half, annexed by the Dutch, is part of Indonesia.] The Australian Capital Territory was established at Canberra in 1927, taking another chunk out of New South Wales.

It seems strange that the once-so-large eastern side of the continent called New South Wales should shrink so dramatically. But at least it could claim one victory. Despite representations from the colony of Victoria for its inclusion, the rich and fertile Riverina district, south of the Murrumbidgee River, was declared to be in New South Wales, and is today one of the country's greatest wine production areas. [Not that Victoria need have worried; its vineyards are both extensive and their wide range of wines highly regarded.]

There were even arguments over the desert areas. There had been, it seems, between 1861 and 1863, a plan to create another state called Albert, which would combine the area north of South Australia and much of the north of Western Australia. This was a logical progression: after Victoria, why not name part of this vast land after Her Majesty's beloved husband so tragically taken by typhoid in 1861, but the idea fizzled out.

It was the new squattocracy – as the sheep, cattle and cereal farmers who took up land to which they had no title were known – who put pressure on Queensland administrators to move its western boundary 3degrees into the Northern Territory. After South Australia had added on the unproductive deserty bit to the west, there was at least a sort of evenness in the arrangement of the states, a neatness that administrators tend to like but take no account of what might exist at the time.

In fact, the states of Australia came into being in much the same way as every other country the British made part of its Empire, when lines were drawn without any understanding or recognition of what the land might mean to the people who lived there. Decisions like this weren't always made in the actual places, but by people in Britain who probably would never see the county they'd taken the pen to. Look at Iraq, occupied by Britain under a League of Nations mandate after World War I. In Europe there were similar illogical divisions, with disastrous consequences in terms of war.

In Australia it probably never occurred to those at the administrative level even to consider the Aborigines. They'd either be the menial workers the new owners needed on the stations, or the Missions – intent on converting them to Christianity of various leanings – would look after them. The priority for those running the colony was to help those new colonials who were willing to do something productive with the terrain. If these people didn't take up this challenge, there was no other way to provide the essential food that the growing communities needed.

Once the British had declared Australia to be theirs, the ownership of the land was taken by the Crown, to be given, sold or leased as was thought politically correct. Arid desert, coastal areas, lakes and rivers became either the King's (George III, George IV, William IV) or, later, the Queen's (Victoria) and nobody gave two hoots that the indigenous people relied on it for food and shelter and spiritual meaning.

The British in establishing their Empire obviously never considered that black people had either intelligence or rights, or souls of their own. The Aborigines' intimate understanding of their environment was gained over centuries, learnt from experience of the way of life of the animals, the growth patterns of the plants, the changes in the weather.

Their strong culture evolved, not based on settling down in one place and growing things, but from travelling a known area, in which they hunted and gathered their food, and moved on when resources needed time to replenish themselves, or when the land needed to revive, or the weather was best left to its own devices.

From generation to generation – man to boy, woman to girl – the traditions and information were passed on, and each tribe or mob, made up of clans, took responsibility for the land and all that was on it. Land was their Manta, their Earth – and still is.

I learnt about this in a remarkable book called *Elders – Wisdom from Australia's indigenous leaders*, a combination of photographs and the words of 17 elders who had been recorded by Peter McConchie (Cambridge University Press 2003). What these elders had to say was illuminating, providing a glimpse of the rich culture of the Australian Aborigines and Torres Strait islanders. It helped me understand some of the things I'd seen and heard in the months we spent in Australia, about the clash of interests – between blackfellas and whitefellas – which are so deep-seated they may never be resolved.

No one knows exactly how many Aborigines, or the number of tribes, there were in Australia when the Europeans arrived. When I was growing up, the exact size of the Aboriginal population must have been mostly guesswork – the 1971 Census, 200 years after Captain Cook landed, was the first to include them. They were the indigenous people of Australia, but not citizens until they were given that 'right' after a referendum in 1967. Today, Aborigines make up 3.3% of the population, yet are so spread around the country that they are rare in the everyday life of many Australians.

In McConchie's book, one elder, a woman, tells how her family was affected by an 1886 law (possibly the first 'Half-Caste Act'), which forced men and women of mixed blood aged 35 and over to leave the reserve which the government of Victoria had set up 'to manage and control the Aboriginal people'. These were the ones who were most able bodied – and without them the Coranderrk people could not survive. The government effectively killed what had become a self-sufficient community. In less than 60 years, that reserve was reduced from 4,850 acres of gazetted land to just half an acre – which is now the Coranderrk Aboriginal Cemetery.

The terrible irony is that the Aborigines at Coranderrk had shown they were extraordinarily capable of doing just what whitefellas did: they ran a school, raised cattle, milked cows, baked bread, grew hops to use for brewing, and made bricks. They prospered and it was that prosperity that the government objected to. Perhaps this is why many Aborigines don't feel connected to 'white' Australia.

6

RULES FOR STAYING SAFE

PROBABILITY OF CHANCE ENCOUNTERS

THERE ARE ALWAYS TALES to be heard about Outback Australia and breaking down in the desert without water. Generally speaking, most people think that this couldn't happen to them. And in all probability they could be right, as incidents of this sort are few, particularly when you consider just how many people must be out there discovering the continent at any one time. Even so, warnings urging travellers to take precautions are necessary.

In 2020 a TV series revived interest in one of Australia's most extraordinary cases involving a terrorised young English woman, an English man who disappeared and was presumed dead, a kidnapper with a dog, and a white van. The Falconio incident in 2001 occurred north of Alice Springs in Central Australia made dramatic headlines – English couple, white van, Red Centre. That could have been us: in our white high-top Toyota Hiace van, but it wasn't.

In 2005 Bradley John Murdoch was gaoled for the presumed murder of Peter Falconio (though his body has never been found) and the illegal abduction of Joanne Lees. It was because she was able to escape and report what had happened on the Stuart Highway that the police were alerted and the search for the killer began. The TV series hoped to reveal what had happened to Falconio, but failed. However, it brought places like Barrow Creek, Aileron and Ti-Tree on Highway 87 to viewers' attention. They were new to us as well as we drove in from the east on Highway 66 via Camooweal, and joined the road to Darwin higher up.

We were very aware that in the UK, people's knowledge of geography, or lack it, as well as discursive reporting in the papers about Australia makes every horror story sounds like it happens just down the road. As we travelled we made certain that we kept our families in the UK and Australia up to date with our movements. Not that they probably took much notice because they were involved with their own lives and there was no reason to think we weren't ok.

But we realised that no one would know exactly where we were at any time over quite a few months and that made us think of the safety aspect of our journey which would take us through many areas which are virtually uninhabited. What would we do if we were driving along and came across a vehicle by the side of the road and a person by it hailed us to stop?

Fortunately the answer came from a veteran traveller we met at a campsite.

– If someone wants you to stop, drive on past them about 50 metres. Open your window and call back "Do you need help?". Do not turn off your engine or get out of your car. If the bloke calls to you and explains what's wrong, you can decide what to do. If he runs towards you, or someone else appears, drive off quickly.

This traveller never considered that it might be a woman who'd done the hailing, but the principle applies whatever the gender. While your instinct might be to stop for a woman it's not a good idea as a man could be hiding behind the vehicle and could jump you if you stopped.

– In my experience if someone breaks down there's usually little you can do. It's best to say you'll go on to the next town and get someone from there to help.

One of the pure delights of the Top End is that you see so few other people; in fact, at times on our journey, we could have been on the moon. Once, captivated by a talk we were listening to on Radio National – the Australian Broadcasting Corporation's all-Australia station – we pulled off the road into a wooded area to hear it more clearly. There in the bush was a van with two occupants who looked most surprised that with all the space available we had encroached on theirs. We exchanged waves and when the talk ended we drove on.

Free or wild camping is popular at the Top End and all over Western Australia. Adventurous people are inclined to stop when and where they want for the night rather than seek out a campsite. Well equipped caravans or campervans travelling together might pull over or go off road into the bush knowing that they were self sufficient with light, water, washing and toilet facilities and food. Because we didn't have 4WD, off road was another world to us and one mostly denied on this journey. We did go off a couple of times but generally stayed on black top. Not that this is necessarily free of problems. One of the unusual elements of northern Australia is that Highway 1 goes through vast cattle stations which are impossible to fence so day or night you are likely to come across grazing animals by the side of the road, or on it.

Road trains fall into the 'outback terror category' for the inexperienced or timid driver. These vehicles are trucks, but with so many trailers added on, they are likened to a railway engine with carriages – the roads are their tracks. They have different permitted lengths depending on the state. The big ones that do the greatest distances can be as long as 50 metres. One I photographed at Camooweal, opposite the last roadhouse in Queensland before entering the Northern Territory, had to curve itself into an arc to fit the parking space.

These trains are the fastest way of moving goods and cattle around this enormous country and are impressive to look at: they are very tall, with lots of stainless steel and snorkels. Whenever I saw one in my rear vision mirror, closing up on me fast, it reminded me of a cartoon dragon, huffing and puffing. They also travel at a fair whack and, because of the load they're carrying, don't like to have to swerve – which is why, if you see one coming up behind, you pull off the road and let it go by. No argument.

As in the UK, you drive on the left in Australia, and the law is very hot on the wearing of seatbelts and obeying the speed limits – always well indicated by signs.

We cut our teeth on road trains on one of the rarest 'sealed' roads we found in our travels, a sort of 'shared' road. We found it when, from Cairns, we made our way inland via the 'must see' ancient lava tubes in Undara National Park, then through Georgetown and Croydon to Karumba on the Gulf of Carpentaria. From here, to get back onto the round-Oz-road, Highway 1, we had to go south through Normanton to Cloncurry. And it was this road that had a central strip of tarmac (black top) just wide enough for one vehicle, with corrugated clay on either side.

The land is flat around here, the scrub dotted with metre-high, terracotta-coloured termite mounds, and there is much wildlife to watch for, like the delightfully elegant brolgas with their grey feathers and long necks, famed for their 'dancing' with wings extended. We saw an adult emu with five small ones and later learnt that this would have been Dad in charge. Mum leaves the off-spring with him to bring up and, when he reckons they're ready – at about 18 months old – he picks a fight, literally kicks them out, and off they go to fend for themselves. How very clever, I thought.

We were admiring a gathering of brolgas, also called Native Companions, when we looked up to see a road train coming at us on the same central strip we were on. Ian was driving and he veered off smartish onto the gritty clay to let it go by. Quite startled, we sat enveloped in a huge cloud of dust whipped up by the truck. When it dispersed, we set off again – and so it continued to Cloncurry. But we had been initiated and knew now what to do.

A note in the diary I kept refers to the high number

of road trains encountered on the Stuart Highway between Darwin and Katherine in the Northern Territory – at one point we came across seven of them in a row. We counted them as they overtook us! This is a busy road as it goes down to Alice Springs and then to Adelaide. With the completion of the Ghan, the 2,979 km rail link between Darwin and Adelaide – a project that took some 130 years, from the time it was legislated for until its first run in February 2004 – perhaps the trains will take some of the goods traditionally transported by road. The Afghanis – after whom the train gets its name – used camels for outback transport once, so things do change.

There are other rules you make to keep you safe. We drove at a steady 90 kph by day and didn't drive after sunset, a sensible precaution because that is when you are most likely to come across wildlife such as kangaroos. They are renowned for the damage they can cause if you hit one or it jumps out at you and lands on the vehicle. Nothing stops the road trains so you'd have them to contend with as well. No, it's a much better idea to find your campsite and settle down long before nightfall.

This advice was given by Alison and Bill at Hervey Bay on the first leg of our journey and we stuck to it. We made sure we had a set destination planned for each day and were in situ and hooked up while there was light in the sky. We also changed over driving every two hours, touched our toes, did a few stretches, had a drink of water or a coffee if we were near a cafe – many of them offer a free cup to the driver – and kept ourselves perked up.

"REST, REVIVE, SURVIVE": everywhere, on every road, signs warn of the consequences if you drive when tired. Ian's favourite, photographed on a Victorian road, was "DON'T SLEEP & DRIVE". All of these are underlined even more by crosses or bouquets of fresh or artificial flowers laid by the roadside where one or more people died.

Each state has its own methods of making drivers aware of this terrible loss of life. At a bus stop in the country north of Margaret River in Western Australia we saw two tiny white crosses on which were the names Leanne and Louise; imagining what tragedy happened there preyed on my mind for a long time. On the limestone coast in South Australia we came upon a grouping of two black and one red posts – red is placed at the scene of an accident to indicate injury; a black post denotes death. What sadness they evoked. On the Nullarbor, three white crosses were planted side by side in the desert scrub. They are sobering sights.

Police and politicians are constantly trying to cut the road fatality rate which, at holiday times, is especially bad. Increasing use of radar and road traps and very high fines for speeding or drink driving are having an effect. Any car can be stopped at random and the driver asked to give a breath test; the consequences of being caught driving after you've been drinking alcohol are high. As wine tasting has increased in popularity the dangers are apparent, but some wineries have taken the sensible precaution of installing machines so that you can test for yourself whether you are fit to drive.

The authorities give fair warning on TV and radio of their intention, and reiterate it by the roadside on big electronic signs which spell out the cost of breaking the law. Spotting one of these makes you automatically look at your speedo to check how fast you are going – every k you are above the limit can add up to a big fine and points on your licence (which then has a knock-on effect on your insurance).

During the big summer holiday, or the long weekends, the penalties can double for a designated period of time, a tactic which appears to be working well, swelling the coffers rather than increasing the coffins.

The safest state seems to be the Northern Territory where there is no speed limit on the open road. There are also far fewer vehicles around this part of the country so that must be a contributing factor to this statistic. I found driving in cities far more hair-raising than anywhere else – in Sydney, especially, everyone drives fast. That's where I had my only ever traffic accident at the age of 20, newly-licensed and behind the wheel of our just bought, tiny Fiat 500, when I went into the back of another vehicle which stopped suddenly. From what I read in one of my former husband's books, I don't think he ever forgave me (though he does, of course, write fiction).

The strict right-lane-must-turn-right rule on all the main roads can be disconcerting if you aren't sure where you are going. It seems remarkable, but we saw only two prangs the whole time we were on the road. Both were in Victoria, and the most serious was on the Great Ocean Road – the stunning views over the Southern Ocean make it a very popular tourist route. Spectacular this road might be, but a lot of it is narrow and winding – diabolical if the sun's in the driver's eyes – and can be dangerous.

Another rule we made was always to fill up when the fuel gauge reached the halfway mark. An optimist would say it was half full but we took the pessimist's view. Even if we knew we were not far from our destination, we stopped at the nearest fuel station. And this proved a wise decision. On a couple of occasions we came to places which had run out of petrol and were awaiting a delivery (which can take time in a big country). This is one element of surprise travellers can do without.

When we signed up with the national motoring organisation (NRMA), we received an extensive list of what should be carried in a vehicle on a long trip. As space was limited in our van we had to make a judgement about the well-intentioned advice. We didn't carry extra water but always made sure we had plenty on board, either bottled or in the van's tank. By following the fuel rule we never ran out (though we got close to it on the west coast where distances between service stations are greater than other states).

In choosing how far we would travel in a day, we were guided by the NRMA road maps showing where we could fill up, and our campsite book which gave us details of sites and facilities. But we could also change our mind if we wished. After we left Douglas Daly Resort in the Northern Territory, the aim was to refuel at Victoria River and stay at Timber Creek, which are both roadhouses and caravan parks – 'roadhouse' indicates that food, fuel and accommodation are usually available. We found we had more time than we thought and, as the *Rough Guide to Australia* described these places as having 'the charm of a gym changing room', we decided there was no reason to linger. We decided to drive on into Western Australia to Kununurra, which meant we had to meet the quarantine regulations.

WESTERN AUSTRALIA IS VERY PROTECTIVE OF ITS agricultural industry – the Kimberley region is free of the fruit fly and intends to remain so – and has strict rules about what you can and can't bring in. Honey is a no-no in all the quarantine areas of Australia, so we never carried any with us. Having eaten what we could of our fresh fruit and vegetables, we chucked the rest into a bin at Timber Creek – and that's what we told the friendly inspector who greeted us at the border. He looked inside the van, opened the fridge door, then said we could go. We were just about to drive off when he suddenly asked if we had any fresh ginger. This we always had, being both good for cooking and for preventing seasickness, and I said Yes. The piece was about 1.5 cm long but I handed it over. (It is a vegetable and really I should have thrown it away with the rest.)

As we drove away we both had the same thought: bet he'll be cooking a Chinese meal tonight. Technically, of course, if we had gone into the state with it, we would have been breaking the law. How well they can police this is another matter. We'd seen the inspector remove a few oranges from the caravan ahead of us – which the couple certainly should not have had – but he let them go, probably with a caution.

Playing it safe in Australia also means being very careful about the sun. The sun's rays damage the skin and cause the deadly cancer melanoma, as well as other skin cancers. When I lived in Brisbane in 1962 I had a blemish on my cheek and a cold sore that would not go away – sores can take a long time to heal in the tropics.

The doctor sent me to a skin cancer clinic and, to this day, I can still see the men and women sitting in the waiting room, different parts of their face and head eaten away by cancer.

Since then, I have been scrupulous with skin protection, and use a sunscreen cream on any exposed skin – face, neck, back of the hands, arms, legs (especially behind the knees) – in winter and summer. But most people think a tan is good for you and regard me as weird, especially in the UK, where sunshine is a prized commodity. No one believes the golden light can possibly be dangerous, even though the facts speak for themselves. Skin cancer is on the increase there, with men as well as women appearing to be becoming more and more susceptible. The melanoma rate per 100,000 people (age standardised) in Britain each year may be low compared to that of Australia – 15.0 to 33.6 – but any increase is frightening.

Australia knows the sun is an enemy and for years has promoted a cancer prevention policy that shows that getting a tan is not healthy. All sunscreens have to be made to a standard (AS/NZS 2604 1998). As this is not always guaranteed with products sold elsewhere in the world, Australians who travel need to remember this and take their own sunscreen with them.

SPF is the length of time the spray, cream or lotion helps to prevent harmful ultra violet A and B rays from penetrating the skin. Australian sunscreens have an expiry date and these are also now included on European ones. It is known that they lose their power to protect over time; manufacturers usually say products have a three-year shelf life but who can remember when a tube or a bottle which has been stored away in a cupboard was bought.

Having red hair and skin that freckles puts me in the category 'likely to burn easily'. I could feel the sun affecting my unprotected skin after eight minutes, so I needed a high SPF to keep me protected. I was never in the sun for very long without a hat or long sleeves but even so I applied sunscreen. I found one at Woolworths, made for sun sensitive skin and broad spectrum – that is, protects against UVA and UVB rays – and water resistant for two hours. In Queensland, I looked for one that protected against both sun and mozzies.

All should be reapplied regularly, especially after swimming or sweating a lot from exercise. While I rarely swam (not being at all interested – sacrilege for an Australian!) Ian did. He has skin that tans easily and a lower SPF lotion allowed him more time in the sun but he put more on when he emerged from the sea or pool. In older people, one of the biggest problems is age spots on face, arms, bald heads and the backs of hands. If you have them already, SPF 50 might prevent them becoming more unsightly.

In Australia parents are made aware of the vulnerability of a child's skin. Children need an SPF 30+ every day. And, say the experts, babies under six months old should not be exposed to the sun at all.

For extra protection on areas where the skin is thinner, like noses and ears, sportsmen and women may use a thick zinc cream, and high SPF lip balm. All this has come about from the Aussie "slip on a shirt, slap on a hat, slop on the sunscreen" education program which was very successful in raising awareness. Fabrics which cut out UV rays are used in school uniforms and sportswear – from Clive Hamer, who had a distinguished teaching career, I learnt that some schools have a 'no hat, no sport' rule. Kids on the beach wear zingy coloured UV-protective togs that cover most of their body, and a hat. Those who aren't wearing this sun-sensible uniform are considered out of the ordinary.

When we were growing up my younger sisters and I, all with the typical fair skin of our forebears, experienced atrocious sunburn in an effort to do what all the other kids did – swim and play outdoors in the sun all day. I have no memory of being told to put on sunscreen. Perhaps it hadn't been invented then. My oldest sister Mildred used to cover herself in a mixture of olive oil and vinegar, so that she cooked like a Mediterranean pepper in the sunshine. I have always wondered if there was any connection between this and her death from ovarian cancer.

Doreen, my other older sister, died from the same cancer which is thought to have started from a melanoma behind her knee, a common site. She had lovely legs and was a 'bathing suit never got wet' type of girl – very popular among the 1940s pin-ups, as the Hollywood beauties of the time were called – but she sun-bathed. Sounds innocuous now, but it was obviously a thoroughly dangerous pastime. Intense exposure to UV before puberty leading to sunburn increases the risk of developing melanoma later in life, say Australian cancer authorities.

Many members of my family had innumerable bumps (lesions) removed from their face – my father had it done regularly – as well as from the head, shoulders, neck, chest and legs, all the result of years of inadequate protection. The most common event is playing sport in the powerful sun which every child does. Aussie GPs are now very aware of the changes to watch for and may perform mini-operations at the surgery, sending a sample to the pathology lab for testing.

Tasmania has the highest rate of skin cancer in the country, thought to be because it is on the edge of the hole that appeared in the ozone layer. This layer had one purpose: to protect the planet from the sun's rays. On this southern island (renowned for its range of weather), the sun can be very fierce when it does come out and you need skin protection.

In Hobart, relishing unexpectedly warm weather, we sought out a table in the sun to have a cup of coffee. Our waiter was most concerned. He was English, originally from Norfolk (there is also a New Norfolk in Tasmania), and he started to tell us graphic tales of what he'd seen happen to people who did just what we were doing. Instant redness, blistering within minutes and peeling. We moved under an umbrella.

Much later we saw an illustration showing the hole in the ozone layer – and Tasmania was right there in the danger zone. It is considered so important that the weather report after the news on TV gives the 'skin reddening' values – even when it is overcast, the UV rating tends to be high. The good news appears to be that the hole is closing up but for those who have lived with it since it appeared, any signs of skin changes must be worrying.

Of course, there's another side to this. We all need the sun, for it is its action on our skin that produces Vitamin D which our bodies use to make strong and healthy teeth and bones. This essential fact was highlighted during the Covid-19 pandemic when people lacking Vitamin D appeared to be susceptible to the virus. And it raised the issue of whether using skin protection products might prevent the sun from working this miracle, and that we could all be in danger of osteoporosis in old age, becoming bent and liable to fractures. The good news is that Vitamin D can be stored by the liver; keep it topped up by letting the sun onto your skin for 20 minutes daily, then slop on the sunscreen.

In the Cradle Mountain-Lake St Clair National Park in Tasmania we chanced upon some tiny bloodsuckers. The day was memorable not because of the weather (which was awful) but because we came across a wombat, lumbering along with its head down – we could almost hear it muttering away to itself as it passed within a metre of Ian.

This animal is mostly nocturnal so we were lucky to see it (though it was so dark mid-afternoon it probably thought it was night). We were walking round the Waldheim Chalet where there's a marshy forest area and an expanse of spongy ground with tall reeds and grasses in which a couple of roos popped their heads up and seemed to be watching us.

About an hour later we felt as though our legs were 'crawling' and when we pulled up our trousers found tiny black leeches, from ankle to knee. We just brushed them off, but if they'd been bigger – they swell up with the blood they suck out – we might have had to rub them off with salt or vinegar as first aid books suggest. To think that 'bleeding with leeches' used to be a body cleansing treatment in Victorian times!

Australia has many wild animals and the first rule that applies to these is that they can never be tamed. Giving food to wild animals is considered foolish, and can be the cause of tragedy. Becoming too familiar with the dingoes on Queensland's Fraser Island, by feeding them, has led to deaths and injuries. Trying to pat a kangaroo or ride a wild horse should not even be contemplated – watch, but don't touch is a good rule. Even that may not be enough. A rogue buffalo attacked a party of tourists in Nitmiluk National Park, south of Darwin, badly injuring two backpackers. These sorts of happenings are rare, but it is best to know that they do occur and to be wary.

Keeping safe from mosquitoes is a hazard in the heat, but they are also known carriers of certain diseases; thankfully not malaria in Australia. But you should keep an eye out for warnings about them. We cycled on hired bikes around Bunbury in south-west Western Australia on paths that took us up over and under bridges along-side a river. Under one of the bridges we came across a sign tacked onto a tree saying 'Ross River Fever is known to be carried by mosquitoes in this area'.

Now this is a horrible illness that you wouldn't wish on anyone. As it was a bright and sunny day, we'd put on sunscreen but it never crossed our minds that we should spray ourselves with insecticide. The problem is that no one's quite sure when the monsters strike. Most people think of mozzies being most active at night, and certainly at that time of the day called dusk, when you're sitting down with a glass of something and watching the most amazing sunsets. But could they be out in the daytime too? It is best to accept that they are.

If you get bitten by one of the little buggers carrying Ross River Fever, or another one called Dengue Fever, you have a nasty time ahead of you with night sweats and swollen joints and no hope for relief until the virus leaves your system. There is no treatment, and you feel sick and out of it for a long time. As I write, there is good news of a Dengue Fever vaccine for people aged from 9 to 45 available in some countries.

What some people get – as a result of the many tiny, and unseen, biting things in existence – is a bad reaction. Your body's fighting force does what it can about the toxin that's been suddenly introduced into your system, but when you give in to that overwhelming urge to scratch, to rub your knuckles over the area as a way of soothing the irritation, you are helping it spread. Next day you'll know it. That's when you see the nasty red welts appear and, in bad cases, this can be followed by infection, for which antibiotics may be needed.

Much worse happened to a young English woman we met in Fremantle who had such an adverse reaction to the bites that she went into anaphylactic shock. This is terrifying as it causes the throat to swell up so the person can't breathe. Fortunately there was a pharmacy nearby and her partner got her there quickly. She was given an injection of antihistamine and her symptoms subsided. We chatted about it in the laundry.

– It gave me nightmares. What if it had happened when we were crossing the Nullarbor.

She and her boyfriend had come from where we were going, and I seriously considered whether I should buy one of these self-administered syringes (shaped like a pen and simple to use) from a pharmacy. Anyone who is allergy prone, has asthma, or has a known sensitivity, to a bee sting for instance, should carry this antidote in the first aid kit. In Australia, you can be a long way from anywhere a lot of the time and you need to be able to help yourself.

We picked up some useful advice on Radio National – a terrific station for travellers as you can hear it in most parts of the country – about protecting yourself from bites. I'd already stopped using soap, which is thought to attract mozzies, and washed myself with shower gel. The news was that a high intake of Vitamin B had been shown to be effective against them. Australia has a B supplement called Berocca (which you dissolve in water) and there's also Vegemite which has a goodly amount of the vitamin. I started spreading it over my breakfast toast quite lavishly. The British Marmite is also a yeast product, which is what puts the mozzies off. I like to think having it every day gave me some protection though, by the time I'd eaten enough of it, we had dropped below the 26th parallel and it was too cold for mozzies anyway.

I'm sure there must have been mosquitoes around during my childhood though they haven't impinged on my memory. They are certainly more of a menace in the northern parts. Ticks I do remember – if we took our golden cocker spaniel for a walk in the bush we always had to check her fur and pendulous ears when we returned. And because I had long hair, my mother brushed it to make sure nothing had lodged there, and carefully examined my scalp. If a tick burrows into the skin it can be very painful and, in some instances, can be dangerous.

If ticks have been on deer – these animals are feral in many places – they can carry nasty Lyme disease.

When you have to remove a tick, you are advised to kill it with a dab of kerosene (or methylated spirit), then twist and pull it out with tweezers (the twisting pulls out the head which, if left behind, may cause inflammation).

As children we never went anywhere with bare feet. Apart from the fact that my father, being in the footwear business, thought shoeless feet was a sign of poverty, standing on a bindi-eye (or bindii) was no fun. The Oxford English Dictionary calls a bindi-eye a small perennial Australian herb with a burr-like fruit – which makes it sound quite tame. But spread through the grass and unnoticeable they are a nightmare for tender feet.

There was also another ever-present danger in the garden: funnel web and trapdoor spiders which live in the soil in cavities that are uncannily finger shaped. They are not found everywhere, only in coastal New South Wales where children learn from an early age not to go poking around in holes in the ground. As dramatic and deadly are red backed spiders which have a venomous bite. The red diamond on their back is a warning sign that is best not ignored. Watch out for them on the eastern coast where they be found indoors as well as out and are most dangerous in summer.

The biggest spider is the Huntsman and your first sighting does tend to give the heart a terrible lurch. It is reassuring to know that it won't harm you but as it is about the size of a side plate it can be daunting. It is a tropical spider that finds its way indoors and chooses a spot high on a wall to await its prey: flies, which are a constant pest everywhere, particularly in dry times. Most

Australian houses are fitted with door and window screens to keep them out, but some still get in so if you had a resident Huntsman all would be well!

It is a pity it doesn't turn its attention to the cockroach, top of the hate list, and found all over the country. There are even ones that fly! They are one of the world's oldest inhabitants and while there is no evidence that they carry germs they are completely unlovable.

Wherever you travel in Australia you'd be well advised to shake out your shoes in the morning before putting them on, in case any of a number of creepy crawlies has sought refuge overnight. There's a particular spider with a white part on its body which is a known carrier of a flesh-eating disease that has caused utter misery. So don't put your foot in a shoe without making sure nothing has lodged inside. Or follow the advice of a New Guinea veteran: leave your socks in your shoes overnight, and check each one when you get up. A good shake does the trick.

Snakes, of course, have a very bad reputation and, when you are doing any bush walking, you must watch where you put your feet. Never step over a log – a snake could be lying on the other side. Snakes are generally shy, but will lash out if surprised. Step onto the log and look down before you move on.

Last but not least are the man-and-woman-eating saltwater crocodiles – salties – which are best avoided at all costs. Inland rivers and creeks at the Top End are not safe for swimming or wild camping too close to the water. Not ever.

7

THE IMPORTANCE OF FACILITIES

KNOW WHERE THE GOING IS GOOD

BEFORE WE LEFT London for Australia we met a couple who had spent three months travelling in an old Jeep from Adelaide up to the Red Centre, then across to Broken Hill and down to Sydney. He was nearly 70, tall, heavily-built and almost immobilised by arthritis; she was a few years younger, slight in figure, and agile – both had been ballet dancers in their younger years. We were amazed at their disregard for comfort.

They told us how they slept out under the stars, how their air conditioning unit packed up soon after buying the Jeep, and how they threw themselves into the pools at the camps where they stopped to cool down. Originally from Adelaide, they had lived for many years in Oslo and had done a lot of travelling around Europe with their children, always with a tent, so they were used to accepting whatever facilities were available. In many Continental countries, these range from highly sophisticated to alarmingly sparse, and we felt it was praise indeed that camping places they'd found in Australia met with their approval.

They'd probably have bought the Landcruiser I'd been tempted by but which would have been totally impractical, and much too hard work for the length of time we'd be travelling. And we weren't concerned that our Hiace didn't have toilet or washing facilities – until we listened to others. My sister Gai and her husband Bob, keen caravanners, carried a Porta-potty in their caravan and, lo and behold, so did Alison and Bill who we met at Hervey Bay.

On the JustinCase principle it wasn't a bad idea. If we wanted to free camp, for instance, there wouldn't be a loo around and there might be unwelcome wildlife if you were squatting on the ground.We didn't know what we might encounter. Burnt into my memory was the time in the late 1960s when I'd stayed at a ruin in Provence that was in the process of being rebuilt from the ground up. It didn't even have the dratted holes in the ground, still found in parts of rural France, cities included. To use the 'facilities' at this building site you took the shovel and went out to the hill behind the house, an area swarming with scorpions. As it was impossible to watch front and rear at the same time when squatting, a serious case of constipation was the most usual result.

Spurred on by my imagination, we checked out camping equipment in Rockhampton. There was a range to choose from, and prices varied markedly. Ours needed to be slim enough to be stowed behind the driver's seat – the last remaining place in the van with nothing in it.

Our choice, called a Portaloo, was like a folded camp stool; when opened, a plastic bag fitted inside. After use, the bag could be emptied and thrown away.

In the event, during nearly seven months of travel, it was only brought into play twice as our constitutions were sturdy enough to survive from 10 at night to 8 in the morning. Both were occasions when the weather was appalling and the on-site WCs too far to get to in a hurry.

The one I remember most was the basic and bleak site at Nullarbor, just into South Australia, which dingoes visited at night in the hope of finding food. We'd seen them on the other side of the road when we arrived in the early evening; in fact, we arrived later than we thought. We had forgotten about the time difference between Western Australia and South Australia – and either there had not been a sign to remind us or we had missed it. Once we were in the van and hooked up to the electricity, I wasn't inclined to leave it for anything. Incidentally, it is much more usual to have unbelievable heat on the Nullarbor, with no rain at all and extreme water restrictions. We only once saw a sign showing a tap, indicating water nearby, so always make sure you have plenty on board.

Our other buys which paid off were waterproof slip-ons (bought from Big W) which we could wear in the shower. Thongs (called flip-flops in the UK, and jandals in New Zealand) would have done equally well, and would have been cheaper too, but neither of us likes the feel of the bit between the toes. Though there wasn't a site we visited that wasn't cleaned daily, there is always the chance of getting athlete's foot or picking up a verruca, both known hazards of watery places such as swimming pools and communal showers.

For athlete's foot, a fungal infection which usually causes the skin to peel between the toes, we carried a tube of Canestan in our first aid kit and some medicated talcum powder. The infection can be difficult to get rid of if the toes aren't kept dry. In medical terms, a verruca is a wart, but that hardly describes the tenderness and pain felt when one of these irritating afflictions lodges on the ball of the foot. Medicated discs which cover the area are the most efficacious treatment, but it may take several changes of disc before the verruca is zapped. Being careful not to get either was, we found, the best option.

After staying at many different campsites I concluded that ablution blocks are mostly designed by non-travellers. I doubt whether the architects or engineers who drew up the plans had actually experienced daily washing in such a fashion. I was told there are rules and regulations about what is acceptable (to meet one, two or three-star standards, for instance), but the amount of space you get in your cubicle varies enormously.

Some have a curtain – at Croydon, a delightful little place in inland Queensland which has its history displayed on attractive street signs – the curtains had cheerful pink candy stripes and stopped our clothes from getting splashed. Others may only have a bench for your belongings and the water goes everywhere. In some places there wasn't a bench at all, just hooks on the back of the door, so there was nowhere to put the foot you were drying with the towel. That's when you get hopping mad. It is the height of luxury when you find a bench with hooks above to hang your clothes on, a splash-proof divider and, inside the shower area, somewhere to put your soap or gel, nailbrush and shampoo.

The trickiest showers are those where the controls and showerhead are placed on a back wall so that the water hurtles straight at you and your arm (or arms, if you are turning on hot and cold at the same time) gets wet when adjusting the water temperature. In warm weather this is not a problem; you just undress before turning the shower on. In chilly weather, I wasn't as keen to disrobe so quickly. Wearing my waterproof jacket until I got the temperature right was the best solution I came up with – at Cradle Mountain in Tasmania, as it happens. Fortunately, we didn't come across many like this!

The best showers were at Cooinda in Kakadu National Park and, while there were no curtains in the cubicles, the space was well planned. Aussies in their own homes are fond of 'wet rooms' where there are no walls to the shower and where the water can run away down a central floor drain. The room is usually big enough so that the clothes you've taken off can be placed where they won't get drenched. Those who make a living by designing shower cubicles in ablution blocks should think the same way.

The better the conditions at campsites, the more popular they are – roughing it is not in the lexicon of travellers today. Most places have a bank of basins, generally separated from the showers, with mirrors above. This could be why we never found any queues for the showers. People went in and out quickly and then finished off their *toilette* at the sinks. All very sensible. And of course, in water-conscious Australia, you leave the tap running while cleaning your teeth.

On quite a few campsites, particularly in large towns and cities, you are given a key to the ablution block, or have to punch in a number (you receive this when you book in). This is supposedly a security measure, to prevent people coming in off the streets and using the showers and loos but, in practice, the door is often wedged open by those who have forgotten the key or the day's code.

Probably the most basic site we encountered was at the Hi-way Inn Roadhouse, at the junction of the Stuart and Carpentaria Highways in the Northern Territory – along which huge roadtrains roared. It was nothing more than a large paddock with scrubby-trees on the perimeter, and the facilities were an unkempt shed with cowboy-style swing doors in the showers and difficult-to-close locks on the loos. But there was water and the cost was low.

There was a bar and food at the roadhouse if we wanted it, but there was no on-site manager, just as there wasn't at Sheffield, a marvellous Tasmanian town with brightly painted murals on most of the buildings. The site was small, with a couple of loos and showers each for men and women. We arrived to find a mother frantically trying to get her young daughter out of the block she'd accidentally locked herself into, taking the key with her. Fortunately, our key worked and out she came with no harm done.

We had been on the road for some time before we discovered the 'en suite site' – where you have your own lock-up shower room, occasionally even a sink and a hob, in a unit alongside your parking spot. These cost a little more a night but we found they were worth it when the weather was inclement.

Our first encounter with this thoughtful extra was in the Northern Territory, at a campsite/resort at Katherine that we called Knotts Landing (after the 1980s TV show) though it is, in fact, Knotts Crossing. It almost spoiled us. The space inside was bigger than the whole of our van and we were able to set up our folding table and chairs, giving us somewhere to eat, sit and read or play Scrabble in comfort in the evenings – all for $22.50 a night!

We were tempted out to try the delectable desserts at Katie's Bistro (my choice was a chocolate heart filled with passionfruit icecream, cream, strawberries and blueberries) where we overheard an Italian, from a coach party, saying that when he returned to Italy after years in Australia he was called a kangaroo.

The Knotts Crossing unit was the most generously sized we came across, but all of them provided privacy and shelter. At Bunbury, south of Perth, we stayed at a campsite called Koombana Bay Resort and our ensuite smelled of fresh paint. It was an unusual design, with a shower area that was capacious enough for five people, but had no basin to wash yer face in. There was space for our table and chairs, plus a sink and kitchen area for cooking. I itched to do some reconstruction: just a couple of simple changes would have made a huge difference.

It was a very pleasant resort, well laid out and well placed to get into the town and for the walks that the council has set up to encourage people to help themselves to health. Heart-smart Bunbury is designed to be discovered easily either on foot or by bike – we did both.

There's a boardwalk that takes you through the mangroves, with information displayed so you can find out more about the area and what to look for around you.

The walk to the Dolphin Discovery Centre is about 5 km. The bottle-nose dolphins come in between 8 and 12 each morning to be fed by the rangers who also keep an eye on the watching visitors, warning them not to try and touch these creatures whose 'faces' always seem to wear a smile. The most famous Bunbury dolphin was Ileuka (which means dolphin in Japanese), a regular visitor to the bay for many years. On this October day Ian waded into the water (as cold as that of England, he said) as Ileuka and friends frolicked around him and several pelicans glided nearby, ever-ready to swoop on any offerings the dolphins missed.

The animals play up to the attention, and obviously enjoy themselves – the previous evening we watched a couple of them dipping and jumping out of the water in the inlet behind the camp where several long racing canoes were exercising. People always talk about the dolphins of Monkey Mia further up the coast, but it is worthwhile remembering that they are also at Bunbury – and it's a very nice place to visit too.

The most unusual experience of an ensuite was at a caravan park about 3 km from Bremer Bay in southern Western Australia. The setting couldn't be faulted, and we liked the way the ensuite sites were arranged like the spokes of a wheel. As we had arrived there mid-afternoon, we had lots of time to investigate the local beaches – well known as viewing points for Southern Right whales (so named because they were the 'right' ones to kill for their high oil content). The white sands were completely deserted and we saw nothing except Customs Watch signs warning of the penalties of illegal entry. At Point Ann there was a very cold breeze – we were, after all, looking across the Southern Ocean to Antarctica – and we decided we'd be better off back at the camp.

What a sight greeted us – the air was fluttering with an invasion of large brown moths and the ensuite was filled with them! I know that butterflies are deaf, and I think moths must be as well, as it took ages for us to get rid of them by flapping our arms and using towels to swat them. Once the door was shut Ian worked quickly to stuff the air hole above it with newspapers and a towel. Eventually we were able to settle down inside though the moths tenaciously kept breaking through, seeping in below and above the door. This was at the end of October and, while no one had an explanation for the inundation, it was not at all uncommon we were told. Moths like these are good tucker, according to the indigenous Australians.

Obtaining a space at campsites around Hobart (indeed any of the Aussie cities) can be tricky. As we wanted to be there for new year, we had the foresight to book at Bowen Park, a Big 4 cabin-park a few ks out of town but on a bus route so that we could get in and out of the city easily. There were just two ensuite sites, and we secured one of them, and felt very lucky to have found it. The cabins are obviously popular with families, as they are self contained, and having an ensuite site put our five-day stay on a par with them.

Apart from efficient ablution facilities, most campsites at the Top End also have pools, not always large, but big enough to allow you to cool off. Probably the most glamorous we found was at the man-made town of Jabiru (in Kakadu National Park, but built to support those people who were working in the iron ore mines before the park was established). Our campsite was spacious, with lots of grassy areas and trees for shade, but the *pièce de résistance* was a most attractive swimming pool with palms, a flamboyant shade sail, a bar and bistro.

By contrast the pool at the town site in Halls Creek, at the heart of Western Australia's dusty outback cattle country, may have been small but was very welcoming after a drive through this arid and deserted region. We didn't realise at the time that we had a tiny connection with this place through our son in law. Tom's father Nick was a long-time employee of the Vestey family from the UK who owned vast cattle stations in this region and also in Venezuela and other parts of South America.

Lord Samuel Vestey, the third baron, had an Australian link: his mother was a granddaughter of Dame Nellie Melba, the country's famous operatic soprano. (Her peripatetic career is remembered by the Oz saying 'more farewells than Dame Nellie Melba'.) Vesty's expansion into meat processing came about via his ownership of the Blue Star Shipping Line, started by his father and uncle, which in the 1930s shipped frozen beef around the world.

After abattoirs and cold storage facilities were obtained Vestey became the largest exporter of chilled beef, much of it leaving from the port of Wyndham to the north of Halls Creek. Following the UK's exit from the EU, a trade deal was struck with Australia which involves the importation of beef, possibly from this very area.

Vestey's Australian assets were sold in 1992 but the prosperous enterprise continues.

If you are looking for a natural swimming experience you should seek out thermal springs. I'd written on my JustinCase list Innot Hot Springs in Queensland, which we discovered on the way from Cairns to Undara Volcanic National Park (where a sign greets you with 'Population nominal').

Innot's campsite has seven pools of differing temperatures, from cold through to hot. The coolest one is swimming pool size; some of the others can only take a few people at a time. Three are used for therapy (which means you sit, rather than swim, in them). The minerals they contain are thought to be of therapeutic value for joint problems and skin conditions, and hence attract coach loads of visitors from Atherton, the main town on the Tableland.

The campsite also has a tennis court and an open-air spa over which groups of green parrots swarmed, their squawks competing with the honking of the Canada geese gathered around the eerie, greyish-brown mud pools just beyond the site. This was our first campsite away from the eastern coast and a wonderful introduction to the inland.

The Northern Territory town of Mataranka became renowned through Jeannie Gunn's autobiographical novel *We of the Never Never* written in 1908 and recounting the life of a pioneering woman. It's on the Stuart Highway, north of Tennant Creek between Daly Waters and Katherine – an area with many World War II connections, such as landing strips for aircraft, and hospitals. The healing qualities of Mataranka's thermal pool were useful in restoring the health of pilots during the war, and to find it after driving through the hot and barren landscape is like a miracle.

It has gorgeously blue water warmed naturally to 34C and is shaded by palms. The extensive and well-maintained grounds of the Mataranka Resort are very popular with holidaymakers (you can stay there, eat there, picnic there), but the pool itself is actually in the adjacent Elsey National Park. It is always open and we paid nothing to swim in it. Which made it especially delightful. Thanks to the Ghan, the train line between Adelaide and Darwin, this part of the Northern Territory just waits to be discovered. But while the train may whisk passengers through in expensive comfort, it is the independent traveller in his or her own vehicle who can stop at will and enjoy the country at its natural best.

Water is a major preoccupation in Australia. At Clairview in Queensland, a quiet and dramatically beautiful site quite reminiscent of Mont St Michel in France. It has 7-metre tides and a vast stretch of sand that remains when the tide is out. There are signs everywhere reminding visitors "Water is liquid gold". Here the loos are septic tanks with instructions about what you can and can't put in them. Everyone relies on corrugated iron tanks for drinking water and bore water (from underground) for everything else, like washing machines in which you have to use specially supplied powder.

Amazingly, in our travels we came across only one site where the showers were restricted by time and abruptly came to a stop. People rarely stay in them for long anyway. In most cases there was a good flow – even at Coober Pedy in South Australia. Here, as in the other desert towns, you wash in bore water and it is useful to have washing gel and shampoo that can cope with it. It took us some time to realise this and my hair looked quite odd for weeks, its texture like that of a horse's mane and standing up as though I'd been electrified.

Campsites make distinctions between where you wash your clothes and your dishes. In the Darwin camp we stayed at a sign in the laundry said anyone washing dishes there would be instantly ejected. Most sites have a campers' kitchen area where you can wash up, or there will be a bank of sinks with hot water supplied. The laundries have very good washing machines, mostly top loaders. They use more water than front loaders, but are less likely to go wrong, have simple controls, and the job's done in 20 minutes. They operate on the coin-in-the-slot method, and prices vary around the country – it cost more when there were fewer machines.

At a campsite in Fremantle the slots were constantly broken into for the money. We sympathised with the park owners. Our only brush with thieves was in Perth where the van's side top window was smashed to allow entry. This window was very small, so whoever got in had to be tiny. The police put it down to opportunistic young kids (it was school holidays). Older children are left in charge of younger ones and, when they come across a sitting duck – as our van was, in a railway car park – they break the glass and slip a toddler through it. Little'uns, it seems, are especially adept at opening doors from the inside.

The other essential at campsites are the loos, and Australia has some that are quite ingenious. This country is the home of the dual flush – one flush for number one, a second for number two – invented to prevent wasting precious water, and popular in British plumbing as well. Australian loo paper is particularly basic, usually a single sheet, but it was plentiful at every site.

If you travel in remote areas you'll come across bush loos which are accompanied by interesting instructions for use. In Cape National Park in Western Australia, the notice said:

"G'day, I'm your OZ BUSH LOO.

1. Lift the seat and wet the inside of the bowl with the brush.
2. Do what you came in for.
3. Wash inside the bowl again and close the lid.
4. Please don't tip brush water down me and no chemical toilets. Yuck! They kill my good bacteria and make me smell. Keep the door closed. Thanks, from the next user."

Right next to this, on the wall behind, was a hand printed message:

"THE 'FLY' ON YOUR SANDWICH PROBABLY CAME FROM THIS TOILET, WHEN THE LID WAS LEFT OPEN BY SOMEONE. PLEASE CLOSE THE LID AND SHUT THE DOOR."

At Georgetown, in inland Queensland, the public loo had a warning placed so you couldn't miss it: "TO STOP GREEN FROGS, please put the toilet seat down!"

From this you might guess that green frogs are a particular menace in the area (though we didn't see any).

There was no mention of cane toads, the ugliest things imaginable and completely out of control in the cane-growing areas, and spreading. They are an example of 'distressful ecology': making something worse when attempting to make it better. The intention, when the toads were imported from South America in the 1930s, was to rid the canefields of a devastating beetle plague. This failed, the beetles remained a problem and the toads thrived, their poisonous secretions from neck glands useful against predators and disastrous for the native wildlife. Never touch one, alive or dead, as you too may become a victim of the poison. There is a constant search to find a way of eradicating this dreaded feral species.

The most modern loo we came across was at Lake Chisholm Forest Reserve on the west coast of Tasmania. It was a serene setting and the composting toilet block didn't look at all out of place amidst the fantastic trees which have stood there for centuries. Such a good idea: a shared amenity – sawdust from the mills is used to break down matter. With tourism a major money spinner, Australia has made providing loos a priority, particularly in remote but accessible spots. Not many people would be keen on using nature's resources in a country where you never know what might be on the ground.

After staying at a few campsites we realised it was important, when booking in, to know how close our allotted area was to an ablution block. If you're in a hurry, even a hundred yard dash is too far. Quite the longest walk was at the site at Coral Bay in Western Australia, which we had booked by phone. Did we want a water view? Yes, we said, not knowing that the facilities were in the process of being expanded as the area was becoming increasingly popular.

Things are generally pretty laid back at campsites. You don't get any feeling of prudery or embarrassment, for instance. I saw women and men in dressing gown and slippers (some women had rollers in their hair). Others were fully dressed, some just wrapped in a towel or sarong. Life at an Aussie campsite is really just like being in one big holiday camp, but your privacy is respected.

8

KEEPING IN TOUCH

MOD CONS AND DOT.COMS

ONE OF OUR first buys when we arrived in Sydney was a mobile phone, using Optus pay-as-you-go, which we expected would help keep us in touch with our family and friends during our travels, including sending text messages for anything important. It didn't work out that way. For much of the time that we were crossing Australia — from east to west and then down the long west coast — there was no signal to be had. Thankfully, at the state capital Perth, when we needed to contact the police after our van was broken into, the mobile worked. As that was the only 'emergency' we had in seven months, we should consider ourselves lucky.

At an early stage we had discussed the idea of a two-way HF radio, which is recommended for people going off road in 4WD vehicles. Really it should be mandatory. The cost of search and rescue missions in outback areas is enormous, and being able to keep in touch would be both time and money saving. As we intended our journey to be very straightforward, the cost of hiring a unit like this wouldn't have been worthwhile. For the more adventurous, however, this radio is especially useful as it is tuned to the Royal Flying Doctor Service (RFDS) which, in the words my father would have used, is worth its weight in gold.

If you aren't well when you're on the move you can get emergency help at any public hospital. In the west, where these are few and far between, there's a generous system of helping a stranger in need. When we were crossing the Nullarbor – during which time the mobile was not operational – I knew I was going to have to seek some medical help for an infection which was causing some discomfort. I hoped I'd be all right until we reached South Australia, but I changed my mind at Eucla, a small town 12 km from the border.

It was seeing a road sign to a nursing centre that made me inquisitive. It was the first such sign I had noticed, and, because I had been a nurse for a short time, I wanted to find out about the Silver Chain Nursing Association which I'd never heard of. The consulting room was part of nurse Maria's home and there was just one other patient, a local with his leg in plaster. After he'd been attended to, I explained my problem and Maria said she could help.

She asked lots of questions about my health, took my blood pressure and temperature, then I gave a urine sample which she tested before ringing the doctor. From the consultation it was decided I needed antibiotics which Maria was able to supply from her medical store. There was no charge, though she was happy to accept $20 as a donation. As I left she urged me to drink more water, at least eight glasses a day (about a litre), saying:

– It's easy to get dehydrated out here. Drive carefully.

I was impressed with the procedure. Maria was cheerful and friendly and, backed by the doctor at the end of the phone, could obviously handle any problem. Hers must be quite a lonely job – Eucla's not a big place, though it has much in its favour after the long stretch of desert, with the first trees we'd seen for a while and a fantastic view over the Southern Ocean (which used to be called the Antarctic Ocean). It also has a splendid multi-armed signpost that left us in no doubt as to *where* we were: Esperance 918km and Norseman 712km behind us; Ceduna 495km and Port Augusta 965km ahead.

The Silver Chain charity, which has as its slogan 'Caring in the Community', has many outposts in Western Australia offering nursing and accident and emergency care – Eucla is the furthest east (1,435km from Perth). It's a non-profit group which started from a letter written to Perth's *Western Mail* in 1904 by a Mr Arthur Grundy who, having chanced upon a silver watch chain in the bush, envisaged a community organisation that linked city and country.

From this idea Silver Chain was born; in 1905, children were encouraged to donate a silver shilling and to become links in a silver chain of friendship. By 1907 there were 1,500 Silver Chain link members and enough money to employ a full-time district nurse – now there are over 4,000 staff and many volunteers to help people in all the states (except Northern Territory and Tasmania) to live their best life at home or in the community. Residents and visitors can rely on the skill and expertise of the Silver Chain Advanced Community Nurse in remote agricultural centres, on offshore fishing atolls and isolated mining communities. And in smaller places, as we found.

In the heart of Australia, people in outlying communities have to rely on the flying doctors. The RFDS is proud of the fact that there is nowhere in the 80% of Australia it covers where a patient cannot be reached within two hours – this is less time than it can take the average city or suburban dweller to contact his or her doctor by phone and get an appointment. The RFDS also has healthcare clinics in various places, which people travel hundreds of ks, usually on unsealed roads, to attend.

If they can't get to a clinic but need a medical consultation, they can get on the phone or radio and talk directly to a doctor. To help this diagnosis from a distance, the person describes his or her symptoms – including pain or injury – and which part is affected, by reference to a 'body chart'. This has front and back views detailing the different organs. It's a bit like painting by numbers, but the chart and symptoms enable the doctor to decide whether the patient needs to be picked up and taken to a hospital or whether he or she can be treated at home, in which case medical help might not need to be sent.

If this latter option is chosen, the doctor prescribes from the 'bush pharmacy', a medical chest of numbered drugs and other medicines which is supplied free by the Department of Health and Family Services to people isolated by distance. The doctor tells the patient which number is apt, and talks through how and when medication should be taken. It's very clever.

The RFDS centre at Port Augusta, South Australia, is a great place to visit. You can watch a video in which you visit inland Australia with a pilot, doctor and nurse so you can appreciate a few of the amazing jobs they do. There's lots of display material about the planes and the people, starting from the Very Reverend John Flynn whose idea came to fruition way back in 1928. At school I learnt about Flynn of the Inland who worked as a missionary with the Presbyterian Church's Australian Inland Mission (AIM) before World War I. At that time only two doctors served 300,000 sq km of Western Australia and 1,500,000 sq km of the Northern Territory. Today the service Flynn started – a combination of medicine, aviation and radio – provides health treatment for people in an area larger than that of Western Europe.

Though it gets regular financial aid both from state and federal governments, it is not sufficient for all the RFDS does. As it has to rely on the generosity of trusts, donations and public appeals, buying coffee and cake in the café or choosing items from the gift shop at the centre is a contribution as welcome as any other.

Also at Port Augusta is the School of the Air which caters for students who live up to 1,000km away, many of them on remote cattle or sheep stations. It provides schooling for children travelling with their families who are employed in highway repair gangs, work in circuses, live in mining camps or are on a trip around Australia. The School of the Air also extends its help to adults who may want to complete their secondary education to improve chances of employment.

In the old days the means of communication was pedal radio, as it was with the RFDS, but today both share the same modern form of high frequency radio, either solar powered or operated by generator. From ages five to 12 children receive correspondence from their School of the Air teachers and daily lessons on-air in all the subjects taught in city and town primary schools. Other modern technology is used, such as video.

The school, in fact, was one of the first in the world to use personal computers linked through the existing telephone network with an interactive video/audio/data system. Secondary students keep in touch with each other and their teachers, using telephone modems, interactive computers and fax machines.

You can visit the Port Augusta HQ and pay to see this happening, watching through glass into a studio where a teacher is giving a lesson. Depending on how much distance is involved, the teachers see their students at least once a year, either by driving a 4WD vehicle or hitching a lift with the RFDS. I was so impressed I wanted to apply for a job! The problem is that there are fewer children being taught this way today and those of secondary school age tend to go to boarding school rather than use the service. But it is a wonderful method of keeping isolated people up to date and abreast of what's happening in the world outside.

The overall plan of the Federal Government is to get Australia networked, providing the internet through libraries. For us this was terrific as, with the mobile inoperable much of the time, we relied on email to keep in touch with family and friends. In the cities there's no problem using any number of internet cafes, but we didn't know what we'd find inland. We first discovered the government plan at Georgetown in Queensland, where we'd stopped for a coffee at Teresa's Museum, a cafe featuring local bits and bobs more quirky than valuable.

When we saw a sign on the library saying *Internet* we went in and found a woman in charge of two monitors (of the computer variety – in Australia, monitors are also very unusual animals, like very large goannas with long legs). She was friendly, welcoming and so chuffed to be doing the job she told us how it had come about without any prompting.

– I was a builder's mate until my partner died. I never thought I'd get another job.

She was full of enthusiasm about National Networking Australia which gave her the necessary training and a new lease of life. She encourages everyone who comes in to get connected. It was fast, and we were on to Hotmail in a flash. While Ian received and replied, I looked around the tiny library for Australian authors, but books by Catherine Cookson, Danielle Steele and Jeffrey Archer filled the shelves. Of course, those of Frank Moorhouse (in whom I had a personal interest), and other prize-winning authors like Thomas Keneally, Peter Carey and Tim Winton might all have been loaned out.

I found the internet in the library at Halls Creek, Western Australia, where at the monitor next to me a young Aboriginal girl was checking out a website for details of how to be a model. At about her age I was discovering the world through an English magazine called *Girl*,

L M Montgomery's lovely book *Anne of Green Gables*, and Elsie J Oxenham's fictional stories about girls at English boarding schools.

Apart from a dark-haired Australian called Bunty who, I seem to remember, promoted Pelaco men's shirts in newspaper advertisements (and went on, in fact, to wed an English lord), models belonged to a rarified world and didn't have the celebrity status of today. For this teenager in the desert they were as near as the screen. I wished her good luck as I left – and I really hope she succeeded in her dream.

The internet was a blessing but we also kept in touch using poste restante, the service run by all Post Offices around the world, and it works well in Australia, so long as you know when you will be where and for how long. You simply tell family and friends to write to you care of poste restante at whatever Post Office – and give its zip code, found in the back of the state phone book.

Mail is kept for a month and, if not picked up, is either sent back or forwarded somewhere else, if that's the arrangement you have made because you're on the move. Internal mail in Australia is notoriously slow, so nothing gets anywhere very quickly. All post from abroad goes to Sydney first, it seems, and is sent on from there. It caused us some anguish.

At Katherine PO, Ian received a letter that required an immediate reply. It came from the Benefits Agency in the UK (sent first to my sister in New South Wales, whose address we had given as ours while in Australia, and she had forwarded it). It didn't pull any punches.

"You have been randomly selected to receive this form to check whether there have been any changes in your circumstances which

may affect the benefit you are getting. The declaration must be filled in and sent back to us in the envelope provided within two months of the date of this letter. Airmail should be used so the form is returned to us in time. IF YOU DO NOT DO THIS PAYMENT OF YOUR BENEFIT WILL BE SUSPENDED."

No envelope was included and the letter was dated two months earlier! The endangered 'benefit' (the quaint English way of describing something you contribute to all your working life) was Ian's retirement pension and, to prevent it being stopped, his only hope was to fill in the form, get it witnessed and send it with a covering letter by fax. Fortunately, a pharmacist was considered of witness status and it was all done quickly.

Would you believe that exactly the same letter and form were awaiting me at Perth poste restante? Amazingly, I too had been "randomly selected" three months before. We repeated the response: another pharmacist, another fax, and fingers crossed. We were at the mercy of this government agency as our pensions were being used to pay credit card and other bills by direct debit in the UK – a sensible system for anyone out of from the country for a length of time. It would have been calamitous if the money wasn't in our accounts.

Neither of us heard another word from the agency (which is now the Department of Work and Pensions) and on our return, while we felt like complaining about the situation they'd put us in, we agreed that the wisest thing to do was to put it down to experience. But it goes against the grain that the retirement pension you've worked for can be given and taken away at will.

Pensions are, in fact, a difficult subject for the British who retire to Australia (or New Zealand, South Africa or

Canada) – their pensions are frozen at the amount received when they make the move, with no annual increments based on inflation.

Once they have settled in these countries, they may find the lower cost and higher standard of living offset that loss but, over the years, the lack of extra income can be a problem, particularly in times of high inflation. Several attempts have been made by British pensioners living in the former outposts of empire to force the British government to alter the system though none has yet succeeded. The Australian government used to make up the difference for British seniors settled there, but no longer do so.

Modern technology – mobiles, faxes, internet – certainly makes life and communications easier today. My past came back with a rush when we visited a museum at Stanley in Tasmania where, on display, was an Edison recording machine which I hadn't seen since I was a junior reporter at Bathurst in New South Wales in the early 1960s. This is the machine on which the newspaper received the national stories from a Sydney agency, with the sound being etched into what looked like an asbestos roll.

My job was to put on headphones and play the roll back, typing up the news to be set in hot metal by the linotype operator. How archaic the machine looked (and probably was way back then as well, as teleprinters were in use). This really was history as none of those machines – recorder, typewriter, linotype, teleprinter – is used now, and the processes of printing and publishing and disseminating news have changed out of all recognition. Knowing about printer's ink, galleys and forms makes you a dinosaur today.

I grew up in a country town and worked in three different country towns, and I found them all very parochial, very closed to outside influences. The newspapers printed local news and any national news had to be warranted. A disaster, such as a murder or train or plane crash, might be given space if locals were involved; the Melbourne Cup, the country's top horse racing event, would make it but not much else. Abroad was everywhere outside the town, and overseas was well beyond anyone's concern. In Queensland, 'south' is below Surfers' Paradise.

But times have changed, and I think the prime catalyst was the arrival of television, which brought entertainment and news – with pictures – into the home of everyone who had a TV set. Now, no matter where you live on the southern continent, the rest of the world can be there, too. Sport is always popular and you can soak up endless hours of celebrities or the soaps, universal levellers that owe much to Australia. My children grew up in London with *Neighbours* and *Home and Away* and today no celebrity list – of actors, musicians, entertainers, writers, painters, sports people – would be complete without an Aussie or four.

I certainly got the impression while we were travelling that Australia was getting closer to being one country rather than separate states – though each state is fiercely proud of its own identity. Local prejudices and interests are still there, and will probably always be there, because the country is just so blooming big – and it must help you feel part of your community if you know what is going on in your own backyard. Certainly, international events have a great influence today than they did when I lived there. News stories involving asylum seekers, terrorism and war affect all Australians, as does the coronavirus pandemic. It was a challenge for the states to come up with ways of protecting themselves while keeping the country connected.

9

PARADISE FOR FOOD LOVERS

TREAT YOUR TASTEBUDS EVERYWHERE

"GOING INTO A HOME" was considered a dire fate when I was growing up, a sign of a family's rejection of responsibility, rather than a practical solution when a person needed close care. Ageing in this way remains a problem in many countries of the world. Dad, trying to make light of it when Mum's father became infirm in his late 80s and Aunty Norah moved him into a Little Sisters of the Poor nursing home, said:

– I can't think of anything better than sitting round all day with people your own age playing cards, telling jokes, watching TV, listening to music, sharing yarns.

My mother, a solitary woman, couldn't think of anything worse. Which made her children feel sad when this was the option she chose in 1987, a year after my father died, when she knew she could no longer live by herself. She wanted independence, refusing to live with me in London, or with either of my sisters, Pam in New Zealand or Gai in Australia.

The Shoalhaven Retirement Village, across the road from his beloved bowling club, and within earshot of a primary school where children's voices could be heard, could have been the sort of place that Dad imagined – but ageing is rarely kind. In its concept the village was award-winning, but theory and reality did not meet. Most people had been forced into living there, affected by body-and-soul-destroying conditions.

There was one section, at ground level, for those who were old and at different stages of wellness; going upwards were floors for those who required constant care. Socialising wasn't a priority. Mum's 'apartment' was on the ground floor. Apart from having occasional health problems, which bedrest usually put right after a few days, she was physically full of the joys of spring in comparison to many others. She didn't even start using a stick for support until she was 98.

Some research I found concluded that people from Manchester have a shorter life than other parts of the UK, but my little mother (she was never taller than 5ft, in the old measure, and shrank as she aged) who was born nearby, in Cheadle, was an obvious exception. At 100, with her hair done, nails freshly painted and wearing lipstick and shoes with heels, she was the centre of attention for her birthday.

She came to Australia at the age of 12 with her parents and younger sister Norah, all of whom lived to great ages. My grandmother, born in Chester, died at 89, my grandfather, from Liverpool, at 92, and my aunt, born in Manchester, reached beyond her centenary as well. Originally, the family was to go to the US on the *Titanic* in 1912, but Grandad – or JJ, as he was usually called –

couldn't get berths and booked them on a boat to Australia the next year instead. It probably ensured their longevity. My mother never returned to England but her genes are spread around the world – in the UK, New Zealand and Canada – through offspring of six of her seven children.

It was a terrific party, though with her long and short-term memories gone I doubt she knew much about why she was being lauded or who most of the people around her were. She certainly didn't know her surviving four children, her daughter-in-law and three sons-in-law who'd gathered at the retirement home for the celebration. But what did it matter. Local dignitaries read out letters of congratulation from the Queen, the Governor-General, Governor, Prime Minister, Premier of New South Wales and all sorts of other figures. Everyone added their puff to help her blow out the candles, so many of them that it looked as though the cake was on fire. My mother giggled and smiled through it all – 'happy demented' was the phrase used.

I always kept in touch with her by phone though it was rare to have a meaningful conversation. During a call in 1997 she said Frank had been to the home to see his frail parents, both of whom needed full time nursing, which I thought very sad. She was pleased that her former son-in-law remembered her though she didn't really recognise him (her sight was badly impaired by macular disease). I was the only one of her children who divorced, but I don't think we ever talked about it. Like the rest of my family she probably thought we had just been too young.

I was quite tearful when we said our farewells as I

doubted I would see her again. A few weeks after her 101st birthday she died in her sleep and I received the news by email, on the other side of the world. What a difference a century makes! In 1901 when she was born international communications were primitive indeed; today they defy understanding.

Before we left Nowra, because the winter's day was warm and sunny, we called in at the local pharmacy to buy sunscreen – I was taking no chances. The woman showing me a selection of products noted my pale skin and red hair.

– Where are you going?

– Around Australia.

– Which way?

– Up the east coast, across the top, down the west coast, across the bottom and then back up here to Nowra.

– When you get into Queensland buy Bushmills. You'll need it against the mozzies, and it's got a sunscreen in it.

– Have you been up there?

Naturally she had, for Australians love to travel. She and her husband had taken a six week holiday in their campervan, driving diagonally across New South Wales to Broken Hill, up to Alice Springs in central Australia, across to Brisbane in Queensland and back down the east coast. Then she added that they'd taken all their meat with them. They'd had a portable freezer, which was charged by their motorhome engine, and in it they had packed enough steaks, chops and sausages to last the whole trip. All I could think to ask was why.

– Fresh food is very expensive up there. We took what we like to eat.

I didn't know what to say after that. From our point of view such a plan was completely impractical on two counts: first, we were going to be on the road for probably two thirds of a year; and secondly, there was simply not a skerrick of spare space in the Hiace. After the high cost of food in the UK the price of meat in Australia seemed very reasonable – but it was no good explaining that to someone who thought it was dear.

We knew there would be vast uninhabited areas but we never expected to be too far away from civilisation at any time. Our plan was to have enough basics on board and to buy fresh foods as we went along to meet our needs. I was sure we could rely on pot luck – that is, one-pot meals which are the mainstay of the camper as store-cupboard ingredients can so easily be combined with fresh to give tasty results.

But I continued to ponder over the woman's remarks. On our way up the east coast, we called in on friends of my family at Hervey Bay who have done a lot of caravanning and I brought up the subject of the meat. Alison and Bill keep meticulous accounts of every trip. They stick to a budget so they know how much they spend on fuel and food. It had been a couple of years since they had done a long trip, but out came the lists. They were able to show us that food did cost a little more when they were a long way from anywhere and the price of fuel varied considerably – which is what the receipts we kept showed, too.

Our most expensive petrol was in the west, at Exmouth, about 1,000 km north of Perth; the cheapest we bought was in the east, at Nowra. This related directly to a special offer from Woolworths, "the fresh food people", where money-off fuel was offered if you spent more than a certain amount.

At every Woolies we came across there was a wide range of excellent food – fresh if you want to cook it yourself, or pre-prepared. Just-roasted garlicky chickens were always a treat. Big W, Woolworths' other half, is a reliable emporium of manchester (bed linen, towels, tablecloths, teatowels, curtains, etc), hardware, car maintenance and electrical goods, as well as inexpensive clothes for men, women and children. We kitted out the van there.

Everyone has smartphones now so won't need to do what we did, use a camera with film that needed to be processed. It was both efficient and cost effective in Big W's instore units – I took about 70 rolls of film and had them processed in batches of 10 as we travelled so we could put them immediately into large albums (costing about $10 each, a bargain). This way we had an up-to-date record of where we had been, before our memories were less sharp.

As a continent, Australia is pretty lucky. Blessed with a range of climates, it can produce every type of food anyone could want and, with the incoming of so many different nationalities, it also has developed an impressive cuisine. But it is a world away from the cooking that I grew up with. My mother mostly made basic meat-and-two-veg meals – as a Catholic family, it was always fish on a Friday with a bowl of bread cubes on the table to ameliorate any bones encountered (the JustinCase principle). My youngest sister hated fish all her life as a result.

Mum was occasionally inspirational – oysters served in a creamy, lightly curried sauce on oven-dried bread was a great invention, and I adored brains in breadcrumbs (*à la milanaise*, as I was to discover many years later), and lambs fry (as liver is known in Australia) with bacon. We even had tripe in white sauce which I remember being very chewy.

From my reading online about wartime rationing, offal, or 'variety meats' as the Americans call animal organs, were much more readily available than better cuts of meat. Rationing began in 1942 when my sister Gai was born and went on till 1950, by which time I had another sister, Pam, and we'd left Sydney for our new Housing Commission house in Nowra.

Britain has much to thank Australia for as the food it produced and shipped over helped prevent starvation during World War II, when rationing there was a fact of life from 1940 to 1954. I was too young for Australia's rationing to impinge on me but I do recall my mother lamenting the lack of rice for puddings.

I loved to eat, and learning to cook naturally followed. Australia's strong baking tradition is a legacy from the world's best sources: the British, with their regional specialities of cakes and pies; Austria and Germany which share a fine tradition of good *brot* (bread) and rich *kuchen* (cake) and *torte* (tarts); and France which produces supreme *pain* (bread) and *patisserie* (pastries).

Cake shops everywhere you go in Oz offer a wide range of treats which would not look out of place in any of those countries, but some are distinctly Aussie: deep, two-layer sponge cakes, dusted with icing sugar and filled with jam and cream; lamingtons, which are squares of choc-and-coconut coated sponge cake; and melting moments, shortbread biscuits joined with a creamy filling.

Many cooks Down Under credit the *Australian Women's Weekly* as their source of inspiration, a magazine which began life in June 1933, and put cookery and food trends among its regular subjects from the start. Over the years it established an impressive cookbook library (which became increasingly more attractive as colour photography and printing methods improved) from which you could cook dishes from all round the world at home.

Sydneysiders had the benefit of Paddy's market where the Chinese – among the earliest people from other countries to settle in Australia – sold vegetables from their own market gardens established on land around the metropolitan area. Sydney, like the other cities, has its own Chinatown, and Chinese cooking must have already been developing its distinctive Australian style when I was growing up. It adapts itself very well to the available ingredients, and in Australia it was seafood.

Many country towns in Australia have small cafes – serving grills and snacks – and milk bars which serve lusciously thick, cold and creamy milkshakes. The real change came after the war with the arrival of the New Australians, as they were known – from Italy, Sicily and Greece who brought the Mediterranean to the southern hemisphere. This incoming had a huge influence on Australia's eating habits. Suddenly we had different food to buy from their delicatessens – in the late 1950s, when Frank and I were living in Sydney's Surry Hills, I tasted my first marinated vegetables, tiny cauliflower florets and carrot sticks, crunchily crisp but with vinegary piquancy. Olives and olive oil were a treat.

There wasn't a big restaurant culture then: Greek and Chinese were the most common. This began to change in the 1960s with the surge of the sporting and returned servicemen's clubs, where gambling and playing the poker machines provided funds for expansion and kept the price of membership low – still the same today, and they're a huge part in Australian life.

When you are travelling you can call in at any of these clubs, anywhere in Australia, and can be signed in as a visitor which gives you a chance to sample the bars and restaurants at exceptional prices. Favourite foods at these establishments include Chicken in a Basket and Hawaiian Chicken (which is Chicken in a Basket plus fried banana) – both deep-fried concoctions with chips. There'll be t-bone steak and possibly Steak Diane, an Aussie dish, dramatically created at the table by conflagration – a splash of brandy added to the peppered steak and whoosh, up go the flames.

Lebanese food is very popular, with its wonderful variety of tastes and textures, strong flavours. Big fat olives, creamy dips, stuffed and rolled leaves – little platefuls of appetizers accompanied by wine. The mezze gave me a life-long love for meals served in bursts, savoured slowly over a long period, never hurried. Greek restaurants had succulent, richly sauced lamb dishes, so different from the roasted leg we had at home, always on a Sunday.

It seems hard to believe that chicken was a rare treat when I was a child (no battery farming then or birds fattened by added hormones), and had to be ordered from the butcher. I didn't see my first garlic clove until I left home and it also doesn't seem possible that, at this time, the main use for olive oil (sold by the pharmacist in a small bottle) was to break down wax in the ear; occasionally, taking a teaspoon or two of it might be a cure for constipation. That it got out of the bathroom cabinet to become a kitchen staple is one of cookery's greatest success stories. Today, self-sufficient Australia produces some very high quality olive oils indeed.

Aussie greengrocers love to show off their colourful merchandise: eggplants (aubergines), capsicums, avocados and zucchini (or courgettes, though Australia prefers the Italian name). It is standard practice to arrange the contrasting hues of fruit and vegetables in geometrical shapes pleasing to the eye in shops and supermarkets. This type of artistry is at its best at the major agricultural shows, held annually in every state, where a geographical district's produce is used to create an eye-catching design depicting bountiful goodness. It is like a huge harvest festival with a storyline to raise awareness of a region – its attraction for tourists, for instance, or prolific production, or inventiveness.

The Royal Sydney Easter Show was the big one for me. Its home used to be Moore Park, on the eastern side of the city, but when Rupert Murdoch bought the land for his new film and TV enterprise, Fox Studios, the Show moved to Homebush, near the site of the 2000 Sydney Olympics. To mark the end of an era a video was made about the Show's history, from 1882 to 1997, a story of enterprise and entertainment.

I can remember the hangar-size shed filled with cakes of all shapes and sizes, their icing and decoration a work of art, and all vying to catch the eye of the judges. Women from all over the state brought these superb structures to the competition, a labour of love year after year. Australia is the home of 'plastic' icing, an adaptable mix that can be manipulated to be draped over cakes or formed into creative shapes to rival reality. This is the icing that today allows all of us to decorate cakes imaginatively and, importantly, doesn't melt in the Aussie heat.

This icon of agricultural shows also had events featuring cattle, sheep, dogs, horses, tractors, marching bands and the magnificent axe men who compete with each other and the clock to fell the 'trees' set up for this purpose. Woodchopping, which remains in the national consciousness because of the importance of timber to the country, was always exciting to watch – and still is.

There were fairground attractions like the big dipper, merry-go-round, bumper cars and ghost train, and all sorts of sideshows where you could win prizes by throwing quoits, balls or darts at objects. Tents would never hold a fortuneteller, for that was illegal in New South Wales (but not in Queensland). But there might be a circus tent and certainly a boxing arena – Jimmy Sharman, the fisticuffs supremo, travelled the country with his troupe of Aboriginal pugilists who would take on local men enticed into going three rounds for a tenner.

(Max Rupert Stuart, an Arrernte man whose sad, and controversial, conviction for rape and murder in 1958 was told in the 2002 film *Black and White* had been a teenage bare-knuckle boxer. He lost his job when he started to drink. No alcohol was a strict Sharman rule. After a Royal Commission the conviction was overturned and he was released in 1973.)

The annual show would not be complete without 'show bags', a commercial tour de force by the makers of every known sweet temptation: Hoadley's Crumble Bars,

Jaffas (orange-coated chocolate balls), Cherry Ripes, Polly Waffles, Caramello chocolate, Minties, Fantales (choc-coated, tooth-clinging caramels with biogs of Hollywood stars printed on the wrappers) and richly flavoured, thick strands of soft liquorice. The idea was to get as many bags as you (or your parents) could afford. On top of that, as you walked around the park, you had to have a toffee apple or a huge puff of bright pink fairy floss that turned to sugar granules in your mouth. This pure indulgence went on for years, not doing my teeth any favours at all.

One of the highlights of going to the show was getting a kewpie doll on a stick to take home. For sweethearts, as Frank and I were in 1956 when we spent a day at the show together, the giving of a doll was a way of showing affection, even making a promise. This was the theme used by Ray Lawler in his powerful play *Summer of the Seventeenth Doll.* Every year for 16 years Roo and Barney have come south to escape the heat of the Queensland canefields where they have worked their guts out for months. Their girlfriends Olive and Nancy have got used to their visits and their absences, and getting a kewpie doll, dressed in white tulle and shining tinsel, as a souvenir from a funfair during their reunion was all Olive could expect from her long-standing relationship. Eventually she realises it's just not enough.

Written in the 1950s, when there were many conflicting interests in Australia, *Doll* is a moving and absorbing play about hopes and realities. In its way it was as illuminating in Australian terms as John Osborne's *Look Back in Anger* was in British, putting its dramatic finger on "the reluctance of people to grow up" (wrote the renowned critic Kenneth Tynan, in *The Observer*).

In rereading the play while we were travelling I discovered that in 1957 Prime Minister Robert Menzies had lost a bet that *Summer of the Seventeenth Doll* would be a flop in Britain. It was the first Australian play to be performed in London's West End with an all-Australian cast and ran for a record-breaking seven months. If Menzies had picked New York instead he'd have won, for the play closed after five weeks. In both countries the Aussie language was a problem and while the British audiences got to grips with it, the Americans didn't.

When we reached Perth in October I was delighted that it was show month and the whole state would have its produce and talents on display. It was a gloriously sunny day when we went and the special guests were the then Governor, Lieut-General John Sanderson and his wife Lorraine. She had been the Girls' Captain of Nowra High – I had been the Vice Captain.

There were sheep dog trials to watch and a sort of mini-circus with performing pigs (the star being 'Miss Piggy' with a tulle skirt round her middle). People in 1950s' gear were taking part in a jitterbug and jive contest, the music of this at odds with that of the country and western singers in another part of the grounds. Cheerful cacophony – just as it had been in Sydney all those years ago!

After looking at the farming machinery and old cars we went into the huge halls. In the main show hall we were amazed at how the areas we had driven through had deceived us. What we thought was a marine desert or scrubby land harboured orchards, vineyards, bountiful farmland. Farming in Western Australia is done on a large scale – holdings are in the hundreds and thousands of hectares – and the state excels in the production of beef, lamb, pork as well as wheat and other cereal crops.

All along the coastline there is an abundance of seafood, the most profitable being the western rock lobster, a crayfish that is regarded as a delicacy and is the basis of a multi-million dollar industry. Inland, in the south among the mighty jarrah forests, you have the extraordinary land crayfish, called marron, for which there is great demand. If you buy a licence (then $15 – probably dearer now) you can snare them yourself in designated areas, but mostly they are farmed. We stopped for lunch at a marron farm in the Margaret River area and tasted the sweet, fleshy meat served with fresh wholemeal bread and home-made mayonnaise.

In eating terms the nearest equivalent is probably the northern *langoustine*, also known as the Norway lobster and Dublin Bay prawn (both now caught up in the fishing wars caused by Brexit, when the UK voted to leave the EU). The eastern side of Australia has the smaller yabby, which is similar to the marron. At a particularly impecunious time in our marriage, Frank and I resorted to catching what we called 'inland prawns' with a length of string with rotten meat attached. Fortunately, it was a productive mud pool, as any Aborigines, if they'd been around Lockhart, would have known. Yabbies have always been good tucker.

I'm glad we didn't even try to carry all our meat supplies around Australia, as that woman I met in Nowra did. Buying our food as we went along, seeking local specialities, was exciting. It might have been difficult if we had relied on eating out. Menus in most towns we went to which had a tourist trade usually featured fare that was fried or grilled. Hamburgers and steaks predominate and the smell of frying onions is sometimes overwhelming. We had some excellent fish and chips and found very good value – as well as originality in using the excellent Aussie ingredients – at wineries. In Western Australia, at the proudly-organic Voyager Estate's superb restaurant in the Margaret River area, the fillet of nan-gai, a local fish, was served with Albany oysters and lime hollandaise, and the boiled potatoes were lightly dressed with pesto, a delicious combination.

And you can come across the unexpected. The cook at the small cafe/bar near the campsite at the Town of 1770 – it calls itself the birthplace of Queensland for it was here that Captain Cook landed to take on fresh water – produced the best seafood pizza I have ever tasted. The base was light and the topping substantial and succulent, quite different from anything I've tasted anywhere.

When I was very young and heard Dean Martin singing his hit song *That's Amore* I thought the words were: "When the moon hits your eye like a big piece of pie" – well, in those days I hadn't heard of *pizza*. And everyone ate pies – they are still favourites today, a tradition in all the states. You see signs for them everywhere. Aussie savoury pies can be square or round, have pastry top and bottom and a filling of beef or chicken in gravy – the Oz way to eat one is to make a hole in the top crust and pour in tomato sauce through the escaping steam.

Some pies have taut, firm pastry; others are soft and squashy. Posher pies might have fillings of venison or kangaroo, possibly lamb or even crocodile. All the makers vie with each other and you could go round the whole continent trying out local ones – each (proudly) claiming to be the best, of course. Round Australia in pursuit of a pie would suit my New Zealand brother-in-law who on every visit aims to find a new one to taste. If you want a life of pie, he reckons Australia's the place – and I think he's right.

10

BEING SENSIBLE ABOUT THE SEA

WHY WATER IS RESPECTED

FOR MANY OF the people who visit Australia, the sea, sun and sands are the big attractions. And sharks are always thought of as being a huge scourge, though, in fact, injuries caused by these are nothing compared to those from diving, stings and barbs from jellyfish and stingrays, dehydration in the sun and sunburn itself. The sea, beautiful as it is, should never be regarded as benign. On this southern continent, to enjoy all that it has to offer, you have to respect its many elements. And know the traditions around it.

Before we started our trip the most common advice we were given was to book a campsite ahead, especially near coast or river or any water. The most popular places come under pressure in the school holidays, when parents, grandparents and offspring take to the roads, in some instances en masse. From the week before Christmas to the last day of January is the time when much of the behind-the-scenes business world, factories included, put the 'closed' sign up – and bosses, workers and children take their summer holiday.

You also have to contend with between-term breaks and these can be different in each state. You need to remember, too, that an Australian school year has four, not three, terms. And people can't wait to be on the move on the long weekends that punctuate the calendar – such as Australia Day (some want it called Invasion Day) in January, Easter, Anzac Day in April, Queen's birthday in June (this name would change if Australia became a republic) and Labour Day in October. You might be surprised to know how far Australians will drive if they want to spend time somewhere – and this Saturday, Sunday, Monday break is set up for hedonists. It's a habit formed from living in a big country where everything is a long way away.

You should mark all these dates clearly in your diary before you set off anywhere so that you can consult a map and choose your sites carefully. We found what we'd been warned about: queues formed outside sites near beaches or where a place has a reputation for getting a good catch. Fishing appears to be a passion with many Australians, despite the fact that it can put them in mortal danger. Choosing to cast off from rocks on coasts makes them prey to the unexpected and horrendous waves that appear without warning and can sweep them to their deaths.

A downturned "tinnie" on top of the car, or a small motor boat being towed, are common sights everywhere. Fishing just off shore is considered an inalienable right. But this recreation can be very hazardous; in Perth a dramatic change in the weather brought tragedy to a family with young children. Their aluminium boat was swept out to sea and overturned in the high waves, with the loss of all lives. They carried no warning equipment and none of them was wearing a lifejacket.

Inalienable rights should have responsibilities as well – the state governments need to have rules about seaworthiness of vessels and safety procedures at sea to make it more difficult, not easier, for owners of these lightweight dinghies, so that tragic incidents like this do not happen. Certainly the government of Western Australia reacted quickly, making it known that something had to be done to ensure that people who use these boats are aware of the inherent dangers of the sea, the precautions they must, not should, take, and know what has to be done in an emergency.

Another alarming event involved two seniors who survived for eight hours in shark- and crocodile-infested waters on the north coast of Queensland after their fishing boat overturned. The two, one aged 77 and the other 82, tried to drag their boat ashore through the mangrove swamp and, according to the newspaper reports, seemed more concerned about breaking their necks by tripping over the extensive root system of the trees than being killed by 'salties', the crocs that inhabit the area. They put their survival down to "the bloke from up there" answering their prayers. And they were lucky, especially as one of the men couldn't swim – not that you would try swimming where crocs are if you know anything about Australia.

In the Northern Territory, three quarters of boats used for recreational purposes are owned by householders, which is a lot when you think how much of this state is desert! But their boating safety regulations, for pleasure craft under 5 metres in length, are clear: a boat must carry an approved lifejacket or buoyancy aid for each person on board, as well as a litre of water for each person, in a secure container. There must be two paddles or oars fitted with rowlocks, a bailer with lanyard (ie, a bucket attached to a rope to empty out any water in the boat), an anchor with not less than 50 metres of cable, a waterproof torch or lantern, two red flares and two orange smoke signals.

If in difficulties, people on board can let off the flares to call for help; the smoke signals are useful to indicate the boat's position when an air search is conducted.

The waters of Australia are magnificent and provide an invigorating playground, but they can be exceedingly dangerous. "The bloke up there" is much less likely to be involved in saving people from difficult situations off shore than the legion of air-sea rescuers who are called out in all weather and at any time of day or night. They, like the strictly trained surf lifesavers on the popular beaches, put their lives at risk for others.

What many might not realise is that most of these guardians are volunteers, men and women who give their time freely in the interests of keeping others safe. The continent's too big for the Federal government to be able to afford to keep an army of such people on the vast coastline where fishing, surfing, boarding and swimming are every-minute-of-the-day activities. Kids in Australia grow up knowing these realities and are happy to be volunteers as adults.

Nearly all schools devote one or two weeks to swimming and water safety lessons at local pools or rivers in

December after the annual exams are over. Teachers are both dedicated and qualified in these subjects and the kids learn techniques and about water conditions as well as looking out for each other while in the water – the 'buddy' system – which means being alert to other swimmers. They are taught freestyle (formerly the Aussie crawl), breaststroke, backstroke, butterfly, treading water and floating.

After the long summer holidays, when the kids return in February, most schools have swimming carnivals so children can display their new water skills. There are also inter-school, state and national competitions as well – and, of course, the Commonwealth and Olympic Games. Swimming, with or without competition, becomes second nature to these kids, which it certainly never did when I was growing up.

My father, two brothers and oldest sister all gained their surf lifesaving medals, which meant they could be part of the team that patrolled and kept an eye on swimmers at Clovelly and Bronte, our local beaches in Sydney. I've only seen pictures of them in those days, the early 1940s, when surf lifesavers dressed in regulation one-piece cossies and caps and took it in turns to be the one who went in to rescue someone in peril. He (surf lifesavers then were mostly males) would pull on a harness, attached by rope to a reel, and run into the sea while the rest of the team picked up the reel and marched it smartly to the water's edge.

Once the swimmer in difficulties had been reached, and turned on to his or her back with the rescuer's hand under the chin to hold the head up, the rope was reeled back in.

It was always something to see, particularly if resuscitation was involved – in those days it was the Holger Neilsen method, which isn't used anymore as the pressure exerted on the back to force water from the lungs could damage the ribs by crushing. Now resuscitation is mouth to mouth and, because of HIV/AIDS and Covid, the rescuer uses a special mouthguard to prevent any mixing of spit or blood.

On many Australian beaches today, rescue from the sea is an entertainment, the basis of inter-beach competition – showing how surf lifesaving has changed over the years. At the beaches round Byron Bay in northern New South Wales I saw the duty lifesaver sitting in a snazzy UV-protected tent. He had binoculars and a walkie-talkie so that he could instantly contact rescue services. And he had a loudhailer to warn people going beyond the bright yellow and red flags marking the 'safe' swimming area.

Where water is involved, you ignore warnings at your peril in Australia. Even when lifesavers can't be there all the time – always check any notices giving times when the beach is patrolled – beaches are generally marked with flags on poles to indicate where to swim.

Rips and currents are notorious, tides extremely untrustworthy on many beaches, particularly near rocks – which is why the flag system was devised. Some beaches, like the famous Bondi in Sydney, have seawater pools, so you can enjoy the salty experience without fear of being swept out to sea.

The Australian Surf Lifesaving Association never recommends swimming from a deserted beach. Not that this is the biggest problem, particularly on the east coast where the big, froth-topped waves are shared by swimmers and board-riders. Overcrowding brings risks of injury, as well as other dangers. The surf can look so benign, but currents are complex and are not obvious to the inexperienced. Far too many visitors are carried out by the sea and drowned.

The gentle lapping of water onto golden sands can quickly become a nightmare. Lighthouse Beach, further south from Byron Bay, is both attractive and popular – but its charm can never be trusted. Locals tell the tale of a young mother who was walking with a baby in her arms along the rock-studded beach while her toddler was paddling at the water's edge. The toddler fell over and was being dragged out by the tide as the mother went to the rescue. Overbalanced by the baby, she fell in and tragically all three were swept away. Such horrible events can happen so fast, especially on beaches that are almost deserted, and often there's no one who can help.

Many of those who get into difficulties are usually not Australian born, a fact which irritates the Aussies, but as one in three Australians were born overseas they might not have had respect for the sea inculcated into them from childhood and won't be as wary of its dangers. Some tourists or newcomers, especially international students, might not even understand the words of warning used on the signs, or even see the signs. All they notice is everybody enjoying themselves in the water, and because they are hot they want to cool off.

Many don't realise how significant the water temperature is. They might not be used to swimming in cold water – and the seas are *not* always warm Down Under – or, in such a big expanse, they misjudge how far they have swum. It is easy to get cold and tired, and cramps are not uncommon. The sea's roughness and high waves can also cause problems.

I have to say I have not bathed in the sea since 1962 when a huge wave struck the Sydney beach of Coogee, picking me up and throwing me hard onto sand which felt like stone. The experience shook me so badly that my capacity to swim, and even my interest in swimming, disappeared. The explanation for this freak wave related to an earthquake in South America that caused a tsunami in the Pacific – and quite a lot of people were injured on the beach. It gave me a fear of the sea which has never left me. My three children swim very well, and with confidence, but I prefer to watch. I found that, at campsites with small pools, when temperatures were in the 30s, just sitting in the water to cool off was pleasure enough.

Unfortunate water incidents over the years have made me aware of what to do if you get into trouble. Most important of all is knowing how to send an adequate distress signal. Waving an arm can be misinterpreted and will not draw attention to your difficulties. Shout for help. Beat your arms on the water. Float for a while then repeat the shouting and splashing, facing the beach or looking towards nearby bathers. Don't try and swim against the current: swim across it is the advice.

Snorkelling looks easy – and, to be truthful, is promoted as easy – but getting out of breath and swallowing water causes the panic that can lead to drowning if someone isn't there to act immediately. We were on a whale-watching excursion off the west coast when we saw with horror one of the snorkellers start to splutter and get into difficulties. There was a small motor dinghy keeping an eye on the group but it was too far away to respond in the time available.

One of the other divers, a woman, showed immediately that she was trained in lifesaving: she turned the man on to his back and, with one arm under his chin, swam side stroke to bring him back to the boat. The captain was quite blasé.

– It's nearly always a Japanese who gets into trouble. Almost one a trip we get. They never think anything can go wrong but.

Scuba diving, which is done in deep water, involves the use of oxygen cylinders and requires more skill than snorkelling. If you want to scuba dive in Australia you have to show proof that you have completed a recognised diving course. Following the strange disappearance of two Americans 9km off the east coast on the famous Barrier Reef at the end of the 1990s, there are much stricter rules about procedures on snorkelling and scuba diving trips.

Taking a head count of those on board is simply not enough. The person in charge is responsible for making sure that all members of the party are there, ticking off each name on a passenger list in the same way as an airline does. Only if this is complete can the boat return to base – but this wasn't the case when the scuba divers went missing.

It was a real 'whodunnit' mystery – which guides on long bus journeys include in their repertoire for entertaining their captive audiences. The disappearance was the inspiration for the 2004 film *Open Water*, which is set in some non-specified diving playground, and has no connection to the area where the two, a man and a woman, vanished. The enquiry into the disappearance went on for 18 months. No bodies were found but body suits and flippers were.

All sorts of weird and wonderful theories emerged, including that they staged the whole thing – not too unusual perhaps in Australia, where a Prime Minister, Harold Holt, was 'lost' while swimming, and a British MP, John Stonehouse, who 'disappeared' off a Florida beach, turned up, miraculously alive, in Melbourne. The PM and the two Americans did not come back to life, nor were their bodies found.

Years ago, I remember hearing the story of a child who was brought up on a boat on Thursday Island, north of Cape York, Queensland, a notorious area for sharks. After seeing his pet cat fall off the side, to try and prepare him for the loss, his parents told him that anything that went overboard didn't come back. What they hadn't intended was that it would strike a fear of the sea in that child which he would never conquer. It took his parents a while to work out why he became distraught if one of them dived off the boat for a swim; what they thought would be a kindly lesson turned out to be a psychological trauma.

FROM THE TOWN OF 1770 – *GREGORY'S ROAD ATLAS* writes it as "Seventeen Seventy" – we made our first boat trip to see whales and to visit Lady Musgrave Island, the southernmost island of the Great Barrier Reef Marine Park. As the crossing here could be rough, we had been advised to chew a small piece of fresh ginger, which takes your breath away somewhat but certainly did the trick. John the skipper, a real character, drove the *MV Spirit of 1770* at a fair lick and we seemed to hit every wave, but he kept the grin on his face and nothing interrupted his humorous banter. Aussies do like to entertain.

He told us he was 77, and then explained that his daughter was in charge of the lunch and his son would be helped by another man to look after the snorkellers and those preferring to appreciate the underwater life through the glass-bottomed boat *Coral Explorer*, which was kept moored off the island. After we had gone through a deep passage into the open sea he slowed down a little, then swivelled round on his stool to face the passengers. That's the reef ahead, he said, and behind us is the land.

– I only tell you this so that if we start to sink you'll know which direction to swim.

The dry remark made Ian remember WC Fields' wry quote: "Laugh early in the day and get it over with". As it happened, everyone laughed a lot that day, nothing untoward happened and the skipper made the Lady Musgrave experience good fun.

Another boat trip, on the west coast, could not have been more different. We were going out from Coral Bay to the Ningaloo Reef, popular for snorkelling and scuba diving (this time to see large and unusual manta rays, as well as hundreds of species of fish and coral), then, hopefully, beyond the reef for whale watching. We started later than expected as it took time for the those passengers who were going to snorkel or scuba dive to get togged up, but everyone was cheerful, looking forward to the day at sea. Pete, the mate, introduced the two 'mermaids' – so named because of their swimming abilities – and, although the sky was grey and overcast, he said the sea would be as smooth as a baby's bottom. I was glad I'd had the forethought to chew some fresh ginger.

Unlike the Great Barrier Reef, the Ningaloo Reef is only a few ks offshore. Inside the reef the water was smooth but as we approached the gap in the reef – through which the skipper had to take the boat – we could see the ocean breaking on the reef quite violently. Some people had gone on to the bows, and Pete called them back into the cabin. The waves in the gap were especially large and vicious, as they were constricted by the reef on either side.

Ian, who's written many books about sailing and the sea, later asked the captain how he could ensure getting safely beyond the reef. The captain said he manoeuvred the boat as near the gap as possible, waited for a wave to come through it, and then gunned the boat over and beyond the wave at top speed – which meant he was out into open water before the next wave arrived. The trouble was, on this occasion, the wave he chose had a what is known as a 'rogue' wave immediately behind it which he couldn't see. The boat, going full tilt, hit it. Or rather it hit the boat which seemed to become almost vertical. It rose and dropped again – throwing everyone all over the place.

I'd been holding on to a rail above my head and felt as though my shoulder had been pulled out of its socket. Ian was a few feet away from me and looking most alarmed. After many years' experience of sailing, he knows how fickle the sea can be – and, from his face, I could tell he was concerned.

The mate came rushing past us and threw a lifebuoy

over the stern. Carita, one of the mermaids, who had been standing on the bow, had been knocked over by the huge wave, gashing her leg on the edge of the anchor as she went overboard – though we didn't know this until later. We watched her ease herself inside the padded ring and start to swim strongly away from the reef, but we could see that it was difficult as the waves were drawing her towards it. A small fishing boat appeared and the mate shouted to the two men on board to pick her up, which they did. They brought their boat close to ours and, when near enough, Carita dived in and swam to us where she was helped aboard.

On the passenger deck two young children were in shock and clung to their parents, crying all the while. One passenger had been scalded by hot coffee, another woman just couldn't stop being seasick. Carita had hurt her neck as well as her leg, and a collar was fitted as a first-aid measure. The captain radioed to shore for a pick-up van to go to a part of the coast where he could get the boat near enough to the beach to offload the injured. Despite their condition, the scalded passenger and the two women swam ashore. Carita, wearing neck brace and a backpack, paddled off on a surfboard, smiling as she waved goodbye. We shook our heads in amazement.

Then we went back to looking for whales. Yes, we saw them with the help of a spotter plane, which caused a *frisson* of excitement when it flew so low over the boat we could see the pilot's face, an action that was somewhat over the top after the earlier incident. And yes, the other mermaid led the snorkellers to a manta ray, but during those remaining hours on board the atmosphere was most uneasy. We tucked into a sausage sizzle lunch cooked by the mate, who served up chardonnay from a cask to accompany the fried sausages, onions, potatoes and eggplant. The bush telegraph got to work as we ate and all the passengers soon knew about Carita's injuries.

That skipper never said a word about what had happened. Ian knew that he'd kept control and the boat didn't broach to, otherwise we would have been swept onto the reef. But the captain never explained, never apologised or made even a lighthearted remark about it. More importantly he made no effort to reassure us – no wonder those kids remained pale and almost comatosed. A passenger overheard him say to someone "Freak waves do occur", but he didn't pass that on to the rest of us. And he should have.

He should have had a duty of care and to do what he could to help people get over the shock of the experience. The mate went round the boat chatting to everyone (though he couldn't bring a smile to those children's faces), and logged the various small injuries – grazes, a turned ankle, my sore shoulder – but the skipper stayed schtum. Pity.

11

"I SEE YOU'VE BEEN TO DARWIN"

START FROM SCRATCH IN THE NORTH

THE BEST PLACE TO get to meet fellow travellers at campsites is usually the laundry block. While you wait for the washing machine's cycle to end or the dryer to stop, you can pass the time of day swapping information and picking up tips about places – for example, the rain's falling there, or the temperature's dropped, or you must go and see. At one site on the west coast, I was removing our clothes from the dryer, and giving them a good shake to remove creases, when a woman, who had appeared to be glued to a glossy magazine full of celebrities and their goings on, suddenly said:

– I see you've been to Darwin then.

– How do you know that?

– Obvious. All those bites on your legs. Everyone who goes to Darwin gets them. I've still got mine and we were there weeks ago.

She rolled up her trouser leg to show the tell-tale red

weals just like those I had on me. Quite reassuring really: at least I wasn't suffering alone.

Anyone going by road around Australia would not think of bypassing Darwin. It is like a pinnacle, a place to aim for. It is not big and full of bustle like other Australian cities and, since we were awaiting mail at the post office (*poste restante*) we intended staying for a week or so. It is an unusual mix: a working city, with a holiday air. Locals, as well as backpackers and tourists, dress in shorts and thongs – suits are simply not suitable.

By the time we arrived, the winter sunshine was just as we had hoped it would be – warm, without being hot or humid. Apart from Sydney and Brisbane (where we didn't stay), all the cities have well equipped resorts and parks for caravanners, campers or travellers preferring self-catering cabins – but they tend to be located some distance from the Central Business District (all cities have this CBD designation). This is not a problem because we found efficient transport systems everywhere.

In Adelaide, for example, Levi Park, just 4 km northeast of the city, is well placed: we could walk to town alongside the river Torrens, take an ordinary bus, or go on the O'bahn, the longest automated busway in the world from which you get stunning views. We stayed northwest of Perth, at Karrinyup Waters Resort, a Top Tourist park, and made much use of the reasonably-priced trains and buses. From Ashley Gardens, the Big 4 holiday village in the delightfully named Melbourne suburb of Sunshine, there was a frequent bus service into the city; once there we used the trams, which are great.

In Darwin we stayed at two sites, both within the sound of Darwin International Airport. Palms Village

Resort, on the Stuart Highway and 17 km from the CBD, is modern, has good facilities, including a pool and bistro/bar, and grassy sites with trees around the perimeter. Shady Glen, in the suburb of Winnellie, 8 km out (or 9 km closer to the CBD), is in a rustic setting with most of the sites under trees.

So that we could sleep with the door open at night, we'd strung a net curtain along the side of the van, allowing any breeze to enter while protecting us from any unwelcome incomers. It never occurred to us that in parking under the trees, and sitting out under them to have our meals, we were courting danger. We burnt citronella candles outside and anti-bug coils inside, along with a few squirts of Raid, and sprayed ourselves with Rid as a protection, but it was to no avail. At both sites we were attacked by whatever it was that lurked in the branches or leaves, perhaps even the roots. I don't think we saw our attackers at any point – they could have been sandflies, ants or mozzies – and they had us in their sights. On me they feasted with gay abandon.

Despite it all, we enjoyed staying put for a length of time – after being on the road for a couple of months we had discovered that short stops, and moving on after one or two days, was unexpectedly tiring. At Darwin we fell into a relaxing pattern of shopping, sightseeing, checking our emails, seeing a film or two, doing what the north is known for – chilling out in the warmth. As we were visitors, we could be signed in to the Fannie Bay Yacht Club where we ate and drank in the balmy evening air, watching the sun go down over the Timor Sea. Internet cafes are two a penny, and you can save cents if you shop around. The one where we spent most time had the delightful name of Didgeridoo.net and we got on to our Hotmail site very quickly. At some places getting connected was quite slow.

Darwin is easy to walk around. Just as on the Continent of Europe, people here like to perambulate. The pedestrianised mall is the main attraction, with lots of shops for browsing, benches to sit on, and places to eat, drink or just relax. Halfway along the mall is an attractive fountain with arcs of water splaying gently on to the walkway – an artistic outdoor shower. I liked the way adults walked round it while the little kids ran through it quite happily. In the heat, nobody cared that they got wet.

There are a few museums to visit, and the pearling one is particularly interesting as pearls are big business in this city. The Chinese market area, a permanent fixture, looks as though it has come straight from Shanghai or Hong Kong. The beach-side evening markets on Sundays and Thursdays are far more ad hoc, spontaneous, hippy-like. They have a world famous reputation for food, crafts and entertainment. They start as the sun is setting, usually just before six o'clock, and the carnival atmosphere continues for several hours.

There's a wonderful buzz about it all, the heady aromas of cooking enhanced by music from different sources – none blaring, which was a real treat. We chatted to a man about the brightly-coloured paper kites he was selling and learnt that he made them himself – he spends six months travelling in his yacht and six months in Darwin. Perhaps in my next life, that's what I'll do too.

Most of the time the streets were quiet and cheerful. Like cities everywhere there are Starbucks and McDonalds, but you can sense that the influences here are more Asian than American. There are also big, sprawling Aussie pubs which look different from those in the southern states. Only once did I come across a scene that could have come from the Sydney that I remember as a young woman, from the inner city suburb where I did my nursing training, where it wasn't unusual to see Aborigines who'd had too much to drink and had reached a belligerent stage.

I was getting money from a hole in the wall on one of the main streets and became aware that I was almost standing between two young women screaming at each other. Their exchange was liberally spiked with 'fucking' (the only word I understood at the start of the fracas), and became more and more heated. One had Aboriginal features, the other – a blonde – was with a male Aborigine and, when she threatened the other woman with 'I'll cutya if I find yiz alone', I thought it best to leave them to it. It probably was a good old-fashioned fight over a fella...

Darwin, which has a year-round temperature in the low 30s Celsius (rule of thumb: double it and add 30 to convert to near-enough Fahrenheit), is a natural magnet for people of all ages. Most visit during the northern winter – the Dry – when days are between 27 and 32, and nights 16 to 22 degrees. It would be, however, a waste of time for anyone interested in a beach culture. The harbour may be bigger than Sydney's, but is not user friendly – among the things you would have to contend with are very high and low tides, crocodiles and stinging box jellyfish.

When we went across by ferry to the Mandorah

Beach Hotel – a local resort for families – we noticed the warnings on the sandy beach that anyone swimming from October to May did so at the risk of being stung. There's a pool at the hotel, so there's no problem cooling off. These jellyfish are known by other names: marine stingers and deadly sea wasps.

They are, according to one website I consulted, Very Dangerous Creatures. Were these the 'bluebottles' I remembered from my childhood, that we sometimes found on the beach, that were also mysteriously called Portuguese man o' war? It seems they are one and the same, and, for seven months of the year, they are a hazard in the seas from Gladstone in Queensland, all the way across the top of Australia to Broome on the west coast – and Darwin falls into that area.

Anyone intending being in the sea where jellyfish might be is now advised to wear a Lycra body suit as a protection, which is what the surfies do. Beach kit these days should also include 4 litres of vinegar as well as wide crepe bandages, the idea being that, should someone come in contact with a stinger, you can drench the affected area with vinegar and then wrap it. If you don't have any vinegar, it is essential to get off any clinging tentacles, using tweezers or twigs in preference to your fingers (so as not to be stung as well), and to obtain medical help for the person as soon as possible.

The most serious consequence of an encounter with a box jellyfish is anaphylactic shock which needs instant treatment with an antihistamine injection. (As I said in a previous chapter, this should be part of the first aid kit of anyone intending to go off road or, indeed, going to the beach in Australia on the JustinCase principle.)

Most people think Oz only has deadly sharks, crocodiles, snakes and spiders, but it's well worth knowing that there is another nasty to be avoided – the stone fish, an ugly, malevolent fish that waits inert in seaweed or mud. Along its back are venomous spines which, if trodden on, cause extreme shock. There seems to be no good reason at all for such a horrid fish, and only the Chinese appear to find any use for it, regarding its flesh as a delicacy. Good luck to them!

As for the sandflies, well, they are there all year, the happy inhabitants of sand and the mangrove trees of which there is a multitude around the whole coastline. 'Mangrove tree' is a bit of a misnomer as it can refer to any tree that can live partly submerged in the salty environment of coastal swamps where temperatures average 24C or more. Excellent examples can be seen on the Daintree River, north Queensland, which has 28 of the 70 types of mangrove trees known worldwide.

Mangrove swamps are the tropical counterparts of saltmarshes and they protect coastlines against erosion as well as being vital breeding grounds for fish, crustaceans and water birds. You can't help but be impressed at the way these trees have adapted themselves to surviving in thick, grey, unoxygenated silt, but why their guardians should be sandflies defies understanding.

Don't think for a minute that Australia is the *only* country plagued by biting insects. In the west and north of Scotland, summer is made miserable for locals and visitors by millions of 2mm-sized midges (*Culicoides impunctatus*, as a scientist might say) which live for between two and four weeks and create hell for the whole of that time. The female bites, to get blood to help her eggs to develop, and at the same time releases pheromones which attract swarms of other equally determined females. If these pesky insects did some good, those who are bitten might be able to accept that they have played their part in some ecological cycle. But these midges appear to have no purpose, being of no importance to other creatures' diet or any other life cycle. A fortune has been spent trying to develop a successful repellent but it hasn't happened yet. And they don't even put mesh screens on the windows there to keep the biters out!

The northern parts of Scandinavia, the Camargue area of France, the central region of Zimbabwe, the forested parts of Canada and the rainforests of New Zealand's south island all have similar insects which, I can say with conviction, nothing seemed to repel or deter. I am part of whatever ecological cycle they have, as they have supped my blood in all these places; I can't believe that anything as annoying can be essential to anything. Humans seem to be their only natural enemies and, worldwide, we appear to be helpless.

Around Darwin, mosquitoes and ants get in on the act as well, hence our many bites, particularly behind the knees. Some I'm sure we got when we wore shorts on a visit to the national park, a large area of natural bushland, on the edge of Port Darwin, named after the naturalist Charles Darwin by John Lort Stokes in 1839. He later became Commander of HMS *Beagle*, which twice circumnavigated Australia, charting the coasts.

In his fascinating report of *Beagle*'s third voyage, Stokes mentions mosquitoes a lot, relating how his land exploration parties had to deal with the constant problems presented by the "ceaseless persecutions of these inexorable assailants". The west coast was worst of all. He resorted to naming one place Point Torment, because of their "vindictive attacks".

From the park – a popular walking and picnic place – you have a clear view of the city across the bay. The first white settlement in 1869, organised by the South Australian Government which then controlled the Northern Territory, was called Palmerston, after the English Prime Minister of the time, but was renamed Darwin in 1911.

It's rare to read anything about the city being a congenial place to be in the northern summer – the Wet – starting in November when storm clouds appear. The general opinion is that monsoonal conditions make for misery. It's a cyclone danger zone too. The worst was Cyclone Tracy which struck on Christmas Day 1974 and killed 65 people, including 16 who were lost at sea, and caused $A1,000 million worth of damage. Ferocious storms had devastated the town in 1897 and 1937, and later, during World War II, Japanese air raids destroyed much of it again, killing hundreds of people in the process.

All this destruction at least has one good side – quite a lot of the city is new and buildings are constructed with ecological dangers in mind (for example, tiles aren't used on roofs – in cyclonic winds, which reach 250 kph, these flying around would be lethal – and roofs don't have gutters either as they'd be useless in the sort of rain they get here.).

Darwin has an interesting history. Because it is so isolated it has always been known as a frontier town – geographically, it is closer to Singapore and Jakarta than it is to Sydney or Melbourne. It began as a trading post for the British Empire – establishing a settlement prevented any foreigners such as the French or Dutch or Indonesians getting a foothold. It was the discovery of gold in 1870 at Pine Creek, more than 200 km to the south, that boosted the settlement's importance and population. Pine Creek today is a tourist attraction, with an old railway and train on which you can take a short ride.

But Darwin also had riches from the sea, in the form of pearls, which made it 'the south sea pearl capital'. Two things make the northwest coast of Australia ideal for pearl cultivation: the extremely active tides (they can measure up to seven metres) and water that is unpolluted. Australian south sea pearls are the largest, most lustrous and naturally beautiful cultured pearls in the world, produced from two oysters: *pinctada maxima* (silver lip or gold lip) and *pinctada margaritifera* (black lip oyster). They come in shades of silver, silver pink and silver white; gold is not so common, but is available.

Darwin is the capital and only city of the Northern Territory, now a state in that it has its own elected parliament, but has a chief minister rather than a premier – described as 'limited self government'. When I was a child, it was under the jurisdiction of the Australian Capital Territory and Canberra, home of the Federal Government. Some of its problems include being a long way from anywhere, its small population, not being self sufficient and having a complicated past, and present, in terms of race relations. It has Arnhem Land in the north and Uluru in the south, both huge areas owned by the Aborigines, and very popular with tourists and travellers.

Much of the state is, in fact, Aboriginal land. Yet in the early 20th century most of the Aborigines who had lived on the area that had become Darwin – the Larrakia people – were confined to government reserves or Christian missions, or were working as stockmen or domestic help on the cattle stations , being paid little or nothing for their efforts. In 1901, when Australia became a Federation, several states and the Northern Territory passed a law "to disenfranchise British subjects who were aboriginal natives of Australia, Asia, Africa or the Islands of the Pacific", a situation that didn't alter until the referendum of 1967.

Though all the Australian cities today could be called cosmopolitan (Melbourne, for instance, has the greatest number of Greeks living there outside of Greece) Darwin was the first that could be called truly cosmopolitan. Darwinians are a mixture of many different cultures and have been there for generations; it was the first city, for instance, to have a mayor of Chinese extraction. The Chinese, who provided the cheap labour needed to retrieve the gold at Pine Creek, so outnumbered the Europeans – there were 7,000 Chinese to a handful of Europeans, says the official visitors' guide to Darwin – that, in 1888, they were banned from the Northern Territory. This ban didn't last long and eventually they returned along with people from Japan, Thursday Island, Timor and the Philippines who were enticed to Australia to be part of the pearling industry.

The Greeks came after the war, mostly from the Aegean island of Kalymnos, having lost their living as sponge divers – this trade disappeared almost overnight when synthetic sponges replaced natural ones. Their diving skills made them perfect substitutes for the Japanese who had been the mainstay of the pearling industry up till this time, but were now no longer acceptable because of the war and Japan's role in it.

The White Australia Policy played a part too, ensuring that no other Asians could be brought in to replace the Japanese. The Greeks now make up about 10 % of the city's population – 148,564 in 2018. With such a background, the city's administrators know that problems can arise when you can't make yourself understood and, to ease this, provide a translating service – for any language into English. The service is available 24 hours a day for the cost of a local phone call.

Today's problems are mostly focused on refugees from appalling regimes wanting to live in Australia; out of desperation, they willingly risk illegal entry rather than going through the normal channels open to people seeking asylum. We saw a group protesting in front of the Department of Citizenship and Multicultural Affairs about Australia's 'race record'. Speakers were encouraging those gathered around to join Families Against Race Restrictions, an organisation which aims to do what it can to help 'escaped' refugees and prevent them being taken back into custody.

It has a surprisingly large membership of ordinary men and women committed to showing kindness to these people who have fled persecution in their own lands. In their view, Australia is a big country, resourceful and lucky, and can afford to be generous in welcoming those who choose no longer to live in places ravaged by war and terror.

It's a difficult problem. Australia must seem like the promised land to many who give all they have or can borrow to the mercenary bandits providing the passage.

The stories of escape are horrendous and heartbreaking, as is their treatment on arrival in Australia and their incarceration in the immigration detention camps situated in non-salubrious desert areas. None of this, however, alters the fact that the citizens of Australia do not accept that these people have a right to enter the country without invitation, without going through the laid-down route.

Australia always has had a problem with immigration. The White Australia Policy allowed in those whose skin might turn brown in the southern sun but were not naturally brown or black – English, Scottish, Welsh, Irish and Continental Europeans, into which category, interestingly, fell the Middle Eastern Lebanese, Turks and Egyptians. The 'coloureds' not likely to be approved were those from the 'darker' parts of the Empire, such as India, Pakistan, South Africa and the Caribbean, and from China.

The indigenous Australians, the Aborigines, were denied citizenship, as were Chinese and Afghanis who had been here almost as long as the first whites, and people from Papua and New Guinea even though Papua was considered part of Australia, and New Guinea was an Australian Protectorate. Woe betide a tourist or student from either country who overstayed his or her temporary permit.

It wasn't until Harold Holt was Prime Minister that it all changed – and look what happened to him. In the year he brought the policy to an end he went swimming off the Victorian coast and was never seen again. Very mysterious. During his time as an elected member of parliament Holt had been one of the few humane politicians to try to ameliorate the divisive policy: non-whites were allowed to settle if they were legally married to Australians and had children; Chinese or Asian businesspeople or educationalists could apply for naturalisation if they had lived there on temporary permits renewed over a period of time.

Darwin does well out of the tourist industry (coronavirus permitting) and is always prepared for visitors. When, after several days at Shady Glen, our bites (mine more than Ian's) became unbearable, we decamped to a self-catering apartment on the sixth floor of a block called Luna Luna, and stayed there for three days until we felt fit enough to move on. There was a swimming pool in the block but mostly calamine lotion and rest was the order of the day. The apartment – really one room with a double bed and kitchenette, plus bathroom, but a bargain at $114 a night – had a small balcony with a view over Darwin estuary and port. It was a perfect setting for a drink as the sun went down. But we took no chances.

Despite the warm evening air Ian covered up with a sweater and trousers, while I wore a long-sleeved shirt, trousers, thick socks and a hat, as I had discovered bumps on my scalp. I must have looked a fright, but what the hell! I went to every shop in town to try and find Ian a plain, light cotton, long sleeve shirt but such a garment was unknown. Regulation gear for men in much of Australia is short-sleeved and inevitably patterned, sometimes overwhelmingly so.

Actually, Darwin need not feel alone in having a reputation for biting insects. Other Aussie places also mark you. Something undetectable seemed to drop out of the trees at Derby in Western Australia, for instance, endowing my arms with itchy, raised areas. The sandflies at Point Samson, further down the coast, added insult to injury when we walked at dusk along the beach in shorts and T-shirts and without hats. *The Rough Guide to Australia* describes this popular spot as having a 'sharp, windswept Atlantic quality even if it does happen to be 320 km inside the tropics'. It certainly does look similar to the west coast of France, south of Nantes, where our family spent many summer holidays. As the guide fails to mention it, let me assure you sandflies are there in abundance.

Townsville in Queensland is renowned for both bugs and beasties, but so are Shute Harbour and Cairns, all favoured tourist spots for young and old intent on discovering the offshore wonderland. Mostly it's the mozzies that get you on the east coast. Some you may see, others you may not. Some don't even make a noise, but you still wake up with bites. In our case we had no terrible after effects, but everyone visiting should take precautions and be aware of the possible dangers.

The domestic Aussie mozzie is a blight on the country because it can spread many illnesses. There have been record numbers of cases of Ross River Fever in Perth, as well as the Kimberley, Pilbara and central wheatlands areas of the western state. It's the same in southeast Queensland and, in other places in the state, Dengue Fever, another virus, is a problem. In 2004, in Central Australia, above average rainfall in February and March resulted in an increase in the numbers of common banded mosquitoes which carry Murray Valley encephalitis, a very nasty virus. Visitors or those intending to camp were warned not to go within 5 km of a swamp, creek or river system.

The most refined form of torture I have come across is to be in an enclosed van and to hear buzzing around your head in the pitch dark with the bug eliminator spray nowhere to hand (I have been told that being inside a mosquito net with mozzies is worse!). But the good news is that clever inventors come up with new ways to repel these insects all the time. I've read about an ultrasonic repeller that plugs into the mains, uses little power and no chemical block. You can also buy an alarm clock and a watch that work on batteries and emit ultrasound waves to ward off most types of mosquitoes. Clothes with in-built repellent are available. I know what to put on top of my 'must buy' list if I should get the chance to do the trip all over again.

12

TREASURES BEYOND COMPARE

ECOLOGICAL WONDERS OF THE WEST

THE FURTHER WE travelled the more I wondered how, in all those years I spent at school, that I didn't find out more about the extraordinary diversity that exists everywhere on the continent of my birth. Nowhere was I more aware of this lack of knowledge than when driving in the biggest state, which covers more than a third of the land mass and is four and a half times the size of France.

Western Australia was nearly part of my past. In 1963, when I was living in Brisbane and trying to decide on where to go next, a coin was tossed: if it were heads the destination would be Perth, if tails it would be New Zealand. New Zealand won. It was a major turning point in my life, and eventually led me to London, so it was in no way disappointing. But it meant that the wonderful discoveries awaiting in the west, over 2,000 miles away (as it was then), were put off for far too long.

The state has treasures beyond compare. You could spend a lifetime finding and appreciating them – in fact, the cry of the free tourist guide available to all visitors is: "We challenge you to discover Western Australia". It is definitely a challenge.

This side of the continent didn't have a promising start. Dirk Hartog is credited as being the first white person to land, on an island that bears his name, in 1616. As the story goes – which I learnt as a 12 year old – the Dutchman, captain of the *Eendracht*, inscribed details of his discovery on a pewter plate, nailed it to a post and sailed away, believing there was nothing to be gained from this barren and scrubby area. He didn't realise he'd landed on an island.

Even today it does seem extremely remote. Halfway up the Western Australian coast, it is regarded as one of Australia's top eco destinations, a virtual paradise with your wellbeing the prime concern. You can stay at the new homestead in an ensuite room, or in the converted shearers' quarters. There's a big kitchen, bar and dining area where meals are served, and days can be dedicated to lazing, swimming or snorkelling. The fishing here, we were told, is magic. You can catch your own fish every day and have it cooked for you that evening. The bays and inlets are home to whiting, schnapper, bream, taylor, mulloway, kingfish – which can be caught from the beach – while mackerel, cod, sailfish and marlin are hooked from a boat.

This part of the coast is very oddly shaped. The island looks almost as if it had broken away from a narrow projection of land, at the tip of which is Steep Point reached by an unsealed road. This is the crossing point for visitors with 4WDs who want to be independent. The island owner transports them and their vehicles by barge at a cost and provides a map so they can explore dunes and beaches, and camp if they choose.

What we did was to take a day trip ($130 a head then), crossing by motorboat from the windswept town of Denham, a popular holiday destination on another of the odd, finger-shaped bits of the coast. (I wrote in my diary that the "wind was blowing like billyo" at the campsite and it was impossible to put up the annexe.)

The journey on *Argosy* took one and half hours, and on board with us was a family who were going fishing after we were dropped off – $85 a head at the time, and a fish guaranteed (both the young boys each caught huge schnapper). It was a stunningly beautiful day with a sky of deep blue.

The island is much bigger than it looks on a map. In the time available we could see only a small part, which didn't unfortunately include the site of Dirk's plate at Cape Inscription on the northern tip. It's very hilly and arid – just as the Dutch captain said – where today goats and sheep run wild. For many years the island's owners lived by rearing sheep for wool and meat, but it is now a World Heritage site with an ecological project that aims to restore it to the same state as Dirk found it. The funding comes from tourism so the ecolodge has flushing toilets in the well appointed rooms.

There's a safari tent camp site and you can put up your own in the national park, on the 'leave no trace principle' (you must take all your rubbish with you when you leave). This is thanks to the deal struck with the Malgana people, traditional owners of Wirruwana (their name for the island).

Dave, our driver and guide, came to Australia from

Bristol, southwest England, in 1964 on the first leg of a round-the-world journey. He saw Perth and decided there was no reason to move on. He works as a guide according to demand, but knows the island well, taking great care with the 4WD on the sandy tracks, hills and beaches, which can be dangerous if you lose momentum and the vehicle gets bogged. He carried a spade, to dig us out if the worst happened, but he wasn't in radio contact with the homestead so, if we did get into trouble, how would anyone know? Fortunately there were no probs (as they say).

Dirk, most certainly more interested in commercial opportunities than sightseeing, missed a lot. The blowholes on the eastern side of the island are spectacular, the brilliant white spume rising high into the air as the powerful crashing waves whoosh into the huge holes in the rocky cliffs. We drove to a cove in which a small number of sharks idled in green waters right onshore. My heart lurched a little at the sight of the fins, but they were tiny. They're called school sharks, said Dave, and no one worries about them, not even scuba divers who adore the wildness of the island.

We walked along a white-sand beach and sat on the rocks to have our picnic lunch – excellent sandwiches, date and orange cake, and coffee – and watched the antics of a party of seabirds that, like us, were enjoying the sunshine. Prominent among them were darters whose actions were now familiar: first the sharp, beak-down dive, then the wide open wing-drying. Dave said there were 16 different birds in the gathering but we were not knowledgeable enough to pick which were which.

Despite the fact that this particular part of the coast

is difficultly placed, another Dutchman, Willem de Vlamingh, found it 80 years after Hartog had marked the spot on a chart. What I didn't know was that de Vlamingh put his plate in place of Dirk's which he took back to Holland where it was displayed in a museum for over 200 years. The Australians would prefer the original to be Down Under, but the Dutch provided a copy which can be seen at the West Australian Museum in Perth.

William Dampier, an odd combination of English naval officer and pirate, was also exploring the coast about this time. He landed near Broome in 1688, and on a later journey, in 1699, he came south and named the Bay of Sharks – now called Shark Bay. His report about the area that he sent to the British Government was so unfavourable that it was probably put away in a filing cabinet (or somesuch) and forgotten.

YEARS WENT BY, AND IT WASN'T UNTIL THE EARLY 19TH century that things started to happen in this huge area described as 'unattached' on maps of the southern continent known as both Terra Australis and New Holland. The French – Britain's natural enemies then and still rivals today, not just on the rugby field – were showing a lot of interest. There was Nicolas Baudin, in *Géographe*, who explored the continent's southwest before sailing on to Tasmania (Geographe Bay is one of the state's highly regarded tourist attractions today).

Later, the captain of *Naturaliste*, Jacques-Felix-Emmanuel Hamelin, and his navigator, Louis de Freycinet, mapped the area. Both men and the ship itself are remembered in names given to parts of the coast. De Freycinet added another element to WA's history when he removed de Vlamingh's plate and took it back to Paris – it is now, however, also in the West Australian Museum, a gift from France.

Where the *Naturaliste* went is today an attraction that is ecologically incomparable. Hamelin Pool, in Shark Bay World Heritage site, is one of the last few places on earth where living stromatolites can be found (there's another, far smaller, collection at Lake Thetis, near Cervantes, in the south towards Perth, and one in the depths around Stocking Island in the Bahamas). These are the link between the prehistoric earth, which had no oxygen, and our world in which we cannot live without it.

Stromatolites are both extraordinary to look at and amazingly difficult to describe. (I found the word in a science dictionary and information is available online.) A volunteer at the small museum at the Hamelin campsite was full of enthusiasm for this phenomenon which went some way to encouraging my understanding of these forms which, millions of years ago, provided the gas that wrought a miracle, allowing other life forms to evolve.

In the museum, housed in the old Telegraph Station, there is a tank in which some stromatolites have been nursed along in a salty bath over a few years. Spend some time here to grasp the concept before you follow the boardwalk on the bay, breathing in the fresh air of the Indian Ocean as you do so. The boardwalk is built over the onshore waters so that you can gaze on these ancient wonders without damaging them – they are exceedingly fragile.

The stromatolites in the shallows are flat and black;

further out where the water is deeper they are taller and bumpy. They look like rocks, but aren't. They have a cycle that relates to light and dark, but are not plants. When deprived of the high salinity, the growth process stops; where this has happened, they are covered in a rusty red crust, thought to be caused by a bacterium.

Stromatolites are dependent on that water and its extremely high salt content – as the waves wash over them, tiny grains of sand are trapped and, over time, this forms a new layer. It isn't a fast process. They grow agonisingly slowly with the help of blue algae (cyanobacteria) and photosynthesis (chemical change caused by sunlight). Perhaps this explains why it took so long for anyone to work out what they were.

As if this were not enough to confound, the 'beach' round here is itself highly unusual. Instead of sand underfoot there are millions of miniscule creamy-coloured shells, the remains of the Cardiid Cockle (*Fragum eragatum*), which have been deposited over 6,000 years.

Fortunately, there are information boards – erected by CALM, which manages this national park – to explain the phenomenon. It is thought that the shells ended up in this one area because of the wind, high temperatures and the way the coastline is shaped – check it out on a map. Parts of the shoreline are, in fact, quarries, with consolidated shells metres thick. Over time the shells became bound together by calcium carbonate which dissolves in rainwater and dries to become a white crystal that's as hard as rock.

For the early settlers, this limestone – coquina or coquinite, as it is known – was a lifesaver. The newcomers couldn't survive without shelter (in this marine desert a tree was a rarity for building purposes) and were saved by the discovery that the hardset shells could be cut into blocks with a crosscut saw (you can see one that was used in the museum).

Coquinite was the construction material for the church at Denham and several station homesteads, none of which we saw, but its most poignant use was as a headstone on that 'beach' at Hamelin Pool. Here a block, with a deep cross chiselled out, marks the lonely grave of 60-year-old Walter Musk who was drowned in the bay when his sailboat capsized in 1911.

As preservation of this area is paramount, blocks aren't dug any more for construction purposes but tiny samples are sold at the museum café. Mine is a reminder of this Aussie eco treasure trove. One day I hope my grandchildren (who are, after all, quarter Australian) will want to see the area for themselves.

Dirk Hartog missed all this, as did de Vlamingh and, I presume, the French as well – although coquinite has a distinctly French sound, in that language the word means knave or rascal and not building blocks, so perhaps they didn't give it its name.

Whatever Captains Baudin and Hamelin were looking for, the fact that they were hanging around spurred the British Colonial Office to action. British presence would be the best deterrent, they decided, and thus the western half of the continent, beyond the 135th meridian of east longitude, was en route to statehood.

The Sydney-based Governor of New South Wales (the name at the time for two thirds of the continent) was ordered to set up a military station on the far side, an extraordinary feat in itself considering the distance involved. That first settlement in 1827 at Albany, in the south, and another in the north at Port Dundas, might have been the end of it, except that the Colonial Office received a good report of the Swan River area, around where Perth is today, which prompted further interest.

With more optimistic information to hand, and the first suggestion that the west wasn't as poor as previously painted, it was time to do some annexing. So it was that Captain Charles Howe Fremantle, in *HMS Challenger*, arrived in 1829 to take formal possession in the name of King George IV. The first settlers and officials arrived from England on *Parmelia* in June the same year, along with the first Lieut-Governor, Captain Stirling, he being the one whose encouraging words brought in the free colonists. He could not possibly have known the riches that were there.

AS WE WERE DRIVING ANTICLOCKWISE ROUND AUSTRALIA we entered Western Australia in the north and the state was revealed to us slowly over quite a few weeks. The idea was that as the heat increased in the tropical Top End, we would make our way down the coast to the more acceptable spring temperatures of what is known as Australia's mediterranean climate, the southwestern region with its vineyards, forests and rich pastures. And that, to a certain extent, was what happened except that, in the year we were travelling, everything about the weather was unseasonal. What the hell. Everywhere we went wonders awaited. Often we changed our plans as we went along, which is, of course, the joy of independent travel.

We spent a few days at Katherine, enjoying a trip through the lush and multi-faceted gorge. We saw an amazing array of Aboriginal rock art and travelled on three different boats, one with a flat bottom, a necessity in part of the terrain. After Katherine we thought we would take the next 300 km at a gentle pace, but we covered it quite quickly, as this part of the Northern Territory is mostly wide open spaces on which miserable looking beasts wander about searching out what food they can. There are no fences to contain these meandering Santa Gertrudis cattle; we saw two that had been hit by vehicles – probably a road train and probably at night.

These cattle are also called Brahmans, a breed related to the Indian ox, and not only do they tolerate high temperatures and resist the accursed ticks but manage to do well on what, to our eyes, looked like extremely parched ground. It was hard to imagine that they could be of any use to anyone, but since the 1950s Brahmans or Zebus have been successfully crossed with other breeds – Shorthorns, Herefords and Aberdeen-Angus, for example – and have contributed to Australia's reputation for producing quality beef.

Driving here is an odd experience. The roads are straight and disappear on the horizon in a purply haze. We'd go for many ks without a vehicle in front or behind and then suddenly there'd be three roadtrains overtaking us in one go – each 50 metres long. It was quite scary at first but soon we became accustomed to their appearance, and pace.

You have to remember one important thing about the Northern Territory (towns excluded): there is no speed limit. However, you are expected to drive according to both the vehicle and the road conditions. We stuck to our 90 kph, which we found the most economical speed.

After stopping at Victoria River roadhouse to fill up and buy a cool drink, we set off to find seven caravans travelling together (in caravan, you might say). Overtaking them was like driving a slalom, or chicane, something we were used to doing in London where cars are parked on both sides of narrow streets with occasional spaces to allow one stream of traffic through while the other one waits. We were relieved not to find any roadtrains coming towards us while we carried out this manoeuvre.

The landscape was a mix of sandy, shrubby hillocks interspersed with scrub much of the time, often with large birds of prey circling overhead, indicating roadkill in the vicinity. Then rugged escarpments would appear atop the hills, looking like the man-made fortresses so common in medieval Europe. There were also fascinating rock formations: big and small reddish-brown boulders balanced on top of each other, a bit like speech bubbles in cartoons. They were enormous. How did they get there? What kept them in place?

Around us was a lot of flat ochre-coloured nothingness, but then we began to notice the boabs, weird-looking trees with a girth out of all proportion to their height. With their large, wide trunks and waving asymmetrical branches, I could easily imagine them as cartoon characters in a child's storybook. Just like the extraordinary termite and ant mounds, which are striking features of northern Australia (the very tall ones are known as cathedrals), these trees figure widely in Aboriginal lore.

According to *The Rough Guide to Australia*, in Aboriginal mythology the tree was so arrogant that it was turned upside down to teach it humility. There is also a mystery about it which possibly goes back to the Gondwana link, when India, South America, Australia, Africa and Antarctica were all one landmass. What the Aussies call a boab is, in fact, a baobab, the only other species of which grows in tropical Africa – the one-time existence of Gondwana is the best explanation as to why each should have its own endemic species.

From Arnhem Land across to the Derby district in the Kimberley, the Australian baobab is found on sandy plains and low stone ridges and, significantly, holds water. There is a striking example at Derby that is not only wide but also hollow which made it, in the past, useful as a temporary gaol. It is, as you might imagine, a popular place for a photo stop.

Sometimes boabs are called bottle trees, but once you see these growing in tropical Queensland you realise how different they are. The bottle tree can grow up to 18 metres high, two-thirds of which is the thick, smooth trunk which tapers, like a neck of a bottle, to branches and foliage which make up the top third.

ONCE WE REACHED KUNUNURRA, A 'NEW' TOWN BUILT IN 1960, we felt we needed to get some perspective on this northern part of Western Australia. The area was the setting for Mary Durack's *Kings in Grass Castles* and *Sons in the*

Saddle, stories of the pastoralists. The homestead built by the Durack family in the 19th century was, unfortunately, covered when Lake Argyle was created as part of the enormous Ord Irrigation Project. A replica is now a museum preserving the story of the early pioneers. Australians are rarely sentimental but this may change if too many treasures disappear.

Though much of the Kimberley area is desert, there are hidden parts to be discovered, particularly if you have a lot of time and a 4WD (which we didn't have). Distances are mind-boggling. There was only one way we could see it to advantage – on a day trip with Slingair, travelling over it first by plane and then through it by 4WD. At 8.30 in the morning the temperature had already started to climb which, according to the driver who'd picked us up from the campsite, meant just one thing:

– You can feel it building up to the Wet.

Luke, the pilot, called the 13-seater plane a caravan. Our fellow passengers were a group on a four-week luxury trip: Cairns, Darwin, Kununurra, Broome, Perth, Adelaide, Melbourne, and seeing all the sights along the way. They were interested to know that we were taking over seven months to follow a similar route. The journeys we took in little planes were terrific. Sometimes we wore headphones to listen to recorded information but on other occasions the pilot chatted away about the history and geography, and explained what to look for and in which direction. I was able to photograph a lot of what we were flying over by holding my camera steady against the window and not using flash (it bounces off the Perspex 'pane').

Our 'caravan' flew for an hour over a massive area with continually changing geology, from flat and arid scorched parts to volcanic valleys and escarpments, brain-like undulating sandstone and mountains.

Then we saw the Bungle Bungles. These extraordinary rock formations could easily be a science fiction city on another planet. OK, so I've seen too many fillums, but these sandstone mounds with their layered construction have to be seen to be believed. On the ground, I photographed a CALM notice, which gives an explanation of their origins:

"The foundations for these towering sandstone cliffs were laid down 360 million years ago. Ancient rivers flowing into a vast basin brought in sediments which gradually compacted to form sandstone and conglomerate. Over time these deposits were uplifted and incised with torrential floodwaters carving out deep gorges. The Range now stands 200m above the surrounding plain."

These rock formations have only been 'around' – in non-indigenous terms – since the 1980s. An ABC crew, making a programme about great Australian areas, met a helicopter pilot called Spud Murphy who took them to see what the indigenous people called Bungle Bungle. That was in 1983, and in 1987 it became Purnululu National Park which today is very big business. It is, however, a fragile area ecologically and its isolation is its best protection. The tropical climate also helps. The park is closed between January and April, which provides a breathing space from tramping feet and off-road vehicles.

We landed at a small airfield also used by tourist helicopters which have an open-fronted area allowing for easier viewing and photo opportunities (but passage per person is also more expensive than in a plane). Waiting for us was a 4WD coach and our driver/guide Kim, a former radiographer, who was delighted to be paid for doing what she enjoyed as a hobby – bushwalking. She drove us for 40 minutes into the park, chatting all the way; then we walked for 40 minutes through bush and escarpments to a magnificent gorge.

Kim pointed out a blowfly tree, and a kapok tree (known as Kimberley snow), then a *grevillea psylanthe* – an endemic plant, only found here in this remote place. Meandering crocodile-style behind her we went between the striated domes which do indeed look like huge beehives. Weathering has left its marks, eating into the rocks, cracking them and allowing lichens to enter. These form a grey crusty surface. What is astounding is the amazing mix of colours that surrounds you.

Eventually we reached an enormous cave, called Cathedral Gorge, which is shaped like an amphitheatre and provided a lunching place for our ham salad, fruit and a drink. Underfoot was the softest, finest and whitest sand (excellent for cleaning jewellery, we learnt – but, of course, you are not allowed to take any away), and in the centre was a pool created from the water that drips from the sandstone above. Alongside it lazed a sand monitor, a smaller version of the monitor lizard I'd seen at Cooinda. It took no notice of us, lying still and enjoying the shade. As we were too – it was all we had until we reached Wilardi Camp, a walk and then a drive away, where afternoon tea awaited us.

The camp has its own accommodation, units sleeping two to four, either old-style wooden chalets or modern safari tents. In the 38C heat I thought there wouldn't be much circulation of air inside the chalets though the tents with their netting walls were more promising. Part of me wanted to stay – not even the temperature put me off this wonderfully strange area.

DESERT PREDOMINATES IN THE STATE, BUT IT ISN'T JUST one unchanging spread of sand. Each one is different and holds treasures of world importance. A prime example is found northwest of the Tropic of Capricorn in the Pilbara region where, on the Burrup Peninsula, is the world's largest concentration of petroglyphs – ancient rock carvings dating back as far as the last ice age. That was a while ago.

This area, which is unbelievably rich in minerals, has been declared one of the world's 100 most endangered sites by the World Monument Fund in New York – the list also includes the Great Wall of China which, in many parts of its extraordinary length, is in a woeful state and needs huge restoration work. The Chinese, recognising its attraction to tourists, will eventually restore it (they do have a huge workforce to call on), but grave doubts exist about what will happen to the motifs on the 22-km long Peninsula, indigenous name Murujuga. These cover the 20,000-year worldview of the Yaburara people, among the country's oldest original inhabitants.

The rock art has been catalogued and photographed, and a programme of preservation was devised by Bill Carr, then Director of the Environment Commission for Western Australia. The biggest threat to the rare collection has been the Woodside North West Shelf Project which erected an incongruous city of steel and concrete halfway along the peninsula, the terminal point for the pipeline bringing natural gas ashore.

It is one of a long line of collisions between cultures in the state, probably going all the way back to the mid 19th century when the first pastoralists arrived, and has aroused a great deal of feeling. Can the petroglyphs be protected from the commercial enterprise? An appeal was made to Unesco to make it a World Heritage site so there can be global recognition of the historic importance and sacredness of the area. So far the paintings have survived the ravages of time but the beast of consumerism may be too great an enemy to resist.

Two of Western Australia's extraordinary national parks, both containing wealth-making minerals, have overcome mining interests and are now protected. The colours of the Kimberley, in the north, are similar, but not quite the same, as those of Karijini, closer to the Tropic of Capricorn. The different earth elements tint the soil and rocks pink, terracotta and red, but it is the array of greens and whites in the plants and trees that provide the contrast. The topography is stunning, with deep gorges, chasms and caves, as well as waterfalls and pools.

Karijini, Aboriginal for 'the hills', is the state's second biggest national park. It too is in the Pilbara region (*pilbara* is an Aboriginal word meaning freshwater fish) and part of the Hamersley Ranges. Here the rocks in the gorges were part of the sea floor 2,500 million years ago! The park, 1,400 km from Perth, is well inland from Highway 1 but is regarded as the jewel of the state and not to be missed. For bushwalkers who prefer terrain that is rough, rugged and remote it is a magnet, with a variety of trails graded in degrees of difficulty.

In any part of Australia it is wise for walkers to know what to expect. In Karijini CALM has put up a notice advising them to wear a hat, sunscreen, sunglasses and sturdy boots and to carry at least 2 litres of water per person per day (very heavy advice). In their day pack should be insect repellent, maps, compass, camera, binoculars, a whistle, first aid kit, notepad, pencil, Swiss army knife, food (including a Thermos – no fires allowed, so you can't boil a billy – and energy snacks such as chocolate, dried fruit and biscuits), swimming cossie and a bag for rubbish. Wow, some pack.

On the gloriously sunny day that we were there with Ally, our driver and guide from Design A Tour, based at the Auski Roadhouse, one part of the CALM notice seemed amusing:

"Be aware that swimming in the cold waters of the park's pools can cause hypothermia, especially between April and September."

And it wasn't kidding. On September 19, at Fortescue Falls, after a 30 minute walk during which body heat rose to what felt like boiling point, there was a discernible gasp from those who enthusiastically jumped into the delightfully blue pool to cool off. Ally thought it was funny, but so did everyone else – when they'd caught their breath again.

Ally's a first generation Australian, born in 1971, a year after her parents emigrated from Bournemouth in the south of England. She'd done a lot of travelling abroad, she told us, but chose to come back to the country which most captivated her. She hadn't long finished her training as a guide and wanted to ensure that we got some insight into at least a little of the million-acre park. 'Little' was the operative word. The day was broken up by walks through gorges and between escarpments, stops for a drink and something to eat, dips into several pools, and chats.

Ally was ecstatic about the trees: the smooth white-barked scribbly gums (the larvae of a moth tunnels through the bark creating what looks like 'writing'); and snappy gums (also called widow makers, as they discard branches at will when dry conditions threaten their survival, injuring anyone unfortunate to be beneath). She pointed out cockroach cassia (one of the first plants to come up after fire and named after the world's longest surviving insect), and a ball of rolling spinifex (spiky desert grass which can self combust in extreme heat). Another name for it is roly-poly, though some people, influenced by the American Westerns, call it tumbleweed.

As we walked we watched for birds, and three types of roo: the blue fliers (red kangaroos, with a blue tinge to the fur), euros (Aboriginal name wallaroos – males are twice as big as females), and rothschild rock wallabies (which look like brown blots against the rocks). Then, while most of the others went off to find a particular pool, which could only be reached down a long slope by holding onto a rope, a few who were feeling less energetic idled in a shallow pool accompanied by pink dragonflies and fireflies which were busily patrolling their patch. The silence was remarkable.

Over the years, one of the most common images of Australia has been a man in a bush hat decorated by corks on strings, their movement supposedly a deterrent to the ever-present flies. There's no doubt these are a dratted nuisance, but there are two pieces of good news. One is that the newer bush hats are much more elegant and have a fine mesh, all-round veil (the fashion conscious might only wear it in desperation). The second is that if you travel in winter there aren't as many flies around.

In fact, it was a shock to come across them in numbers at the Pinnacles, just north of Perth, in October. We started doing what everyone does naturally all through summer in Australia, waving our hands like fans across our faces to prevent the flies settling on the mouth and eyes. They weren't big blowies, but little, irritating bush flies which were all over our sweaty backs. Gail, our guide, had warned us about them:

– You've got the moisture and they want it.

This Limestone Desert gained a little notoriety, a sort of bum's rush, when Scottish comedian Billy Connolly ran naked through the 4 metre-tall pillars as part of his Down Under television series made in the mid 1990s. One of the dunes is moving towards the area at a metre a year and one day that video footage will be a record of what was once there and is no more (and I don't just mean Billy Connolly). Fortunately, people come to Nambung National Park not to copy him but to see this very rare place

where the creeping sands make constant changes to the landscape. The sand dunes do, however, look very tempting, and Gail tried to ensure that no one made the mistake of trying to run down them.

– They are deep, unstable, and could be covering limestone. It is very easy to break a leg. Walk, don't run, down them.

There were two young Japanese backpackers in our party and they took absolutely no notice. More by luck than judgement they reached the bottom without incident, though they built up a terrifying forward propulsion in the process and had fear written on their faces. But it turned to exhilaration – they like a challenge, do the Japanese. And it doesn't always end well: they feature highly in the accident statistics here.

You can't stay in Nambung National Park but you can drive to the park and pay an entrance fee. We'd chosen to take the tour from the campsite at Cervantes – the nearest to the park – because part of the 19 km road to the Pinnacles is unsealed. We'd been warned that care should be taken to avoid vehicle damage on this road, so the Hiace stayed put. It is also more interesting to be shown this incredible place by Someone Who Knows. Like all the guides we met, Gail loved her subject and was keen to impart facts and figures (remembering that being precise about anything so old is rather difficult).

The formation of this desert, with its huge mobile dunes, began a long long time ago: sea shells were broken down into lime-rich sand which was brought ashore by the waves and carried inland by the winds. In the park, if you look to the west, white caps of the breakers indicate the near Indian Ocean. The limestone pillars, some of them up to six metres high, were only exposed in relatively 'recent times' – Aboriginal artefacts at least 6,000 years old have been found there.

Seeing these reddish gold pillars spread out over a vast vista is a weird experience. Gail explained that they are the fossilised roots of long-dead trees and shrubs around which the limestone formed over many thousands of years, starting during the last ice age. With the sand shifting all the time, pillars disappear and reappear; to the early Dutch sailors, who viewed them from the sea, they looked like the remains of an ancient city.

She pointed out, to the east, the sandy pinnacle-less area that extends for hundreds of metres. To the northwest, the dunes are whitish in colour; it's a young system, in process of formation, and a stark contrast to the much longer established brown/yellow sand of the Pinnacles. But it means the desert is expanding. It was hard to imagine what it all might be like from one year to the next, as the shifting sands, powered by the southerly winds, uncover the limestone shapes in one area and cover those in another. In fact, Gail told us that she was often surprised at how different it looked each year.

If Captains Baudin and Hamelin were to return to the southwest of Western Australia today, they would find one of the most prosperous areas of the state and one of those ironies that cause amusement – unless you are French. Here, in the area known as the Margaret River winegrowing region, vineyards producing world-recognised wines are dotted along the coast from Cape Naturaliste (named after Hamelin's ship) to Cape Leeuwin (after a Dutch boat that was in the area in 1622), where the Indian and Southern Oceans meet – a great spot for a photo opportunity. (We turned our picture into a stamp using a post office service so we had a truly original addition to our Christmas cards.)

Inland are vast state forests with sky-reaching specimens of karri, jarrah and other eucalypts – and an amazing aerial walkway through the 'Valley of the Giants', from which you look down on them – but it is the 140 km-long coastal strip that astounds. For walkers and hikers, it is described as "a windswept limestone ridge, perched on a basement of ancient and resistant granite rocks...the backbone of the Leeuwin-Naturaliste National Park". For wine lovers it could be one long indulgence, from Busselton to Augusta.

The success of the Australian wine industry is, in a way, a direct result of a French decision to allow quality wines made in particular regions to have particular names. Only in France could there be Burgundy or Bourgogne, Sancerre, Côte du Rhone, Côte d'Or or Champagne, to give a few examples. This strict ruling caused havoc in the viniculture industry of other countries, but also, stunningly, opened up the world of wine.

The Aussies, doing exactly what they are renowned for – calling a shovel a shovel – chose to make their wines known by the grape name, starting a fashion that gives wine drinkers an understanding of the different tastes of a single type or a combination. The French, hit hard by wine imports from the New World – a designation for Australia, New Zealand, South Africa, South America and California – are realising their labels and description of bottle content need to change with the times.

We had a joyous few hours at a Cape Naturaliste winery, an unrivalled setting looking over Geographe Bay, where the owner was full of praise for his Coat Door range. And very nice it was, too, just a glass each taken with a selection of breads and dips (eggplant caviar, salsa and tsatsiki) in the modern restaurant, built high with big windows to give extensive views over rose gardens, vineyards and sea. The label, with a drawing of a door and a coat hanging on it, must become a collector's item.

That the Wise Winery, situated in one of the world's most out-of-the-way places, might want to arouse the ire of the French is typical of the Aussies. The French like a legal fight – they pursued the South African winery that produced Goats Do Roam through the courts – but the best lesson for them might be to join in this revolution. As every winegrowing region we went to in Australia has spectacular rose displays (an attractive defence system: any vine-threatening bugs will attack the roses first), it would seem that Down Under they've discovered the secret formula for the days of wine and roses.

13

THE URGE TO CHASE SUNSETS

GLORIOUS COLOURS ON LAND AND SEA

THERE SEEMED to be two criteria by which travellers we met in various parts of Australia judged the places they liked most: either how good the fishing was, or the quality of the sunset. Fishing didn't attract us, though we appreciated the sense of it when we were in the Northern Territory, staying at Cooinda in Kakadu National Park, and our neighbours showed off the day's catch, a very large barramundi. This is a much prized fish, having good texture and flavour, though there are many others in these southern hemisphere waters that bring a glow of satisfaction to the face of the amateur angler. Black jewfish, cod, groper, saratoga, threadfin, schnapper – all are good tucker, for free.

We were impressed by this family who were well into their adventurous 12-month plan to travel around the whole country with their children, a girl of 11, a boy of 10, and a 20-months-old toddler. With his white blond hair and tanned skin, the little one looked a miniature version of the Aussie surfies we'd seen on the east coast beaches. After years of talking and dreaming about it, the journey became possible when the father sold his business (so there were no money worries) and the oldest child was in her last year of primary school. It was now or never, they decided, so as not to disrupt her secondary schooling. They rented their house in Melbourne and off they went, 'on the wallaby' as they say in Australia. (I think that only applies if you have a swag on your back, but you know what I mean!)

Their mobile 'home' was well thought out: a caravan with double axles for greater stability, a self-inflating tent for the older children, and a tinnie with outboard motor that travelled on top of the powerful Shogun. The caravan had a large annexe – motorised, so there was no fiddling about with poles and guy ropes – which gave them a protected outdoor living area.

Here the children did their daily schooling, overseen by their mother. As set sections of the schoolwork were completed, they were mailed off and, at pre-arranged places in the itinerary, the next lot would be picked up at the Post Office, along with comments on progress and marks for work done previously. Written guidance was provided for the mother so that she felt confident supervising and advising, if the children needed help.

As a home education method I can't think of anything better. If this family is anything to go by, to broaden a child's mind you should start young – though broadening the mind is obviously good at any time. Australia boggles the mind as well!

Dad would sometimes take the older children to the nearest water to catch the evening meal; easy when you have a 4WD. In Kakadu there are many barra-rich freshwater billabongs, like Yellow Water, in the South Alligator river system. Their Shogun – with exhaust snorkel so they could cross flooded areas – enabled them to go wherever they wanted without being restricted by the condition of the roads. We were realising by now just how much of Australia can only be reached successfully by off-road vehicles.

The caravan had solar panels and a generator so that the family wasn't dependent on campsites – they had only stopped at Cooinda because of the need to do some housekeeping and washing, what we called our 'make do and mend' days. And, of course, to socialise with others on the road, which the kids needed as much as the parents. That's the best way of exchanging information.

The parents were full of praise for the gorgeous sunsets they'd seen, as well as the fishing. They were going clockwise, the opposite way from us, and had come across so many amazing places as they drove up the west coast that they were several weeks behind their original schedule and were hurrying to get to Darwin to meet grandparents who were flying there specially to see them. They were beginning to wonder if a year was in fact long enough to see all there was to see.

I had just a year of Australian history at school, but it could never teach me what these children were learning, discovering the history and geography of their own country while following the curriculum provided by the education system as a correspondence course. School stuff in the mornings, enjoying their environment after lunch – a most satisfactory formula.

The area which had slowed their progress, only in a

physical sense, was Indian Ocean Drive, which lies between Cervantes and Exmouth. It has many unique attractions: a limestone desert (Pinnacles, near Cervantes); a bright purple betacarotene lake (Dongara); a turquoise sea (Cape Range National Park); prehistoric stromatolites (Hamelin Pool); dolphins, dugongs, the rare and extraordinary giant whale sharks (Shark Bay), a barrier reef with 220 species of coral (Coral Bay); wildflowers in bloom on sandplains all year round. How did all these – and more – escape me when I lived in Australia?

Of course, Western Australia could be a country in its own right – it is 2,527,633 sq km (according to *Gregory's Road Atlas*), almost as big as India. The distance from Perth, the state capital, to Wyndham, at the Top End, is over 3,200km. It has an incomparable coastline (7,000km long) and a vast inland that encompasses an incredible diversity. All schoolkids learn about the goldfields of Kalgoorlie and Coolgardie, due east from Perth, for it was the discovery of this precious metal that attracted people from around the world hoping to make their fortune, and influenced the way Australia developed.

My only contact with this part of the west was through knowing Sheila Hawkins, illustrator, author and painter, who was born in Kalgoorlie in 1905, came to England in 1932 and lived in London. I met her through her daughter Anna du Polnay, artist and former actress. Sheila was a war artist of World War II whose archive – including drawings of the Australian Forestry Units working in Scottish forests – is kept at the Australian War Memorial, Canberra. Her drawings of Australian animals, done for her many children's books, are captivating – some of her work is preserved at the Mitchell Library in Sydney, and in Adelaide at the South Australian State Library as part of the Children's Literature Research Collection. She died in 1998.

To get back to the sunsets: we had had our first sight of how extraordinary they could be on Fraser Island, off the east coast near Hervey Bay in Queensland. The town, about four hours' drive north of Brisbane, is known as 'the whale watch capital of the world', particularly from late July to early November. Fraser, thought to be more than 800,000 years old, is the biggest sand island in the world. Australian author Patrick White set two novels here: *The Eye of the Storm*, which he completed in 1973, the year he was awarded the Nobel prize for literature, and *A Fringe of Leaves*.

The island, long and narrow, is edged by pristine cream-coloured beaches and dotted along its length are freshwater lakes, creeks and streams. On the eastern and northern sides are 30 sand 'blows' – huge drifts with dunes, which move just as they do in a desert. Most mysterious of all is how the lush rainforest which covers much of the centre survives, how the giant kauris and other eucalypts, she oaks, strangler figs and paperbark trees manage to grow so tall on sand which has few nutrients.

The acceptable explanation appears to be that over thousands of years nutrients were blown in by the wind, were harnessed by plants and, after a long slow process of recycling decaying wood and plant matter, eventually a sustainable base was provided for an array of plants including bloodwood trees, banksias, pandanus palms and grasses, as well as the trees and vines in the rainforest. However it occurred, the island is stunning.

Because it has World Heritage listing, it is carefully managed. Guided tours travel by ferry from Hervey Bay – only a set number of vehicles is allowed on the island at any one time. It is a National Park, and you have to pay an entrance fee plus, if you intend camping on the beach, the cost of a permit.

Those in 4WD vehicles are given a map on which the driving and other tracks are marked. Buses, cars and walkers have their own designated routes to avoid any chance of accidents – Fraser has its own police constable to keep an eye on the visitors. You can stay several days if you want time to explore and enjoy the atmosphere, either at a resort or caravan park (these have ensuite sites and are naturally very popular, so it's essential to book ahead).

It is a 'must see' place and people flock to it; even in the second week of July there was already a lot of traffic. We travelled in a 6WD mini bus that took 16 passengers and was driven by our guide Richard, a former policeman, an entertaining fellow who also cooked us a barbie lunch (I had sea perch fillets with herb butter, and Ian had T-bone steak, both delicious). He was one of a growing number of eco rangers, men and women who retrain to be part of the tourist industry aiming to protect the country's superb natural resources.

Through his two-way radio he heard that seats were available on the small spotter plane that uses a part of the beach as a runway. Would we be interested? Would we! (It costs between $A80 and $A150 per person, paid by credit card. Our pilot completed the transaction on the wing of the tiny Cessna.) The 15-20 minute flight provides an overall view of the island's many parts, with a perspective we could never get at ground level. It was the only real way to understand what a sand blow is, and how extensive they are on the island. And there was a bonus: we saw our first whales, two humpbacks cavorting off the coast in the clear water.

There was no sight, however, of the dingoes, the major wildlife on Fraser, and a danger for the unwary. They set their place in the island's history in 2001 when one young boy was killed and another badly injured, causing the rangers to cull those dingoes scavenging the picnic areas.

Signs everywhere warn that dingoes are wild animals and should not be fed, but the words are far too often ignored, making a tragedy more than a possibility. In Australia the important lesson to learn is that not everything can be tamed and wildlife should be respected.

All in all, it was a very long day, which brings me to the point of this particular tale. In Queensland in winter it gets dark early (no daylight saving) and from Fraser Island the sunset is over water, not land. Returning on the ferry, my camera caught the golden orb spreading its glistening rays over a brassy sea. I had become a sunset collector.

As we drove into the Town of 1770, further up the coast, we found roos frolicking in the bush by the roadside in the special light that announces the end of day in the tropics. We arrived just in time to get the last place at an idyllic campsite right on the beach when the nightly displays are a melange of orangey gold, yellow and inky blue-black smudges on a turquoise background. People start gathering along the shore under the palm trees from about 5.30 so that they can sit and watch the drama of the sun going down. It sort of falls out of the sky at 6 o'clock.

We also had another view of the sunset over water when we took an evening ride on a LARC – acronym for 'lighter amphibious re-supply cargo' – vessel, once a military transporter and now surplus to requirements, except in a tourist sense. Painted a distinctive raspberry-and-cream pink it is a great attraction. As the authorities designate it a boat on wheels, the 'driver' has to have his sea credentials. It's very smooth. First we bowled along the brownish sand, then moved seamlessly on to the water, following the coast for 10 minutes or so before heading back to land with the glow of the setting sun behind us.

Travelling through Queensland's canefield country, we saw the sky filled with smoke from the fields being burnt off after the harvest. When the rays of the setting winter sun hit that smoke, they create a dramatic array of patterns and colours. This is a sunset with an aroma, for you can also smell the burning. Some splendid skies can be seen when the weather's been warm and dry for weeks. This is the time, too, to see willy-willys, Aboriginal for a storm or whirlwind. These tall, typhoon-shaped wind gusts appear and disappear suddenly, moving corkscrew-style across wide open spaces gathering up topsoil and plant debris in the process. By the time you think of taking a photo, it's over.

We saw a lot of scrub that had been burnt as we crossed the state, but we didn't see another perfectly painted sky until we reached Katherine Gorge in the Northern Territory. There, high on the balcony of the modern and commodious visitor centre on the campsite in the Nitmiluk National Park (you don't pronounce the 't' in the Aboriginal word), we sat with our cold white wine and watched the golden rays light up the fluffy clouds above the eucalypt-clad hills.

In the wet of 1998, we were told, the water in the Katherine River rose to just 13cm below the balcony we were on – which must have meant that there was a lot of rain that season (about 100cm usually falls between November and February). Fortunately we were there in August, in hot but not too humid weather, and well before the rainy season.

The next notable sunset was on the Kakadu floodplains in Australia's largest National Park, measuring 20,000 sq km. It is an outstanding place. The two-hour wetlands cruise left at 4.30 in the afternoon with Scott, our driver guide, making us aware from the start of the paradise we would find. On all sides there were birds: tall and stately jabirus and brolgas, a tiny jacana stepping fastidiously across the lily leaves, a rufous heron watching us from a branch, and a number of different sized egrets poised on the banks and branches. Darters stood with their wings opened wide to dry them, as a blue-winged kookaburra, known as the howling jackass, flew by. Quite a few very large crocodiles lay around on the banks, obligingly opening their snouts to reveal their terrifying teeth.

The evening light was beginning to alter as Scott turned off the engine so that we could appreciate the delightful silence of the paperbark forest. Despite some competition from coughing, talking, and feet moving on the metal floor of the boat, I was spellbound. Nothing could really spoil the pleasure of the water's stillness, the orangey-green mix in the mirror-image reflection of trees and mangroves. The sun set as a perfect red orb against a pink and blue sky, the result of deliberate burning taking place in the park, whispered Scott.

Setting the trees afire is done simply because some seeds, as a protective measure in a harsh climate with water problems, are encased in a hard wooden capsule that will only open in flames. The indigenous people, with their deep understanding of the land and their reliance on it for food, would burn when it was considered necessary. After the horrendous fires of 2019 in so many parts of Australia, the whole subject burning off was seriously debated and decisions made about future practice.

In inland Queensland we drove through a wooded area that suddenly erupted in fire, set alight from a small plane we heard passing overhead. Within minutes the road ahead was clouded by smoke, and flames were racing in the trees on both sides. It did give us a bit of a turn, but we kept on driving, and it was soon behind us. We were very glad that the incendiary method, whatever it was, had landed where intended and had missed the Hiace. If it hadn't, imagine having to explain such a mishap to the insurance company!

Sunsets in Western Australia are stunning. At Port Hedland, the exact halfway point of our round-Oz journey, the coloured sky was enhanced by the lights from the BHP iron ore factory twinkling on the bay. At full moon, between March and October, there is a natural phenomenon called "Staircase to the Moon": pockets of water are caught in the sand ripples so that it looks like a golden staircase. To see this, make sure you find out the approximate full moon rising times via porttourist-park.com.au

The next additions to our sunset collection weren't far away: Broome, 80 mile Beach, and Kalbarri (where there's a similar staircase effect on the gently rippling waters of the Indian Ocean). Much further south, at Bunbury, the sky patterns were affected by the natural magnetic pole phenomenon called Aurora Australis. (In the northern hemisphere the colourful movements in the Arctic, mostly green, are created by Aurora Borealis.)

When we reached Tasmania, which is even closer to the Antarctic, the fantastically fiery skies at Hobart were far reaching and vibrant. In South Australia, at Renmark on the Murray River, the ever-present pelicans (whose beaks hold more than their bellies can, says the rhyme) made a fine silhouette against the rose-pink and aqua sky as it gradually lost its light.

There is one sunset that people willingly pay to see, and we did too. It happens at Uluru – or as a taxi driver told us wryly in Alice Springs "Ayers Rock, as the Aborigines call it" – and it was part of a six-day coach trip we took to the Red Centre from Adelaide. We'd missed the Red Centre when we were in the Northern Territory and this was going to be our last opportunity to see the famous monolith.

It was the final trip of the season, in November (after this the heat is too great), and the coach followed the Stuart Highway. Our first overnight stop was Coober Pedy, a rare place that surely has no equal in Australia. Here, 850km north of Adelaide, in what appears to be almost featureless desert land, is a Precious Stone Field measuring 4,954 sq km. Since the first opals were found in 1915, only 10% of it has been worked yet it has made Coober Pedy the largest producer of opals on earth.

The landscape around the town looks as though giant moles have been active, leaving behind cone-shaped piles of reddish sand. These are called mullock heaps and are the by-product of the search for opals. Little ones may be failed attempts, bigger ones indicate promising results. Anyone can stake a claim and dig; if unproductive, you repeat the process. For many, digging for the semi-precious gemstones becomes an obsession. One of the pastimes of the hopeful – visitors and those down on their luck included – is to sift through these heaps, 'noodling' as it is known, looking for the gorgeous-hues that may have been missed. Some areas have been fenced off since a couple of tourists fell into a shaft and were killed. It is, however, the underground pursuit that makes Coober Pedy extraordinary, and exceedingly eerie.

Half of the 2,500 population, made up of 45 nationalities, live below ground, in houses with all mod cons including – would you believe it? – swimming pools and squash courts. Here, too, is the Desert Cave, the world's only underground international hotel, where visitors generally attest to having their best night's sleep ever – it is quiet, cool, airy and dark. No natural light reaches down this far.

There's an underground church, run cooperatively by the protestant denominations . The Catholic Church of Peter and Paul, however, is above ground (interestingly, the priest covers an enormous parish, stretching to the borders of the Northern Territory and Western Australia, travelling by small plane and 4WD vehicle).

Sandy, our guide, was fascinating. She was born in Coober Pedy and was the youngest person to hold a bomb licence, having learnt the skills of controlled explosions from her parents who, like her, are opal miners. She rubbed her arms as we walked along the three to four metre high circular tunnels forged out by TBMs – tunnel boring machines – then said:

– I get goose bumps when I get near opals in the rock.

She ran her fingers over the wall surface and showed us the very fine, white powder that came off. The powder, soft and silky to the touch, is allorite, which sells for about $2 a barrel. Sandy said a French company used it in a masque to restore skin tone, a bottle of which costs $150. At the time I thought someone was missing a trick but I bet it's now been corrected.

Having kept us riveted by her tales of the intricacies of explosions and the effects of different explosives (she said it was against the law to take dynamite into pubs at Coober Pedy, an understandable precaution), she went on to describe opal mining as a reasonable proposition, particularly if the area mined becomes your home. Houses below ground are called dugouts – you can have a tour on YouTube by geobeats; semi dugouts have some part above ground. I found a 3-bed semi dugout going for $A155,000 online.

The air in the first level remains at a constant 24C, the level below is 18C; there's no need for heating or cooling in an underground house. All sewage and waste goes through pipes to a large, deep hole which an average-size family fills in about 20 years, after which another hole is dug and pipes are rerouted to it. When you walk round the town you'll notice the trees – they are planted on top of the old sewage holes and, this being Oz and the land of the much-appreciated pun, are known as lava-trees.

The houses have kitchens, bathrooms, lounges and bedrooms like homes anywhere though, of course, there are no windows. The walls, sealed to give a matt finish, don't need any support, as the stone is laced with silicon. Only in one other place in the world does this occur: under the pyramids in Egypt. Another link with long, long time ago Gondwana?

We didn't see any, but postcards indicate that there are spectacular sunsets here in the desert, as there are fantastic electrical storms which light up the sky for quite a while. As we headed north, our driver told us how highly rated the sunset at Uluru was. From the roadhouse at Erldunda, where we stayed, we still had 250 km to go on the Lasseter Highway into the National Park, and it is a very busy road. Planes fly in from many places as well – Darwin, Brisbane and Sydney were all mentioned – and the passengers are brought by bus to the permitted viewing area at about 5.45 pm. There were 10 or so buses parked with ours. It was surreal.

Tables were set up, laid with white cloths on which were placed silver buckets with the chilling champagne (or probably an excellent Ozbubbly, like Seaview), flutes and plates of nibbles. We felt quite miffed as we heard the corks popping and wondered why we hadn't brought our own. As we were in an indigenous-owned area where the distribution of alcohol is strictly controlled, the driver probably decided not even to mention this aspect.

The well-dressed passengers looked very glamorous

sipping and snacking in the flattering and fading light, but within minutes everybody took up their cameras to catch each subtle change of the rock against the opalescent sky as the sun dropped below the horizon. Of course, I was snapping away too, but I had my ears opened for the comments around me, in French, American, Japanese, Chinese and English, all of which, literally interpreted, added up to "Fantastic".

It was over far too quickly. The rock became a shadowless, deep, impenetrable brown and everyone lost interest. Suddenly the tables were cleared away and people were being encouraged back onto their buses. Some would be going back to the airport, about 20 km away, their day-trip over; others would be heading for the extremely expensive Ayers Rock Resort at Yulara and would be bussed back to Uluru very early next morning to see the sunrise as well. I wondered if bubbly was served then too. Probably. It would be the only accompaniment suitable for such a wonderful sight.

Did we climb the monolith? No. But of course we kept meeting people who had. The Aboriginal owners, for whom much of the area is sacred, have never been in favour of such climbs and their decision is now law. Then, your age and weight, your level of agility, the speed of the wind – it was very windy on the day we visited – or the temperature of the sun were all given as reasons why it wasn't possible, and because it was after eight o'clock in the morning. But at least we were able to walk right round it, seeing its many nooks and crannies.

Not being able to climb it won't put visitors off. That 384metre-high-rock is one huge business, as is the whole National Park. It includes Kata Tjuta, 36 strange landforms made of composite rock and lava which are collectively known as the Olgas (explorer/discoverer Ernest Giles named the range after a German princess, but the Anangu Aboriginal description 'many heads' is more apt). The area attracts more visitors than any other National Park in the country – Yulara town itself can cater for 5,000 a day.

Our driver, a knowing fellow, said that one day people would be able to drive from Sydney to Perth via Brisbane, Mt Isa, Alice Springs, Uluru and Coolgardie, about 4,000km of bitumen. That's a lot of blacktop to maintain, I thought then. But the cross-continent highway (from Cairns to Perth) is now in existence – considered worth it to the lucrative, money-spinning world of tourism. This was before the pandemic and who knows what may happen in future. In creating the road though, it wasn't so much gold at the end of the rainbow, more a sunset.

14

AN ENCHANTING LAND OF ANIMAL MAGIC

WATCH FOR WONDERFUL WILDLIFE

OUR DRIVER, during the coach trip we took to the Red Centre, told us that someone wanted to turn parts of the country into a huge safari park, along the lines of those found in some countries of Africa. He proposed several reasons for this. Quite a few of the African animals were under threat, and this would be one way of ensuring their survival. Australia has a lot of unused space, enough of it similar to the African habitats to make the idea feasible. Australia is just one country, with no language problems or difficult border crossings (this was before the Covid crisis). Australia has no malaria-carrying mosquitoes (though some spread viruses) and a very low HIV/AIDS rate.

If the plan went ahead, the old Africa would be the new Australia, and visitors would be able to see the spectacular animals without having to compromise their health or get caught up in heated political situations. Well, you can see why it might be thought a good idea.

Of course, there would be some major problems to overcome, like, for example, keeping the new animals to one area without creating a zoo and, even more important, protecting the existing wildlife.

Having lions wandering about hunting prey in the outback sounded like a pretty wild idea, but on this extraordinary continent you shouldn't rule out anything on the grounds that it would be impossible. That word is not in the Aussie language. Our driver – who covered a huge distance in the six days of our trip, more than we could have done in our van, even with changing drivers every two hours – kept himself, and us, awake by talking. There is the possibility that the safari idea could just have been something he thought up for our amusement.

From his almost ceaseless commentary we gleaned fascinating insights: the rugged MacDonnell Ranges "were once as high as the Himalayas", and campers at Ellery Creek Big Hole, a very deep waterhole, "don't get any sleep at night because of the howling dingoes".

He was an ever-rolling compendium of interesting facts. The opal town of Coober Pedy, for instance, is Aboriginal for 'white men down hole' (which is an exact description of what goes on in that unusual town). At Alice Springs, as we drove around the Tom Brown roundabout, he said this was Australia's exact centre – it was 1,000miles to the sea in the north (Arafura), south (Great Australian Bight), east (Tasman Sea/Pacific Ocean) and west (Indian Ocean).

Like the other passengers we kept watch on the desert landscape expecting to see the supposed hordes of camels and water buffaloes that are said to have taken over this region and pose a huge threat to the natural habitat of

Australia's own animals. Wherever they were, they weren't where we were, sad to say, but they are the legacy of the many incursions that have occurred since the country was taken over by Britain in 1788.

Water buffaloes came in, courtesy of the Indonesians, in the 1820s, and they were very useful to the early settlers in the Northern Territory for hauling carts and wagons. A few camels had been brought in during the 1840s, and they proved their worth after gold was discovered at Bathurst (New South Wales), Ballarat and Bendigo (both Victoria) in the 1850s. Camels could go where bullocks couldn't, taking supplies to isolated areas where the gold diggers lived in horrendous conditions, hoping for riches.

Two dozen of the beasts were imported for the 1860-61 Burke and Wills' Great Northern Exploration Expedition, which went from Melbourne to the Gulf of Carpentaria, along with an Afghani handler called Dost Mahomet. They got there all right but on the return journey Burke and Wills died of exhaustion and malnutrition. This tragic failure was seen as a lack of understanding of the country, not of the use of camels, and, with so much necessary exploration on the agenda, a recruiting drive in India and Afghanistan resulted in the arrival, in 1866, of 35 Afghani camel handlers and 124 camels. In 1886, 259 more were brought from India, and thus the camel population increased.

Donkeys, nimble-footed in dreadful terrain, were also imported as beasts of burden; harnessed into teams – numbering up to 30 – they were very useful in the hot, dry and harsh interior. The Afghanis, who made a huge contribution to life in Australia's inland, used both lots of animals to carry mail and supplies to areas, such as cattle stations, which were inaccessible by any other means.

Inevitably, other transport methods took over, and most of the animals were released to go their own way (though some camels were retained on stations where very large areas and the boundaries have to be maintained). This land was now their land and they thrived.

Buffaloes particularly relish the coastal plains that become swamps in the wet season and are at home in the freshwater floodplains of the Top End. These creatures have so long been a feature of Arnhem Land that they are part of Aboriginal stories and culture. For the Aborigines they're also good hunting. Buffalo meat is becoming more available to everyone as well. It's like a gamey beef, and tender.

Of course, these very large beasts with their moustache-shaped horns are not all roaming where they please. Some are earning their keep by producing speciality milk, yogurt and cheese – which in Italy would be known as buffalo mozzarella. These foodstuffs are much in demand in Aussie restaurants and home cooking, and so the buffalo has earned its place in the new world.

As for the camels, well, who could have foreseen that central Australia would one day have the last remaining herds of wild camels in the world, one and two humps? Today there is an established trade exporting the most common ones, dromedaries, back to the Middle East. One desert is like any other, I suppose. My experience of them in Tunisia many years ago was a distinctly off-putting emanation from front and rear, and a minor temper tantrum to rival any two-year-old child who's frustrated or thwarted.

Perhaps life's more to their liking in Oz, as tourism has latched onto these desert animals successfully – the domesticated Australian camel is quite big business. The annual Camel Cup Races at Alice Springs in July have become a fun event, drawing visitors from abroad as well as from the other states. If you choose to, once you're in Red Centre, you can go camel trekking for two or five days and get a very close-up view of the West MacDonnell Ranges (whose colours inspired Aboriginal painter Albert Namatjira) or the Simpson Desert.

Our first sighting of a camel chain attraction was at Lighthouse Beach in New South Wales and, by the time we reached Broome in northern Western Australia, we had seen quite a few. Here you can take a camel ride on the white sands of Cable Beach, a particularly popular activity as the sun is setting. Traffic is held up as the brightly adorned camels make their way in a single line through the town, their passengers perched atop and rocking with the stately, swaying gait.

It was the same in Hobart, too. In fact, in Tasmania from October to April, you can take short walks or overnight treks in the bush or on the beach on Bruny Island, where you have a wonderful opportunity to experience what wilderness really is and perhaps to see wildlife that tends to be shy. The island remains unspoilt; in parts like this you may not even meet other travellers, just as you can drive for many ks on its east coast and see neither cars nor people.

You also don't come across any roadkill – because this island is the home of the Tasmanian Devil. We didn't find one in the wild, but learnt all about its unusual qualities when we visited Bonorong Wildlife Park, an animal sanctuary near Hobart. Two newborns, which had been found lying beside their dead mothers on the roadside, were being reared – carefully – by rangers. About the size of a small dog and covered in black hair, the Tasmanian Devil is not endearing to look at, and you certainly couldn't call it lovable or cuddly. It makes a most unappealing noise and moves at an amazing speed.

While they are at the sanctuary, until they can be released back into the bush, the devils are treated with extreme circumspection by the rangers lest they find themselves slashed by long and knife-like talons. It's tricky. The rangers must form a one-to-one relationship with the animals without exciting their digestive system. One young man, sporting a cut on his face, said he must have changed his after-shave or his mother must have used different washing powder for his clothes. Whatever it was, the devil didn't recognise him and lashed out, fortunately just missing the eye area.

The nocturnal Tasmanian Devil has appalling eyesight which is balanced by an extremely acute sense of smell, and teeth so sharp and strong they can crunch through bones, hide, hair and flesh. In terms of survival, the animal doesn't need to see its prey but, through its olfactory processes, finds it and tucks in, getting nourishment from all its parts. These devils are nature's vacuum cleaners and mop up anything they find. They don't hunt living animals and dispose of dead ones efficiently.

There has been concern about the devils in recent years as their numbers have been affected by a virus. The wolf-sized Tasmanian Tiger (Thylacine), a different animal, with different survival skills and habitat, has been extinct since 1936, and it would be terrible if the devils were to follow suit. They are distinctive and have no counterparts anywhere in the world, so their survival is of great importance.

One of the most heartening stories of rescued Australian wildlife involves neighbouring New Zealand. Towards the end of the 19th century Sir George Grey, a former governor of South Australia, New Zealand and South Africa's Cape Colony, bought Kawau Island off the northeast coast of Auckland and stocked it with animals that reminded him of his postings. Zebra, antelope and kookaburras found themselves in a new setting along with tammar, parma and brush-tailed rock wallabies. The wallabies in particular flourished and, despite regular culling and exportation to zoos around the world, by the end of the 1990s had become a problem. Testing their DNA, however, brought one of them, the tammar, a new future.

The tammar wallaby is a small and rare animal; only two of three types have survived in Australia, both in Western Australia. The type Sir George took to Kawau had died out in South Australia, but the DNA of the relocated animal proved its ancestry. Thanks to a joint project of UCLA (the South Australian Department of Environment and Heritage) and the Marsupial Cooperative Research Centre, the direct descendants were reintroduced to their original habitat, hopefully predator free as it was in New Zealand.

This relocation is part of an ambitious programme called Ark on Eyre which aims to try and preserve or restore unique flora and fauna under threat on this South Australian peninsula. Quite how the 60 or so New Zealand-raised tammar wallabies take to this new environment is another matter – but their progress will be tracked, as they'll be wearing radio collars which allows them to be monitored.

The extraordinary array of wildlife is one reason why Australia is so highly regarded by travellers. But the country is hard pressed to cope with the range of feral – wild – animals that are growing in numbers.

Two in particular have been disastrous. In the early days of white settlement, foxes were brought in to give the newly-arrived 'gentry' something to hunt, and rabbits to give them something to shoot. Foxes have been responsible for the extinction of more Australian species than any other animal (except humans). Rabbits are not cuddly bunnies out there, but are considered vermin, as are cats and dogs that are feral.

These animals have proved impossible to eradicate. The legally lethal myxamatosis worked for a time, but the rabbits became immune to it. Frequent culling is seen to be the most efficient answer – ironically continuing the hunting and shooting aspect – though viruses and specifically targeted baits (known as 1080) are being tried. The baits should not harm indigenous wildlife and notices are displayed in areas where they are being used.

Two of the most unusual preventative measures were the rabbit-proof fence that stretches for 2,000km through the western state's desert, and the 1.8 metre high one at Cameron Corner, where the borders of Queensland, New South Wales and South Australia meet, which was put up to stop rabbits entering Queensland from the south. At 4,580km, it is the world's longest, and today protects sheep from dingoes. Should you go through one of its many gates and don't shut it after you, you face a $1,000 fine.

Conservationists feel strongly that every effort has to be made so as not to further endanger indigenous wildlife. No pet dogs are allowed in any of Australia's National Parks, for instance, and there is a costly penalty for breaking that rule. Rabbits cannot be kept as pets in Queensland and all the states are most strict about domestic cats and dogs, putting the onus on owners to make sure the animals remain in their care. Dogs that become wild and mate with dingoes are a further complication.

Tasmania is especially concerned about feral animals. The word *fox* strikes fear in all hearts on this island for it has taken determined action to make it fox-free (the island is also dingo free, not by design but naturally, as they never crossed the Bass Strait). It takes very seriously indeed anything that threatens its status as an international, natural, environmentally friendly playground. And it's taken a cue from New Zealand with regard to brush-tail possums.

Australia 'gifted' 200 of these in 1837 to begin a fur trade across the Tasman. It went wrong when wearing fur fell out of favour with the fashionistas and the possums proliferated. They wreak havoc on the forests on both islands, every night destroying 21,000 tonnes of native vegetation. Culling has been inadequate and today there are about seven million of them (well outnumbering sheep). But the Kiwis are fighting back, taking the utilitarian approach: find a way to make use of them.

Their solution was to combine possum fur with

merino wool to create a superbly soft, light, thermal fabric. It goes by a variety of names (including MerinoMink, Possumwool, Eco-fur) and designers have been enthusiastically using it for hats, gloves, socks, insoles for shoes, scarves, skirts and sweaters. As sales increase, so will demand for this ever-adaptable possum product which, in turn, should give the hunters more encouragement to bring in more pelts. As the Kiwi plan could be an acceptable way of controlling the numbers and helping the environment, Tasmania is producing these unique items under licence. And it has a culling programme too to reduce the animal numbers.

AUSTRALIA ALSO HAS A PROBLEM WITH HORSES. THEY played a large role in how the country evolved, so history is on their side. Many have a soft spot for them because horse racing is a favourite pastime. The Melbourne Cup, run on the first Tuesday in November, is almost a national holiday – everything stops mid-afternoon when the race is shown on TV and broadcast on radio.

Into the box marked 'Things I didn't know when I was growing up' must go the fact that Archer, the first Melbourne Cup winner, in 1861, came from the south coast of New South Wales. Bred at Braidwood but trained at Terara near Nowra, Archer was taken by his jockey Dave Power to Melbourne. It took three weeks, with Dave walking and riding Archer the 880 km (in those days 550 miles). After the win, he then had to walk and ride the horse back home.

The most legendary winner of the Cup was Phar Lap

whose enormous heart – weighing 6.2 kg, about 50% larger than a run-of-the-mill racehorse – is preserved in formaldehyde and remains on display at the National Museum at Canberra. His was a story to bring tears to the eyes. Bred in 1927 in New Zealand, the chestnut gelding came to Australia as a two year old. The world by this time was in the grip of the Great Depression and in such poverty that all forms of gambling were a temptation, indeed a hope. If you had a win at the track, the family could eat, the kids could have shoes. Everyone needed a champion and, in Phar Lap, they found a hero.

Phar Lap, whose name comes from Thai and means 'lightning', raced in 51 events, being first past the winning post in 37 and placed second and third in five. On the Saturday before the 1930 Melbourne Cup, someone took a pot shot at him, but on the Tuesday he went on to win. Nothing daunted this wonder horse: he grew to a mighty 17.1 hands and earned nicknames like Big Red and the Red Terror.

As the best horse in Australia, Phar Lap was invited to run in the Agua Caliente Handicap, in Mexico, which had a purse of $US50,000 – big bickies then and not so bad now. He was taken by ship across the Pacific to San Francisco and then transported in a horse van the 640 km (400 miles) to Tijuana. Despite the fact that he had to carry the heaviest weight and was racing on soil rather than the grassy Aussie tracks he was used to, the Big Horse from Down Under won easily by two lengths and in record time!

After this, his owner decided to get as much as he could from this amazing animal, and he entered him in various American races – but it was not to be. Phar Lap became ill very suddenly and died in April 1932. He was only five years old. What a disaster. All sorts of theories abounded about his death – he was poisoned, killed by gangsters, etc –and that added to the sadness. In fact, only in 2001 were these suspicions put to rest when it was proved he died of a nasty digestive disease.

When Big Red fell into the skilled hands of a New York taxidermist, he was portioned up for posterity. His skeleton – which the Aussies are trying to get back – went to the Dominion Museum in the land of his birth (now called Te Papa Tongarewa, Museum of New Zealand, in Wellington), his heart to the National Institute of Anatomy at Canberra (now the National Museum), and his hide was superbly, and realistically, stuffed. It remains today one of the most outstanding and esteemed exhibits at the Melbourne Victoria Museum.

There have been other great horses of course, some also born in New Zealand (including Ethereal, the 2001 Melbourne Cup winner), but Phar Lap is embedded in the national consciousness. So is Norseman, the stallion that stamped its hoof on a particular spot in Western Australia and led its owner to gold. In sculptured form, the horse welcomes you to the town that bears its name at the western end of the Nullarbor.

I have never been a rider, but my interest in horses came about through my father who was, in the old parlance, an SP bookie – which meant he took off-course bets on the horses, dogs or trots anywhere they might be running, using the starting price odds. It was illegal – and I think my father was delighted to give it up when the regulated tote and betting shops came into being in 1965, allowing off-course investments to be added to the on-course for odds and dividend calculations. [The tote, known as the TAB, was in fact invented in Australia in 1909: called the Julius Apparatus or Totalisator, between 1948 and 1955 it was installed at 99 race tracks worldwide – the last one ceased operation in 1987 at Harringay Dog Track, in London.]

Dad inherited the SP business through his sister's husband when I was about 11, and while Saturday was the big day, trotting and dog racing meetings on week nights forced the family out of the house when bets were being received. It was hardly arduous for us as we went to the pictures – three times a week until I was 17, right through the Intermediate Certificate and the Leaving Certificate years (which my teachers would have been horrified to know).

Sometimes Dad would leave my much older brother Bill to it and he'd come with us – and usually slept through both films, waking at the interval (before the main one was shown) to have a Peter's icecream. His chronic asthma stopped him sleeping well when lying down, but he was fine sitting in the Roxy's plush chairs.

He got very angry with me once when he heard me tell my friend Rhonda that he was a boot maker and a bookmaker. Rhonda, who lived across the road from us, was a policeman's daughter – I had no idea until then that what he was doing was against the law, or even what SP stood for. But I adored the drama of it all, the secrecy. It was just like the world of Damon Runyon (a favourite writer who made American crooks sound lovable), and I felt I was living out that same intrigue Oz-style.

Quite how he organised the business I don't know; he had to have phones and numbers, somewhere to operate from, a way of collecting the betting money, getting the starting prices, returning winnings to the punters – all this, and avoid the police too. Some bets were laid in the hotel, but most were made by phone and, at this time in the 1950s, there was no dial-your-own – all calls went through the Nowra Switchboard. I have no doubt he charmed those ladies of the phone lines – probably repaired all their shoes for free.

And he bought a car. Now in their 50s Mum and Dad learnt to drive so every Saturday they could get to a small hut down a dirt road in the bush near Bomaderry where there were wooden benches and two phone lines which some phone engineer must have creatively accounted for.

I was the cockatoo, the lookout at the back window watching for any sign of the police. That 20-minute journey was always nerve-wracking; Mum, Dad and Bill were like scalded cats, very on edge. It was a relief to drop them off, pick up my sisters and go to the pictures. Then we'd repeat it all again when Mum went to pick them up.

Sunday was 'doing the slips' day, and my turn for mental arithmetic. Dad, who'd taken the starting prices from his Sydney contact by phone, spread all the bets, itemised on slips of paper, on the kitchen table. He had an incredible facility for doing maths in his head, being lightning fast at working out who'd won what and who was owed what. It was my job to add up collections of bets, all those in one name, much more slowly than he could, but at least it was one less thing for him to do. Well, not really, as he had to check my additions, but I felt I was of some use.

By the time I entered my teens he got help from another source – a hefty table-top calculator with a handle – so I was made redundant. I think Dad was glad when he pulled that lever for the last time, long after I'd left home. He took the responsibility of it all very seriously, living under a lot of pressure, with much money involved over many years, including bribes which had to be paid to prevent being caught. The police in many states must have done very well out of SP bookies before the law was changed.

Mum always hated Mondays, when he settled up with the punters down at the pub. When things had gone his way he came home for tea very merry; when they didn't and the long shots had cleaned him out, he was in no mood to be argued with. My mother was the "Wait till your father gets home" type of parent, and they were the times when we were likely to witness the harshness of his temper.

THERE WAS AN UNUSUAL LEGACY OF MY FATHER'S bookmaking days. One of his punters who built up rather a large debt was a dentist, and my two younger sisters and I were walking examples of the payback. Our teeth – long damaged from indulgence in sweets from showbags and lack of enforced brushing – got the gold treatment, which was particularly noticeable when used for front fillings. I had mine replaced when I came to London (the gold paid for the cost of the treatment), but youngest sister Pam kept hers as a reminder of those days.

She and I, at different times in our teens, were also

our benefactor's dental nurses. I worked for him for just a few months between leaving school and starting my nursing training in Sydney. These were the days when drills looked fearsome, with a reel and belt system that was operated by foot – the job of the nurse – and made a terrible noise. Local anaesthetic was rarely given. Aargh. Just thinking about it makes me feel the pain!

If my father were alive I can't imagine what he'd think about the present-day TAB and internet betting, with quinellas, trifectas, doubles and the rest. But, of course, he'd have known well that gambling and sport are entwined in the Aussie way of life. In Adelaide we found a 24-hour sports bar, with huge screens spread around the walls showing every type of sport, from racing, to rugby, cricket and basketball – eating, drinking and betting all under the same roof day and night.

Though attendances at the dogs and trots are today much reduced, horse racing has remained in favour because it has much more of a social quality to it, with big-money race meetings taking place in all the states' capitals, as well as country towns inland. People go to the big races to be seen, just as they do at Ascot, Epsom and Cheltenham in the UK. And racing in Australia is a remunerative activity as the country produces so many excellent horses.

The animals are revered, which adds to the anguish many Australians feel about feral horses that are damaging national parks in several states. Wild horses in Aussie parlance are called brumbies though where the name came from isn't certain. There was a James Brumby, a soldier with the New South Wales Corps, who arrived on *Britannia* – the same ship on which my ancestor was imported – in 1791. It is thought Brumby was in charge of some horses in the colony and, when he moved to Tasmania in 1804, he left some behind. When locals asked who owned the horses they were told: "They are Brumby's". Seems quite plausible. Then, at the end of the 19th century, in the foreword to Banjo Paterson's poem *Brumby's Run*, brumby was said to be Aboriginal for wild horse.

Many believe brumby refers to a Clydesdale shire and Arab cross that came about when the redundant draught horses, once used for hauling logged timber on Fraser Island, off the Queensland coast, were let loose and mated with pure bred Arabs which had swum ashore from a wreck in 1884. Their numbers gradually increased and problems arose when evidence was found that these hoofed animals were endangering the very rare environment of the world's largest sand island. Under Native Title law, the brumbies actually belong to the island's indigenous owners; one website says this is the Dalungbar tribe, another says it is the traditional land of the Butchulla people. They objected to brumbies being removed or sold, but both happened. There is doubt about how many brumbies are left on this World Heritage site.

Whatever the derivation, or correctness of the name, for most people wild horses are brumbies – and they have become an Aussie icon. When, because of the damage they do to the parks, the wild horses are culled, there is countrywide outrage. The most vociferous happened in 2000, just after the Sydney Olympic Games, when it was learnt that the animals were shot from helicopters and left to die where they fell. The incongruity was the fact that one of the memorable opening scenes at the

Olympic stadium had been a reenactment of the Aussie pioneers riding the horses they relied on.

The web is full of sites about saving brumbies. From one I learnt that the Franz Webber Foundation in 1989 turned an abandoned cattle station of 50,000 hectares into a native reserve and brumby sanctuary. It's between Katherine and Darwin, if you're up that way.

At the southern end of the continent, the Coffin Bay National Park – 30,000 hectares on the west coast of the Eyre Peninsula, not far from the home of John and May who got us started on our round-Australia journey – has a difficult problem. Ponies, whose ancestry can be traced back to Timor ponies brought to the area in the 1840s, have been running wild and harming the massive sand dunes, native woodlands, swamp and ancient limestone. In ecological terms, those horses cannot be as important as the land they are destroying. But someone has to make the decision to get rid of them.

The situation brought about by the existence of all these wild animals could probably be turned to advantage as part of the tourist attraction – and do the country some good at the same time. There are already safaris in central Australia for people who like to hunt, during which the environmentalists' commandment "Shoot only photographs" is not applicable. In Queensland, however, hunters have deliberately released feral pigs and rabbits to give them game to hunt, a kind of eco-terrorism which results in unacceptable environmental damage and the danger of spreading diseases.

Probably the animal most visitors want to see is the cuddly koala – or native bear – which has become a distinctive symbol of Australia, simply because it looks unlike any other. After the horrendous fires of 2019 they are in deep trouble, with numbers very low indeed.

On our journey we stayed plumb in the middle of an area of New South Wales designated the Koala Coast, at Lighthouse Beach near Port Macquarie and we thought we'd see these furry marsupials everywhere. We didn't. The closest we got was hearing from Bob, my brother-in-law, that he'd been caught in a traffic jam on the way home because a mother koala with her baby on her back had taken up residence in the middle of the road and everyone waited patiently until she moved on. What courtesy.

Koalas live in certain types of gum trees and are picky about what they like to eat, sticking to just one type of leaf. Unfortunately, long before the 2019 fires, there was a clash of interest between their needs and those of humans. The trees the koalas prefer are being cut down to make room for new homes on this very popular coastline. I'd told Ian how, in 1962, when I'd driven to Brisbane, I could remember passing through well-wooded areas where koalas perched precariously on the end of branches – this time we saw no sign of them. Even on Magnetic Island, off the Queensland coast, which supposedly has many koalas, they weren't there when we were looking.

After the 2019 fires, there was a determined effort to revive the fortunes of these small creatures and if anyone can do it, the Aussies will. Port Macquarie now has a Koala Hospital dedicated to their care and conservation.

Another animal in need of protection is the cassowary, a rare and extraordinary bird with a very big reputation for wreaking havoc with its powerful legs. I don't remember ever knowing about it when I lived in Australia, but on our journey we drove along the Cassowary Coast, as the area around Mission Beach in Queensland is known. The birds are endangered because they wander on to roads and get killed. In the region between Ingham and Innisfail signs warn you to drive carefully, and slowly.

We found a space at the Hibiscus caravan park at Wongaling, which has a ginormous stone cassowary at the front, and went for a couple of afternoon walks in the nearby Licuala State Forest. Here we found the animals' tell-tale dung – which is something to behold. The cassowary gobbles up huge seeds but doesn't digest them. They exit at the other end, and in this way the bird is able to spread trees around the forest. After we'd found lots of dung heaps, but no sightings of the animal itself, we decided to return at dusk and wait.

There's a delightful educational part to the forest created for children by the Department of Natural Resources, which manages the park. "Cassowaries for kids" explains that the birds are part of the emu family, what their tracks look like, how to identify dung and why they are endangered. We hovered around the perimeter of this kids' area, and the light had almost gone when we heard rustling and then saw a cassowary ahead. I felt goose pimples all over.

Taking advantage of a sturdy tree trunk to hide behind, we watched as it grazed. A couple of metres high, it had black feathers, a bright blue face, head and neck and red wattles. It was intent on eating, but every so often would raise its long neck and head and focus its big eyes on the surrounding trees. At one point we thought it was looking directly at us, and neither of us hardly dared to breathe. I certainly couldn't use my camera as I didn't want to draw attention to where we were.

Later, we both said we'd been thinking of the tales we'd heard: of seven people who'd been killed by them; of someone seeing two cassowaries fighting on a beach very early one morning attacking each other with their legs. We stayed for a few minutes then, in the darkness, very quietly backed away. As we walked along the road to the camp the moon was beginning to rise and there was no sound at all. Seeing that cassowary was one of the most wondrous moments of our trip.

From the Unique Australian Animals website I discovered the cassowary's link with Gondwana: it is one of the struthioniformes called Ratites, all flightless birds, that lived on the joined-up landmass. This has been proved by modern DNA which shows that ostriches (South Africa), rheas (South America), kiwis (New Zealand), emus and cassowaries (Australia and New Guinea) are of the same order. How wonderful that all are still there to be appreciated.

Not all the animals people come to Australia to see are land based. Whales are a big draw Down Under as they have set routes up and down the east and west coasts to the spawning grounds well to the south. My sister Gai was overjoyed to discover that, from her balcony at Lighthouse Beach, she had a wonderful view of the humpbacks way out in the Tasman – at one time of the year going north, at another going south. And the numbers are increasing.

When we reached Airlie Beach, the other name for the town of Whitsunday near the Great Barrier Reef, we took a whale-watching trip which was made enjoyable by the presence of experts who were good at explaining about the animals and their actions.

We left from nearby Shute Harbour in a SeaFerries catamaran which acts as a scheduled ferry taking passengers to Crocodile Island resort and South Molle and also picks up those going to see the whales. We hadn't thought to chew our fresh ginger but when the sea became choppy the crew offered everyone a ginger herbal tablet and it must have worked as we weren't sick. The captain was, of course, a joker (must be part of every job description in tourist-minded Australia).

– It's just a little bit of motion on the ocean. Nothing to worry about.

Humpbacks had been seen about 5km offshore, and the engineer positioned himself on the cabin top to watch through binoculars for the telltale spume. When it was sighted the captain turned the cat in its direction. What an exciting hour it was. And completely frustrating at the same time. The animals were marvellous, putting on a show with hefty peduncle 'slaps' – bringing their huge tails down splat on the water. This is what the male does to get the female interested, it seems. We saw several lots of two, putting on great displays. One performed a huge leap in a corkscrew motion so that its whole body was out of the water. The cries were coming thick and fast.

– There's one over there!

– There's one over here!

People ran from side to side, from bow to stern, as the whales popped up all around the boat. And the frustration? That came about because I couldn't be in every part of the boat at the same time and capture on film the stunning sights we were seeing. I seemed to click the shutter just a nano-second too late...

We were sitting outside the van that night (it was the third week in July), talking over the day's events, when a bush stone-curlew, an unusual-looking bird with long legs and large beady eyes, came and stood beside us as though it was listening. It was completely motionless for a few minutes, then wandered off. Above our heads there was no moon, but the huge black sky glittered with the countless stars of the Milky Way. Under the southern stars, life appeared idyllic.

We had also seen dolphins on our cruise – whales are often accompanied by them – and they put on a performance for us as well. Dolphins are delightful creatures which have a reputation for calming and healing; swimming with them is frequently promoted as a life-changing experience. It may also be one of the most dangerous things a dolphin can do as it is susceptible to viruses humans carry – very important now since the emergence of corona viruses. In those areas where dolphins are a tourist attraction there will usually be a ranger or a sign which will say: "Enjoy by looking, but don't touch".

When we were at Esperance, in southern Western

Australia, we took a half-day-trip to Woody Island via the Bay of Isles. The skipper steered the boat thrillingly close to steep rocks over which strident waves were breaking as Australian sea lions and New Zealand coal-black seals somehow clung on. After a walk around the island, we watched a tractor carrying on its fore-hoist a very large – and dead – turtle.

It was thought to be over 100 years old and was being taken on our boat to the marine authorities on the mainland. Turtles are endangered worldwide. There are only seven species of ocean-dwelling turtles left in the world and six of these are found in Australian waters. Was it old age or a virus that killed this one?

Which brings me to one of the ocean's oddest animals, the dugong. Also known as a sea cow, it is like a huge slug with flippers and a whale-style fluked tail. Related more to an elephant than marine mammals, the dugong can grow to about 3 metres in length and weigh up to 400 kg. They live on plants, grazing on coastal meadows of seagrass in sheltered tropical and sub-tropical waters, and are slow procreators, so there aren't a lot of them around. We missed seeing them on the east coast and tried again at Shark Bay in Western Australia.

The pretty catamaran *Shotover*, with its big sails, goes out twice a day from Monkey Mia, and does a sunset cruise too, to see the dolphins and dugongs. To top our layers we were given bright yellow waterproofs, which ensured warmth, as the boat headed out to where the dugongs are known to graze. Boy, was it windy! While the dolphins played around us, the dugongs – if they were there at all – remained out of view. The cheerful skipper did a good job convincing many of us on board that if we concentrated hard on what looked like brown scum on the horizon we might see the creatures coming up for air; they need to surface to breathe and can only hold their breath for a few minutes underwater. Ian swore he saw them.

Dugongs were the animals the early seafarers called mermaids – how on earth did they find them! As with elephants, grazing takes up most of their day so they quickly submerge to get to food. They're too shy, and hungry, to hang about for any length of time, so it would be a miracle if one was seen atop the water. Still, it was an entertaining outing and I bought a postcard showing a mother and calf – taken underwater, naturally – so I know exactly what I missed. This was one for Ripley's 'Believe it or not'...

15

IN SEARCH OF SNAKES AND REPTILES

WHAT YOU MAY, OR MAY NOT, FIND

SNAKES, or Joe Blakes as they are often called, are, of course, the big Australian scare story. They are supposed to be everywhere. Sad to say we travelled over 26,500 km in our van and had difficulty seeing any.

Ian was particularly keen to see as many as possible, but only in the wild, not in a zoo or nature park (that would be too easy). We followed every lead. We were told that in north Queensland the taipan and green tree snakes are viewed frequently, so we took a day trip to Cape Tribulation and the Daintree, the oldest rainforest in the world; cycads (tropical plants that look like palms) growing here go back to the time of the dinosaurs. The annual rainfall is about 6 metres and, according to our cheerful guide Andrew, in 1996 1.5 metres fell in five days. Fortunately, it was not in the month of August, which is when we were there. The weather was warm and sultry, but I'm glad we had our waterproof anoraks with us – among the huge trees, the temperature drops dramatically.

Andrew took us on several short bush sorties, telling us to watch where we walked and to keep our eyes open.

– Remember the snake that climbs is a good snake. Only those on the ground will hurt you. The good news is that there are no hibernating snakes in the Daintree.

One of the party saw something slithering away, which Andrew said was a common tree snake. We missed it. Then Andrew sighted a most unusual animal, a Boyd's desert dragon, which posed long enough on the tree trunk for me to photograph it (see it on the back cover). A contrast of green against brown, it looks like a leftover from an ancient time. Andrew was impressed.

– You're lucky to see that. It's rare.

During a short cruise on the Daintree River, with mangroves to both sides, little freshwater crocodiles idled on the grey-mud riverbanks. These freshies, as they're called, are only found in Australia, can live to be 100 and aren't, we were assured, dangerous to humans, though how you would feel if you found one in the same stretch of water you were swimming in is another matter. They're danged clever animals, which is probably why they survive so well. They can slow their heart to one beat a minute and they have an extra valve that allows them to shut off the blood supply to the extremities. Self conservation is the objective.

This area of north Queensland has a magnificent array of wildlife. We saw many brilliant-coloured kingfishers – the azure, and the sacred, which is yellow and blue. In a clearing, we spied a jabiru. (Botanist Joseph Banks gave this graceful stork its Brazilian name – it obviously resembled one he and Captain Cook had seen in Brazil, on their way to the Pacific to observe the transit of Venus in 1769, before coming to Australia). Our boat's skipper Alan produced a white-lipped green tree frog which had jumped on board, and it sat quite unperturbed on a stick being passed from passenger to passenger while cameras stored memories for the future. But we didn't see a snake...

Jabiru is also the name of the town specially created for tourists in the Northern Territory's Kakadu National Park (where the film *Crocodile Dundee* was made). At the campsite there I overheard a family describing an olive green python they had seen. Dad and his two young sons couldn't stop talking about it, and I had to find out where they'd been.

– Douglas Daly Resort, south of Darwin. It was huge. Ya gotta go.

This was inland from Highway 1, but we didn't have to think twice. For the sake of seeing a snake, it was worth going out of our way for – though we did have to break one of our rules and drive on an unsealed road to reach it.

Douglas Daly turned out to be a rare find, one of the remotest campsites. It had a swimming pool as well as a river with its own 'thermal' pool, bubbling up from an underground source. There are free-camping places along the riverbank, mostly taken by those whose sole purpose in life is to catch fish to eat. In this particular instance, in such delightful surroundings, I could see why such a pastime would be tempting.

The resort may be off the beaten track but is a welcoming watering hole for 'locals' who may not live within cooeeing distance of each other but will drive up to 100km for a meal and drink. Eager to find out where the python might be, we were in the bar about 6 o'clock – happy hour, so drinks were half price – quizzing everyone. A bandicoot wandered in and was fed some chips by people at a nearby table (so much for the signposted rule about not feeding wild animals).

As we walked back to the van later, our way lit by a full moon, wallabies hopped around us, and the fearless bandicoot even came out as though to say goodnight. It's an interesting looking marsupial, quite like a rat in shape, and now much in need of protection: two of the species, the pig-footed bandicoot and the rabbit bandicoot or bilbie, are extremely rare.

We spent a day walking in the scrub by the river and tried out several unusual swimming spots, but there was no sign of the python. One of the resort owners was quite matter of fact.

– It comes and goes. It was out near the pool the other day. Gave someone a bit of a shock. You gotta see the bowerbird's house but. That's pretty rare.

It was on the road leading to the river, though the occupant, the Great Bowerbird (*Chlamydera nuchalis*), was absent (we did eventually get to see one at Katherine Gorge van park). The bird uses its strong bill to build the arched walls with twigs and leafy branches, creating a tunnel up to 120cm long and 45cm high (according to the *Field Guide to the Birds of Australia*), but the one we found was a shadow of its former self.

The male bowerbird is the acquisitive one, collecting all sorts of things to put in the bower, anything brightly coloured or shiny being particularly attractive, along with pieces of glass, bones, shells, flowers and fruits. It is all part of the wooing of the female, and it must be something indeed to see him in action, delivering the object in his bill, his head lowered, feathers ruffled, crest expanded, and hissing as he bounds to the bower. Some display!

We stayed to have the resort's special Sunday night meal of roast buffalo (excellent with roast potatoes and pumpkin, and a bottle of Shiraz) and headed off the next day, checking out first that the python had not revealed itself. At least, as we slowly drove back along the teeth-chattering road, we saw emus and kangaroos in the scrub around us.

ON THE BUS TRIP TO CAPE LEVEQUE (NAMED AFTER A French explorer, but the pronunciation is Australianised to *Leveek*), the driver needed especial skill on the atrocious red clay road and never seemed to take his eyes off its ever-changing undulations. Then suddenly he called out:

– Big brown on the right hand side.

The bus almost tipped as everyone on our side rushed to the opposite windows to see the snake go slithering off. We just got a glimpse.

At the southern end of this huge state, at Esperance, to the north of which lies Norseman, the start of the Nullarbor Plain, we took an Aussie Bight day-trip in an OKA, a West Australian-designed 4WD which really could be described as a transport of delight for its 16 passengers.

The plan was to travel along the beach and through

the sand dunes to Cape le Grand National Park. With great aplomb and the Aussie dry sense of humour, Frank the driver/guide said he was still learning to drive the OKA but he was sure, if he could get to the top of the dunes, we'd be able to get down the other side. It was thrilling, particularly when the we climbed what looked like an enormous boulder – 35metres high – set against a deep-blue cloudless sky. The vehicle seemed to sway slightly at the top and then hurtled down the other side! After this the dunes were a doddle. At the top of these shifty sandhills we had a choice: either sandboard down or go in the OKA. I went down sitting next to the driver – dramatic!

Up he went again to instruct those who wanted to board down – which Ian did. I stood at the bottom of the golden dune photographing his descent. Eerily, though we'd seen no other people up to this point, a couple of powerbikies appeared, playing loop-the-dunes. We watched them jump their machines high into the air and then disappear down into the gully, after which they'd suddenly appear atop another dune, their engines roaring.

Eventually we got back on board and drove on to join the road leading to the park. Everyone was chatting away about what we'd just done when Frank yelled

– Big snake on the road! It's a tiger!

He stopped the OKA and jumped out, all of us scrambling behind, but too late. Another snake not seen. The tiger's the one with the big reputation, the most lethal Joe Blake – it takes about 30 minutes for its venom to kill.

Though we had no luck seeing these reptiles, we did

come across two animals called monitors that appeared to be a cross between a snake and a goanna. The sand monitor, about two metres long, came running on its short legs into the campsite at Cooinda (in Kakadu National Park), and I had the presence of mind to get a picture before it disappeared. I did the same, too, at the Bungle Bungles, with the water monitor, a shorter version, which slunk along on the talc-like sand in the cave where we were having our lunch. I haven't read anywhere whether they are harmless or not but, according to the Oxford Dictionary, if monitors are around, so are crocodiles. Best not swim anywhere there then!

In the UK we saw a television documentary with Steve Irwin working his way across the Red Centre with his wife and first child, then a baby, in search of snakes. He was mostly on his hands and knees creeping up on one or on the balls of his feet ready to jump away from a deadly example whose tail he had clutched in one hand. In his remarkable accent he recounted how he'd learnt about the reptiles at his father's side when he was growing up.

[His father opened the Queensland Reptile and Fauna Park when Steve was eight; he was about nine when his father taught him how to catch a crocodile by hand, a talent which eventually led to his successful *Crocodile Hunter Show*, shown worldwide on TV. His death in 2006, after a stingray injury while filming on the Great Barrier Reef, was truly shocking – even though people had been spellbound by his filmed encounters with dangerous animals.]

If there's not yet a word for 'love of snakes' it could be Irwinamia, which covered both his passion and mania.

It gave me the creeps just to watch him in action. He seemed to have no trouble at all finding these 'shy creatures' and obviously has amazing vision, as he was able to spot them from a great distance. And to think we went across the Nullarbor and only saw a couple of pretty manky dingoes!

His area of operation was further to the north of the treeless plain, it is true, and the parts he went to could only be reached by 4WD or a quad bike, a mini-tractor-style vehicle, which he'd brought with him. Leaving his wife and child, he took off on this, going up and down the dark orange sand drifts and rocky escarpments with ease. It was safer and far more comfortable to watch it on a screen than following in his footsteps, or tyre tracks.

But I did have an encounter of my own. As a feature writer for *TV Times* Brisbane in 1963, I was sent by the editor to the Atherton Tableland to interview locals who, thanks to the erection of new transmitters, would now be able to receive television. How excited would they be to have the opportunity to watch the 'soaps' of the day, *Dr Kildare* and *Bonanza*, not just to hear the news but to see pictures of the places where it was all happening? It was my job to find out, but first the photographer and I had to find the people.

We drove for many miles (in the old calculation) encountering no habitation. We talked to some of the timber workers in the forest and eventually, in much more open land, we came to a farm where the mother of two small children invited us in. While the children went outside to play, we sat talking in the lounge room about the programmes she could look forward to. I became aware of a scraping sound, like sandpaper on a rough surface, which naturally distracted me.

– What *is* that noise?

– That's the python, out the back on the concrete. Loves rubbing its stomick over it.

– Where are the kids?

– Out front. They don't go near it.

To say that my blood went as cold as the reptile's would be an exaggeration, but only just. I looked out the window and saw it lying there and, for me, that was as many snakes as I ever want to see. These pythons aren't supposedly harmful but my sense of self preservation makes me doubt that information. If one wrapped itself around you it could squash you to death...

In the article I wrote for *TV Times*, about the placing of the transmitters, I described the men responsible as modern day pioneers, having hacked their way through some of Queensland's roughest and toughest areas. Finding the best sites was a problem, because the towns lie in pockets between a lot of mountain ranges. The men had volunteered after the Postmaster-General called for 'adventurous employees' to be part of the exploration group.

From 1960 to 1963 the four-men survey teams, plus a draughtsman and trainee technicians, camped out for many weeks, mapping and photographing possible areas and, in the process, climbing the state's highest peaks. By September 1963 they had climbed Mt Stuart and Mt Elliot (Townsville), the Eungella Range and Mt Blackwood (Mackay), Mt Goonaneman and Mt Woowoonga (Maryborough) and Bartle Frere and Bellenden Frere (Cairns).

I wrote: "They had to enter the domain of the deadly

taipan snake and poisonous spiders, battle through fierce monsoonal storms where the rain is often measured in feet and yards." [50 years later rainfall may be metricated but it is still as heavy.] They found the 'good tucker' of the grass tree to top up their dwindling food supplies, and tapped vines for water.

They couldn't have known then that these survival techniques would one day form the basis for some of the world's most popular TV programmes. Or, even more mind-boggling, that celebrities would be flown in from the UK and placed in a natural setting much like this (across the border, in northern New South Wales) while TV cameras focused on their every thought and action in a far-from-glamorous environment. Who'd have believed that millions of viewers would be riveted to their screens watching this so-called reality. In the 1960s, this would have been the stuff of science fiction!

A weirder 'reality' also existed. In the 1950s if you read the *Cairns Post* you would never know there were snakes in Queensland. The proprietor of the town's only newspaper was so proud of his home state he refused to publish any story detrimental to it. In his paper no one ever got bitten by a snake or died of snakebite.

But fatalities there are and, frightening though they might be, Australia's extraordinary range of reptiles is something visitors want to see, which is why the reptile houses are exceedingly popular in all the zoos around the country. Though we were thwarted in our intention to see them in real life, I have a photograph I took at Kulgera Pub, one of the desert roadhouses on the way to Alice Springs from Adelaide.

On one of the corrugated iron walls was a huge

poster showing the dangerous snakes of the Northern Territory – all curled-up squiggles of many colours and textures (indicating they were probably dead at the time of celluloid capture). From the family Elapidae, meaning they are front fanged, some I recognise as those Steven Irwin loved and had held in a spine-tingling way as he talked about them on TV. I prefer them as a photograph; even looking at it makes me shiver.

Though death by snake bite is very rare, when you travel independently in Australia, as we did, you will be advised to carry a snake-bite kit as part of your first aid equipment. But do you know what that comprises? Nothing more than a crepe bandage and some form of splint. You bind the limb that's been bitten so it is immobilised – this slows the spread of the venom – and get to a hospital as fast as you can.

THE REAL RULES ARE WHAT *not* to do: don't suck or cut the wound, don't wash it or put on any antiseptic. Most importantly do *not* apply a tourniquet (if done wrongly this can cut off the blood circulation). Keeping the person still and calm and obtaining medical help as soon as possible are the essentials of treating snakebite. And if you saw that Joe Blake, try to remember its colour or markings – the doctor will want to know so the right anti-venom can be given.

16

ECOLOGY AT THE CROSSROADS

BE IN AWE OF THE NATURAL WONDERS

THE WORLD WAS aghast in 2019 as television showed fires raging all over Australia, causing death and horrendous destruction of homes, forests and wildlife. Over and over again we watched as planes scooped up water from the Pacific and dumped it over the burning land. It was an awful sight.

What happens to the continent in the future may well depend on water – there just isn't enough of it in the southern half of the country (as there isn't in many parts of the world, including the Mediterranean area). After Antarctica, Australia is the driest land mass on earth – almost a huge desert island. It has 12 surface water drainage divisions, which is the way scientists describe the way the rivers run, called basins. The two biggest, Lake Eyre and the Murray/Darling, are similarly sized and economically significant. The pictures of the Darling, almost empty of water, were unbelievable. Climate change is predicted to increase drought frequency and severity and the whole river system suffers — including the animals, fish and birds that rely on it for survival.

The Darling, Murray and Murrumbidgee Rivers, the three largest in Australia, with their many tributaries, cover about 1 million sq km, about a sixth of the continental landmass, which is just too big for most minds to grasp. The MDB, as the river system is known, extends from Queensland to South Australia, New South Wales and Victoria, and it is the lifeblood of industries such as dairy, cotton, rice and horticulture (particularly burgeoning viticulture and viniculture which have made Australian wines popular worldwide).

And don't forget tourism – this brings loadsa money Down Under (certainly until the coronavirus pandemic), and keeping this voracious industry going puts pressure on the resources which may not be replenishable. Marketeers use the catchy slogan 'once it's gone, it's gone' as a selling method; I can only hope that my fellow Aussies won't let that happen to the country's unique features.

Arthur W Upfield called the Darling Basin "the gutter of Australia". In *Madman's Bend* (published in 1963) he wrote: "Unlike the Murray, of which it is a tributary, it [the Darling] has character and atmosphere. Though it runs roughly 600miles [966km] from Walgett to [the junction of the Murray at] Wentworth, it so twists and turns that its overall course is 1,800 miles [2,898 km]. It is shaded and sheltered from the summer sun and winter winds by massive red gums forming an almost unbroken avenue".

This is the self-same place, in New South Wales, where, because of erosion, the river's banks are giving way, sending tens of thousands of tonnes of soil and rock into the water, taking with it hundreds of the statuesque gums described by Upfield. There is also algae to contend with, sick-making bacteria that erupt in the low-flow conditions – its spread on water is called a 'bloom'. In 1991, bloom poisoned more than 2,000km of the Darling. With the Big Dry now a fact of life in Oz, lack of water in the rivers will encourage even more algae to proliferate. It all sounds dire.

In my growing-up years I was always aware of the importance of water to Australia – and even today I won't let a tap run for any length of time – but I don't remember knowing about wetlands, or their significance. To my surprise I discovered that within the MDB there are 30,000 of them, as well as flood plains and billabongs (the Aboriginal word meaning a pool separated from a river, an anabranch, and heard most in the opening line of the anthem-like *Waltzing Matilda*: "Once a jolly swagman camped by a billabong..."). These biologically diverse ecosystems provide breeding and feeding habitats for waterbirds, fish, invertebrates and plants.

I found out about this firsthand when, for my birthday treat in November, we went to Banrock Station, a choice I'd made because we drank their wines in the UK and, from their labels, knew of the company's policy of using a percentage of its profit to maintain its wetlands. Banrock is at Kingston on Murray, South Australia, and is an impressive set up with a modern visitor centre providing great views of the property.

We ate lunch on a huge deck under glamorous and practical shade sails, looking out over the land which has been rescued by an ongoing programme of tree replanting. Later we walked to the wetland area to see how many more birds we could identify from our bird book.

It's been a lot of hard work and Banrock is a success story. The tragedy is that it is not happening everywhere, that many natural water places are drying out as a result of human activities, and are being affected by pollution from agriculture, chemicals and untreated sewage. Extensive clearing of native vegetation – including the felling of 15 million trees in the MDB – has allowed rainwater to leak through the soil into the groundwater. As groundwater levels rise this causes widespread salinity problems – salt rising to the surface destroys the land for agriculture and wildlife.

From Renmark – where, from our riverbank campsite, we watched stately paddle steamers pass by, one of the features of travel here – we took a half-day trip on the Mighty Murray, an eerie experience as the river in this part of South Australia is dotted with the trunks of dead, ghostly-grey gums. The engine was hushed as we almost glided along on the murky waters listening to a CD of local bird sounds. I bought the CD because that wonderful birdsong is now at terrible risk of disappearing because of what's happening to the river.

To give you an idea of how bad things are, look at this one paragraph of the Adelaide Declaration, made in 2003, by state and commonwealth Members of Parliament:

> "We acknowledge that since European settlement, the environmental and ecological state of the river has measurably deteriorated and as legislators and

decision makers we are united in the view that we must take joint and individual responsibility to act with urgency to restore the River Murray to health."

"Since European settlement" means since 1788, not a long time at all in the grand scheme of existence, but the mishandling of this valued waterway has been disastrous. Fish in particular are in trouble. The Murray cod – almost a supernatural fish, the subject of many tall tales – can live to be a hundred but is under threat because of alterations to the natural flow of virtually all the rivers in the MDB. European carp and other introduced fish are now declared pests because they are predators, and it is illegal to return one to the water if caught. As I've said, fishing is a big pastime in Oz.

When we began our journey, with the intention of following the shape of Australia, we didn't get to Cape York Peninsula, at the top of Queensland. We were thwarted, first of all, by the distance involved and how much time such a detour off Highway 1 would require, and secondly because a 4WD vehicle is essential for much of the terrain.

By all accounts it is a fascinating area, with many rivers that, with the huge rainfall in summer, become raging torrents. The peninsula has the world's biggest reserves of high-grade bauxite (used in the manufacture of aluminium) at Weipa, but also has thriving beef cattle and grain industries, as well as rainforests and sandy plains. With part of the Great Barrier Reef offshore, the Cape has become a special spot for tourists and pleasure seekers who have more money to spend than the backpackers. All, however, is not well.

There is, for instance, grave concern about what is happening to the mangrove forests, the main protectors of coral reefs and sea grass beds, and the prime nesting sites for migratory and other birds. Mangroves were once thought to be useless but are miraculous trees: they have tangled prop roots – leg-like roots that come off the trunk – which can get a grip in unstable soils, can withstand currents and storms, and 'breathe' air through their extraordinary aerial root system which have cells that water or salts can't enter. Freshwater is as precious to a mangrove tree as to a desert plant, and the tree expends energy to rid the water of salt.

Mangroves, which only take root near the mouths of rivers or along a shore, can be badly affected by large oil spills, but on this Queensland coast the biggest threat to the forests is the growing demand for prawns, or shrimps as they are also known. Thousands of hectares of mangroves have been cleared to make artificial ponds in which prawns are farmed – it brings in very big bickies. 'Don't come the raw prawn with me' is a favoured Aussie response when someone thinks he or she's being told fibs, but in this case the truth about prawns is unpalatable to anyone concerned about the environment.

Ecologically, the Cape is at a crossroads – will it be protected or be a victim of destructive development? The Wilderness Society, a conservationist watchdog aiming to defend Australia's 'wild' country, believes the Queensland government should do more to diversify the region's economy, particularly in aspects such as eco and cultural tourism.

According to the society, Cape York Peninsula is an 'ark' of biological diversity, one of the world's great wilderness areas. The eastern coast has the last strongholds of old growth rainforest and the least damaged section of the Barrier Reef. The western side has a near continuous line of wetlands, to rival the Northern Territory's Kakadu in terms of migratory birds.

ENVIRONMENTAL AWARENESS IS GROWING, BUT CAN changes be made fast enough to prevent further damage? The Lake Eyre Basin (LEB) in central Australia is a role model for what could be achieved when people manage change rather than be victims of it – and, although the population of the area is very small, all those involved are volunteers, determined to be stakeholders in their own future.

This is a really old part of the world, where spectacular fossil finds – dinosaurs, giant kangaroos, Australia's only freshwater dolphin – have opened a picture window on the past.

The LEB is twice the size of the state of Texas and although we didn't appreciate it at the time, we were at its tip when we stopped at Camooweal in the north (Queensland/Northern Territory border), and at its base when we drove towards Port Augusta and the Flinders Ranges in the south (north of Adelaide). Just look at a map to see the sizeable chunk of land in between the two, both on Highway 1!

It is the world's largest internal drainage system, covering about 1.2 million sq km of arid and semi-arid land. It is 15 metres below sea level and is usually a huge salt pan containing little or no water – the annual rainfall is 125 mm. Summer temperatures, in the shade (if you can find any), regularly reach 50C (far too hot to convert to Fahrenheit!).

But every 30 years or so – twice, or perhaps three times, in a lifetime – Lake Eyre fills spectacularly. The highest recorded level was in 1974 – it would take 45 days for the waters of Europe's longest river, the Danube, to produce that amount of water, though South America's Amazon could equal it in three days. The lake becomes a breeding ground for many species of birds, fish and invertebrates, a sight that is one of the great wonders of the Land Down Under.

The big rivers that feed the LEB are the Cooper, Diamantina and Georgina, all flowing through what is called Channel Country or Heartbreak Corner – extremely harsh desert land where the states of South Australia, Northern Territory, Queensland and New South Wales meet. Channel Country has deep spiritual significance for the Aborigines. In the early days of white exploration many died in the tough conditions here, yet the indigenous people knew the area through their trading routes which followed the permanent waterholes – billabongs and gnamma holes – of these rivers. According to the website of the WA Museum, one of the main sources of water for the Aboriginal people were 'gnamma' holes, natural cavities found in hard rock, particularly granite outcrops. These act as natural water tanks, which are replenished from underground stores and rainwater runoff. Gnamma holes vary in shape and depth, and the hole's small surface area helps to minimise evaporation.

ONE OF THE MOST NOTABLE CONSTRUCTION FEATS OF THE track for The Ghan, the train from Adelaide to Darwin (completed in 2004), is the bridge that crosses the Finke – 15 spans, each 30 metres long. It is one of the oldest rivers on the planet, forming in the MacDonnell Ranges in the Northern Territory, near Palm Valley – which has gum and cabbage trees found nowhere else in the world – and runs hundreds of ks to flood out in the Simpson Desert, which makes it part of the LEB.

[To digress slightly: one of the reasons why building the track took so long – apart from the fact that it is a long way – was that the sleepers had to be made of cement. Termites make a meal of traditional wooden ones. They are a menace Down Under: one in five houses has termite infestation, causing more damage than fire, flood, storm and tempest combined, and you can't insure against them. About the size of half a matchhead, a termite can pass through a 2mm crack and get stuck into the timber, the main building material in Australia. If you had enough money to build with Cypress pine you'd be OK, as this is unpalatable to them.

The termites make huge mounds above ground in northern Australia, but in the cooler areas they build completely below ground. Subterranean termites are also called white ants but aren't ants at all; they are related to cockroaches and have a similar 200 million year history. You can see what you're up against if you live in this part of the world.

Fortunately, a remedy has been found, by a scientist who was a teenage refugee from Eritrea. Berhan Ahmed sought asylum in Australia when he was 22. In Melbourne he did a master's degree in Animal Science and worked first for the CSIRO (Commonwealth Scientific and Research Organisation, also known as Australia's national science agency) and then the University of Melbourne's Institute of Land and Food. He found that a layer of specifically-sized crushed rock placed beneath a house's concrete slab created an impassible barrier for termites.

He also works with the Yolungu community in the Northern Territory whose indigenous knowledge might help the country to live with termites. According to Berhan Ahmed, anything is better than spraying: organochloride sprays are carcinogenic, indiscriminating and non-biodegradable. This could be another climatic disaster in the making.]

The LEB website (www.lakeeyrebasin.org.au) explains the strategic plans for the management of water and natural resources with the involvement of the Community Advisory Committee, made up of residents of this vast region who represent local interests (pastoral, indigenous, mining, conservation, tourism).

They have found that managing change also involves picking up the pieces after thoughtless travellers (ever increasing in numbers now that there is both the desire and methods available to reach outlying places) who leave litter, start fires or have poor hygiene practices. Chances are it is going to get worse, not better.

After a visit to Coongie Lakes, one of the many waterholes along the Cooper River near Innamincka – aren't these names just wonderful! – Joc Schmiechen, a committee member, wrote:

"...the unfortunate downside is the impact on the most accessible and desirable spots. The onus is on caring and

responsible visitors, who outnumber the ignorant few, and take on the job of cleaning up the mess rather than complaining and moving on. If we are to have any hope of managing and enjoying the fantastic heritage we have in the Lake Eyre Basin, those of us who visit have to do our bit"

In such dry surroundings, it's hard to believe that beneath the LEB is the world's largest body of freshwater called the Great Artesian Basin, containing (it is estimated) as much water as 17 Sydney Harbours. It is into this that bores are sunk, often 1.6km deep (a mile in the old measure), a water-retrieval system that, because of Australia's water crisis, is now carefully monitored to reduce water flow and wastage. The water is too high in minerals to be used for agriculture but those living on the land rely on it for survival. It is a precious resource.

WHEREVER YOU GO DOWN UNDER YOU SEE GUM TREES of all sorts of shapes and sizes. Eucalyptus, of which there are 800 species (only three, coolabah, jarrah and karri, have their original Aboriginal names), is well suited to an arid land, thrives where the mean annual temperature doesn't drop below 15C (60F), and grows where few other trees survive – on rock and sand. If you do a lot of travelling in the world (as I have) you'll find that many countries have these trees too, and that they are not unique to Australia.

In a tiny grove on Cyprus, called Aphrodite's birthplace, I came across an impressive gum, standing proud among acacias and smaller eucalypts. In parts, this island on the eastern end of the Med looks as though it could have broken off from Australia, for it also has streets of pink and white oleanders and huge-flowered hibiscus, walls clothed with vivid orange/red lantana and, inside an ancient castle in the north, superbly colourful jacarandas.

In an area of ongoing excavation of mosaics at Paphos, around the House of Dionysus (2nd- 4th Centuries AD), the scrubby land covered with dried grass, everlastings and thistles, looking across to the sea, is uncannily like areas of southern Western Australia. The plants were so familiar, I could have been back in Australia – but the plants aren't Australian at all. In fact, plants being transplanted willy nilly from country to country have caused more problems than anyone might have imagined.

Since Captain Phillip arrived with the First Fleet, an estimated 28,000 garden plants – among them roses, shrubs and bulbs – have been brought in to make Australia more like the old countries the 'new Australians' came from. The effect on the country's ecology has been disastrous. It's an ever-present problem that's affecting every state and involves everyone, as it stems from their own back yards. Many imported plants have become 'weeds of national significance' that require search and destroy operations – using planes, boats, quad bikes and 4WDs if necessary – in areas where their invasive tendencies are a threat to local flora and fauna. Strewth.

On one website, when I was checking out information about environmental and agricultural weeds, this statement rang alarm bells:

"Slow incremental change is leading to an impoverished future where our grandchildren will surely not know what the natural Australia we knew was like."

What 'natural Australia' would that be? The one created by the settlers who wanted to establish English, tropical or Mediterranean-style gardens? The one of my childhood, when suddenly it was illegal to pick native plants such as waratahs and boronia in the bush? From all accounts, since 1788 Australia hasn't been in any way 'natural'.

Many of the plants you may think of as typically Australian are foreign. Exotic frangipani originated in the American tropics, hibiscus was introduced from India, bougainvillea and jacaranda from Brazil. It is hard to believe that the deep-purple flowering tibouchina or lasiandra (also from Brazil) haven't always been there. They certainly look well entrenched in New South Wales towns like Grafton, which has a jacaranda festival in November, and Lismore, which has a tibouchina festival in March, when the trees are at their most glorious.

The most common suburban brighteners – two species of coral trees and flame trees that have vivid lipstick-red blossom – are natives, as are the macadamia tree, producing what were called bush nuts in Queensland, the melaleucas with their whitish pink or purple flowers, and bottlebrush whose name describes its red flower perfectly. And there are lots of others too – all threatened by the diabolical effects of the determined invaders (rubber vine, prickly acacia, mesquite, prickly pear, para grass, mimosa pigra, boneseed, gorse plus lantana and blackberry), some of which were brought in for pastoral reasons, and got out of hand. Another, a plant called Scotch broom, is displacing the natural plants in the World Heritage listed Barrington Tops National Park in the Upper Hunter Valley, New South Wales – 85% of this rainforest, near one of Australia's most productive wine areas, is declared wilderness.

One of the reasons it all went wrong was thoughtless dumping of garden waste. The pink and white gladiolus – Dame Edna's favourite flower, according to Barry Humphries – also called watsonia, grow wild everywhere, well established by roadsides in southern Australia. Until we knew better we'd thought how pretty they looked – but they are among the many plants introduced as ornamentals that are regarded as noxious weeds.

Just as the leaves of oleander, an introduced shrub, are toxic to humans and many grazing animals, at least 23 common weeds are decidedly unhealthy, causing serious respiratory problems and rashes, especially in young children. Rye grass, parthenium, ragweed, plantains and privet have been linked to a high increase in asthma in the young Down Under. This respiratory condition is a major problem in older people, too: along with emphysema and bronchitis, it is the fourth most common cause of death, after cancer, heart disease and stroke.

When the whites arrived in Australia they brought with them illnesses that decimated the Aborigines. Measles, typhoid and sexual diseases took a dreadful toll. What a sad irony that they themselves fell foul of the plants they brought in to soften the harshness of the landscape. It seems that gardening, like cigarettes, should carry a warning about being dangerous to health Down Under.

17

NOT JUST THE CLIMATE IS COMPLEX

YOU HAVE TO TAKE A VIEW

BECAUSE AUSTRALIA IS SO big and so varied it is very, very difficult to provide a complete picture of the continent. Even the word 'scenic' takes on new meaning when you find, as we did, a sign at the Nullarbor Roadhouse offering 'scenic flights'. Empty fuel cans, painted white over the rust, edged the landing strip; the scrubby and very flat surrounds were barely green; and discarded machinery suggested that a venture had failed here, and not in even the recent past. At one of the more elevated spots, after Madura Pass (which is like an oasis), from the lookout you get a panoramic view of absolute nothingness – which in itself is impressive. 'Scenic' is not always pretty as we were to find elsewhere.

Because the Nullarbor is what it is, an extraordinary treeless plain, people want to go there. It might not have charm in any usual sense, but I'm glad it is on Highway 1 and was part of our roundOz trip. We weren't in a hurry and took four days (with three one-night stops) to drive from Norseman in Western Australia to Ceduna in South Australia – where we collected a certificate from the Tourist Office to show we had completed the crossing.

We were well stocked with water, food and cash (there are no banks on this part of the Eyre Highway), and found the 1,256-km journey different from anywhere else we had been. With many road signs warning of the chance of meeting emus, kangaroos, camels and wombats, we were all eyes!

The land is scrubby, and granite rocks dotted here and there looked remarkably like the shorn sheep we'd seen in the paddocks around Esperance. Emus were particularly abundant – indeed, one veering out in front of the Hiace when I was driving was our only encounter with an on-road animal that might have ended in the all-too-common roadkill. It flapped its feathers and fled away on its long legs as my heart fluttered, but all was well on this occasion. We encountered something dead on the road every 30 km or so, mostly roos.

Along this route is Balladonia, which in 1979 found its own fame, thanks to a part of the American Skylab crashing there from space. Where it actually landed, on the roof of the roadhouse, is now a museum. It is such an odd sight you need no other reason to stop and refresh. From here to Caiguna – where we stopped – is the longest 'straight' in the country, 146.6km (or 90miles) without a curve, which excites those who might harbour a dream of being a racing car driver.

A little way along is Cocklebiddy, northwest of which is one of the world's largest cave systems. The Cocklebiddy cave is a major attraction for speliologists, who tend to be intrepid explorers – a French group went to an historic depth of 6.4km, in 1983, a record broken in 1995 by an Australian going 20 metres further.

It is hard to imagine when you are on this treeless plain that below your feet are vast limestone caverns, rockfalls and subterranean lakes that extend for several hundreds of metres, many ks away from the sound of the sea.

SOUTH OF COCKLEBIDDY IS THE EYRE BIRD Observatory, on the Great Australian Bight, which we really wanted to visit but had to resist – 32km there and back on the gravelly clay road would have been excruciating for the Hiace and passengers.

The state of the roads can defeat curiosity in some rural parts of the states. In Western Australia, because the road surface was unsealed, we never made it to Mount Augustus, well inland from Carnarvon (north of Monkey Mia). It is a monadnock, or residual hill, claimed to be both bigger and older than Uluru which is, geologically, a monolith – meaning one stone.

To the north and west is the Pilbara, one of the oldest geological areas in the world which also has huge deposits of iron ore and natural gas. The only way we could see it all was to take a flight over the Hamersley Ranges to learn about the local towns.

Tom Price is named after an American who started the mining industry here; it is west of Karijini National Park, and can be reached by sealed road. Wittenoom, on the other hand, can't. Named after the first Colonial Chaplain, an Englishman, it is, in effect, a ghost town, having been 'closed' since 1966 when the government bought the area and shut the infamous mines that produced asbestos. *Daily Mail online* reported in 2020 that the town just has one resident who refused to leave. A deeply poignant photo shows miners taking part in an asbestos shovelling competition in 1962; all but one man died from exposure to the deadly mineral.

It was said you had one of the best paid jobs in Australia if you were an asbestos miner. From the 1930s to the 1960s men worked three eight-hour shifts every day to bring out this fibrous mineral that found application in many different spheres. The miners wore paper masks but, as these restricted their oxygen intake, they pushed them to the top of their heads, a fatal decision, as many of those men were to die of mesothelioma, a lung disease that is even more lethal than asbestosis. The town is no longer on maps.

The NSW Housing Commission house I grew up in had walls of fibro, a construction material made of asbestos – even today I wonder whether this affected my father, a life-long asthmatic. After the war there was a desperate need for new housing all over the country and the large grey sheets were, in fact, a breakthrough in building, providing inner walls as well as quickly erected, weatherproof cladding that could be painted. Nobody thought it was dangerous in the late 1940s when my father applied for and 'won' the house in the Housing Commission draw. Now it is treated with extreme care, and there are strict laws about removing and disposing of it.

Danger lies in its milling or cutting for this produces dust and tiny fibres that can be inhaled. They lodge in spongy tissue, hardening it over time, so that the lungs lose their ability to expand and contract, making breathing more and more difficult. And it wasn't just the miners who were affected – the wives who washed their husbands' working clothes were also exposed to the fibres and faced the same diseases.

Claims for compensation for asbestos-related illnesses, not just in Australia, have been costly, but what's been paid out is little compared to the fortunes earned by the mine owners and construction companies which used this material. As mesothelioma can take many years to develop, claims may be expected for years to come. New South Wales Governor David Martin died in office in 1990 of mesothelioma, which appeared 45 years after his time as a seaman in World War 11 when he came in contact with asbestos lining pipes aboard ship.

IN MANY PARTS OF AUSTRALIA PLACES WHICH DON'T appear to have obvious attractions for tourists face an ongoing struggle to stay alive. But no one gives up without a fight out west. If you want a vibrant community you need ideas for drawing in visitors and a good business plan. An example is Jerramungup, in the Southern Wonders Region of Western Australia, on the edge of a vast pastoral region created by soldier settlement after World War II.

Here townies and farmers got together to raise $A1.3 million to build a centre which is their pride and joy. Of course you don't go to Jerramungup by accident and although it is on Highway 1 to get to this part of the state you have to have been coming from somewhere, usually a great distance.

Perth, the state capital, is 440 km to the northwest. To the northeast is Kalgoorlie, famous for its rich pickings in the 19th century, and still producing gold today, and to the east beyond Esperance lies the Nullarbor. Way to the southwest is Albany, the state's first settlement and now a sizeable town with a population of about 40,000. It was from here that convoys of the Australian Imperial Force set off to play their heroic part in World War I. Wearing their distinctive slouch hats, the Diggers, as they were known, became part of history at Gallipoli in 1915 where, between April 25 and December 20, more than 7,800 of them died.

Anzac Day – April 25 – is always marked by a holiday, to honour those who fought and gave their lives on that distant shore, as well as all those who served in other wars. I remember well those dawn ceremonies I attended as a child in Nowra, wearing a white dress and old-style matron's headwear – the uniform of the Junior Red Cross. I couldn't have fully understood what it was all about, but I remember my tears falling when everyone repeated the line "At the going down of the sun, and in the morning, we will remember them".

People come to Jerramungup because it is the western gateway to the Fitzgerald River National Park which, in ecological terms, is a treasure-house, and is a hugely popular holiday destination. And if the visitors are staying awhile they, like the residents, can use the entertainment and sporting complex. It is impressive, more so when you consider the population of the shire as a whole is only about 1,500. But we are in sports-mad Australia where young and old play outdoor activities like golf, tennis, bowls, hockey and cricket. Jerramungup has its own Aussie Rules team, too. The complex can cater for all this, plus concerts, plays, and conventions.

The town's name is Aboriginal, meaning 'place of the tall yate (eucalyptus or gum) trees which grow through the mist' but the town itself was only formally declared in 1957. By 1958 a quarter of a million acres had been cleared of trees and 141 farms established between Jerramungup and Ravensthorpe to the east. Fields were ploughed and seeds were scattered to bring an abundance of cereal crops, with the help of trace elements. Cattle and sheep flourished.

But times are not always good. Farmers have had to contend with years of ongoing drought and locust plagues (we drove through one on the Nullarbor). There is a crisis from rising salinity, the result of decades of ill-considered clearing, burning, ploughing techniques and grazing. It is noticeable how few trees, yates or others, there are. The area has been struck by some of the most erosive winds known in world agriculture and there seem to be no clear solutions to land degradation, though the recent growing of lucerne as a cereal crop is improving soil structure and stabilizing the water table.

People here are used to the Big Dry, as longlasting drought is known (the annual rainfall, if it comes, is about 10cm), and adverse conditions are not exceptional. Farmstays can help make ends meet and for travellers like us it was great to stop and talk to people who lived in a way that contrasted with our own. Near Ravensthorpe we had a b&b stop with Barb and Harold Cronin at Chambejo, in the house they built themselves.

He was born in New South Wales but in the 1960s, at the age of 18, he grasped the chance of cheap land – two shillings and sixpence an acre in the old calculation – and went west. Son Christopher had an adjoining property, and the two were farmed as one. Barb, a porcelain painter, regularly won 'best of the show' at Perth – that year her winning piece was a tall, raspberry-pink lustre vase decorated with grey dancing brolgas. It was exquisite.

Barb draws her inspiration from her surroundings, the many-splendoured birds and the rich collection of wildflowers. In spring (September to November) much of the state is transformed by these blooming wonders – we saw many, from Kalbarri all the way round to Jerramungup, but we were told it was a disappointing year. The six china dinner plates she made for me show some of these western glories. I treasure them.

WE WENT INTO THE NEARBY FITZGERALD RIVER National Park, land which early explorers described as "worthless". On this 330,000 hectares of wilderness more than 1,800 species of wildflowers are in bloom all year, though spring is the best time to see them. They are not blaze-of-glory flowers, but gently attractive.

In the park you need to tread carefully on the verges and look closely among crevices, gravel pits and dunes. The area's symbol is the Qualup Bell (*pimelia physodes*) whose pink and cream flowers nestle amid the rocks in the pessimistically named Barren range that follows the coastline and seems to rise straight from the sea. Here in arid conditions are plants that are found nowhere else in the world, among them 70 types of naked orchids.

Much of the central park is accessible only on foot, and walking can be rewarding if you come across bush wallabies, kangaroos, ring-tail possums and emus, as well as dozens of different reptiles. If you're really fortunate, you might glimpse two small and very rare marsupials: the tiny insect-eating dibbler, and the little tammar wallaby. Both have had a tough time surviving foxes, feral cats and fires.

Oddly, in an area is known for its peace and quiet, it is home to 200 or so bird species, according to West Australian ornithologists. Twitchers just love it. Early settlers reckoned Australian birds were songless – and many are by UK standards. But it is not just sound that a bird-watcher seeks. Here, in what's called mallee country (mallee is a Victorian Aboriginal word meaning scrubby land covered in dwarf eucalypts) you may come across the rare and unusual birds that scrape up twigs to form a mound which is an incubator for their eggs.

The malleefowl is one of only 14 mound-building birds in the world and one of three species in Australia. We saw the orange-footed one on Dunk Island, off the Queensland coast, but missed the malleefowl of Western Australia.

The park has a superb stretch of coastline, from Bremer Bay to Hopetoun, with several vantage points to view migrating whales – the Southern Right and occasional humpbacks – with their calves from June to October. Beyond here, across the Southern Ocean, is Antarctica to which this coast was once joined when it was part of the vast continent of Gondwana. But that really was a very long time ago, before the moving tectonic plates pulled them apart.

ANOTHER FARMING COMMUNITY TOOK A DIFFERENT PATH when faced with saving their town. Sheffield in Tasmania, about 3km from the ferry port of Devonport, saw some prosperity while the nearby vast hydro-electric scheme was under construction, but when it was completed the workers moved away. The town became rundown and the future looked bleak. Then came the brainwave: let's do what the Canadian town of Chermainus did and create an outdoor pictorial history book in full colour. So, instead of the sterling silver, on which the Yorkshire town after which it is named became known, this Sheffield found fame from the huge murals that adorn every possible wall, depicting different facets of the community's growth from the early days of settlement.

The work began in 1985, and between then and 1997 artist Peter Lendis completed 24 dramatic, larger-than-life scenes of times past, in a picture-book style. The first, called Stillness and Warmth, is a tribute to Gustav Weindorfer who was responsible for nearby Lake St Clair/Cradle Mountain being declared a national park. The scene – about 8 metres by 3 metres – shows him in his wooden hut, described by this entry in his diary:

"When the ground is all covered in snow, I build a big fire, open my door, seat myself very very quietly in front of the blazing logs and presently they come in one by one, the wild animals without their usual fear of man or one another and share... the warmth."

It was outside his very hut that we encountered a wombat, so the animals are still there. Over the years much has changed, however.

After facing a copyright problem – the townspeople might own the walls, but the art on it belongs to the artist – SMART (Sheffield Mural Arts and Rural Tourism) went for even more artistic works. There are now over 50, all painted by professional artists, and every year there's a Mural Fest, a 10-day event with artists demonstrating their illustrating skills. The three works voted best are displayed for a year in the new town square created as part of SMART's aim to make Sheffield one of the world's top five mural towns.

A British visitor might find local geography confusing: here, Sheffield is in the Kentish District. Equally unusual is a piece of town art, showing town and district, which could be a good indicator of how Tasmanians see their world. Bass Strait is shown south of the land, but the direction finder points to the north, to where those in the mainland would put south. Perhaps in this particular part of the island they think the rest of the planet is the wrong way up.

Northwestern Tasmania is an ecological wonderland. Where the forest meets the sea, the water runs brown with tannin from the superb Sassafras trees, and constant washing over the boulders on the shore has made them both rounded and tanned like leather. They glisten in the sunshine on beaches that are completely deserted, the sand strewn with bleached timber, natural detritus from the forest. The fallen branches and trunks are taken out to sea with the tide then brought back again. It happens regularly, twice a day. When you stand on that beach with its talc-soft white sand, it looks as though it has been going on forever. Not many people actually come to this part of the world, which is probably why it is so captivating.

At the top west point of the dauntingly named Cape Grim (it was where a massacre of Aborigines took place in 1828) a notice explains that right here, high up on the cliffs and looking over the Southern Ocean, is the most unpolluted part of the world. It is a boast that's backed by evidence, as the air is tested every week.

Not far away, at Jim's Plain Rain Farm, they bottle the "purest water from the purest place in the world" and sell it to America for $4 a litre. In the United States, which has the highest obesity rates in the world, they will spend a fortune if they think they are paying for good health.

Cape Grim is on one edge of a private property called Woolnorth whose vast acreage, 22,200 hectares, was given to the Van Diemen's Land Company by Royal Charter from King George IV in 1825. Woolnorth's major shareholder for many years was New Zealand's largest dairy farming company, Tasman Agriculture Limited, a thriving enterprise combining dairy and sheep farming with tourism.

Visitors can take day trips to now renamed Woolnorth/Temdudheker (where there are two impressive wind farms) during which they will learn about its history and setting. Or you can stay overnight and be pampered as well. The old homestead, called Top House, reminded us of an English country house hotel with rooms of chintzy furnishings and panelled surrounds. But there the likeness ends. The house is a bungalow, the rooms are enormous and from the big picture windows you look out through rows of tall purple agapanthus to the rolling grasslands.

In another direction lie 500 hectares which are in the process of reafforestation. There are three huge sand blows on the property, a sign of an encroaching desert, and no one seems able to stop them. Eight years after 1,000 trees had been planted on one blow, there was no sign of them.

The last four Tasmanian tigers were captured at Woolnorth and sent to the Domain Zoo in Hobart. Their photographs were displayed in the dining room at Top House along with striking life-size carvings of a tigress and cub in Tasmanian pine. Ian's head almost fitted inside the mother's mouth!

The tigers are thought to have been extinct since the 1930s, but some Tasmanians like to believe that the animals sought refuge in the dense forests to the south. This is national park land – some of which, it was said, has not been explored even by the ever-active forestry department. The major flaw in this theory is the fact that the tigers – so named because of stripes on the back – were creatures of the grasslands.

Spare paddocks on Woolnorth have been hired out for the production of one of the most lucrative world crops: opium poppies. Glaxo Wellcome Australia take a three year lease on the land (not just here but also in other parts of Tasmania), surrounding it with electric fencing, and keep it under strict security. Prominent warning signs are ignored at your peril. After the harvest nothing is grown on the land for two years and all traces of the crop are removed.

The world demand for morphine is high (40% is produced in Tasmania), and there might have been poppies for peaceful purposes if the pharmaceutical companies had got together and done something about Afghanistan at the end of the disastrous war there (though the amount of security needed might have been on the same scale as an invasionary force).

On a part of Woolnorth is a white-sand beach, looking out over Bass Strait, on which lies the wreck of the *Colliloi*, beached there in 1932 after springing a leak off nearby Hunter Island. Many of Tasmania's native animals make their home in the area: bandicoot, wallaby, wombat, echidna, sugar gliders, quolls and Tasmanian devils. Most of them are nocturnal.

The property has 23 farms and 30,000 cows. Each dairy has a robotic milking system by which 80 cows are milked twice a day. On one dairy there are 1,700 cows, which means about 650 are robotically hooked on and off per hour – there's a steady stream of big milk tankers taking it away for export. The shearing shed is enormous, with 13 stands for shearers brought in on contract to remove the fleece, an activity that takes place in January and March. At shearing time the place bustles, we were told.

[Not all goes well at Woolnorth Temdudheker. When the Chinese company Moon Lake took over in 2016, after approval by the Turnbull government, it promised to add jobs, invest $A100m and allow the construction of a fence to help prevent the spread of deadly face tumours among Tasmanian devils.

Not all of this happened. At the time of writing, a damning report in the *Sydney Morning Herald* exposed problems, predominantly about animal welfare and over-stocking of cattle causing effluent systems to fail and damaging nearby waterways.]

THIS AREA OF TASMANIA IS VERY REMOTE, BUT I HAD NOT expected to find it so silent. Up to this point, wherever we were we'd been aware of the birds and their exciting range of sound, from the 'laughing jackass', better known as a kookaburra, to the startling squawk of the cockatoos in the bush. In downtown Sydney at dusk, the noise the mynahs (imported long ago from India) and starlings make in the tree-lined streets leading to Circular Quay can drown any chat.

The bird book on which we relied (the Graham Pizzey and Frank Knight *Field Guide to the Birds of Australia*, Angus & Robertson) includes 778 species, making Australia the most bird-rich country in the world. It is a naturalist's dream and we were proud of the number we managed to find, recording each sighting and where it occurred on the relevant page in the book. Despite going right round Oz as we did, many pages were unmarked (and that has to be a very good reason to do it all over again!).

Though we heard the occasional owl and, on one memorable occasion at a campsite at Derby, Western Australia, the delightful song of a willy wagtail in search of his lady, nights were generally quiet. With one exception. What I did not expect was the sound of night-time coughing, wracking harsh noises, indicating lungs struggling to expand and contract.

Often it was the only noise we would hear in a camp after dark, and how odd it seemed in the wide open spaces in air unpolluted by any manufacturing. But it was a sound I knew well: my brother-in-law Les, a life-long smoker, spent his last years suffering the miseries of emphysema, his every breath relying desperately on the oxygen he was hooked up to. He was, he used to say sardonically, waiting in the tow-away area.

Most of the way up the east coast we travelled in parallel with a man who was driving a John Deere tractor around Australia to raise funds for a cancer charity. "Barnestorming for kids with cancer" said the sign on one of the caravans which his entourage set up at a campsite – and, naturally, people went over to talk to him. It was a good way of gathering donations. We must have taken different routes inland because we didn't see the group again until Darwin when they set up just near us at the Shady Glen campsite. Only there, when I saw him sitting on the tractor, did I realise that this man was a smoker which seemed ironic in terms of the challenge he had taken on in the fight against cancer.

Of course if you are a smoker, taking your home with you gives the freedom to puff away without restriction wherever you go. On the open road you won't come across rules that prevent you lighting up – as you might in hotel rooms, for instance, which is a nightmare for smokers on holiday. The travelling smokers sit outside their caravan or campervan and fill the open air with the nicotine fumes that haven't stayed within them. Fortunately, Australia is a big place, and the fumes dissipate into the big skies, hopefully damaging nothing else.

Some people might not notice any of this, but other

ex-smokers – like me – are universally attuned to coughs and the smell of nicotine. It is also a sad fact that I took my first puff in a hospital, in the first weeks of training to be a nurse. Then, in the 1950s, when our lives were ruled by British and American *fillums*, smoking was regarded as very sexy, very glamorous. The cigarette packets were made enticingly feminine, and we fell for it. On the verge of 18, with three years to go before accepted adult age and with our lives ahead of us, we made the fatal decision to smoke.

What fun it was, all of us together in the Preliminary Training School at Royal Prince Alfred Hospital in the Sydney suburb of Camperdown. For three months we lived in long dormitory-style huts – we'd come back from our day's lectures and, still in our blue uniforms, sat around on the beds and smoked.

There were over 60 of us in the intake, young women from all over the state, plus two from Brisbane and one from Hobart, much of a muchness in age but not in experience. I was not only naive but, as the daughter of a former smoker who struggled to live with chronic asthma for most of his life, I was stupid.

Someone handed me a lit Peter Stuyvesant – a firm that resoundingly collapsed many many years later, which seems only right and proper now – and I put it to my lips. I'd seen enough movies to know you inhaled and having done so found myself sitting on the floor. It was like a momentary blackout, a loss of oxygen caused by the inhalation of the cigarette smoke.

The other girls thought it very amusing. I didn't like being laughed at. I took another puff and a smoker was born. The temporary collapse should have been a warning, but wasn't, as I went on smoking. It never occurred again and I moved on to many different smokes: tailor-mades, roll your own, even a small pipe and cigars before stopping for good in 1989.

But smoking was the fashion, and it was synonymous with sophistication (a word which in those days implied superior style but then, as now, meant false). The ones I liked best were in a smart red flip-lid box, with a European name De Rezske. They made me feel part of the bigger world. We certainly tested the market – there were no warning notices around then, or known information about the harm tobacco could do. Black Sobrani were the essence of elegance. The cigarettes were black and came in a flat black box lined with fine tissue paper. A sister box had nicotine sticks coated in a palette of pretty pastels. Both types had gold tips, so having a smoke did not feel like an addiction.

We weren't allowed to smoke while on duty, so it was a treat to look forward to when our shift was over. Each time I lit up it felt like an occasion, but it really was the start of cloud cuckoo land. When our training was completed and we went into the wards as First Year Nurses, we were earning £2 a week.

From this we bought our own shoes, stockings and suspender belts – tights were a mid-1960s invention – but were given our uniforms and meals, and each of us had a room in the newly-built nurses' home, called, as you might expect in those pre-Pill days, the Virgins' Retreat. How did we manage on so little?

I couldn't afford to take the train from Sydney to Nowra – actually Bomaderry, as this is the railhead – so, about once a month, my father would send the price of a ticket. It was a dirty, dusty journey on the old steam train (being blackened with soot was something you accepted) but it meant I could enjoy some cossetting on my days off.

Big, freshly-caught-and-cooked prawns, and oysters in their shell, bought at the fishermen's jetty on the Shoal-haven River, was a treat that I have not lost the taste for since. Learning to shuck an oyster was probably my first culinary skill – even in England I keep a blade in the kitchen drawer on the JustinCase principle, though it's hardly had any use. Mum would cook me fillet steak and egg for breakfast, another indulgence – no one talked about cholesterol then. That also started in the 1960s.

Australia is a land of plenty, "God's own country" as journalist Donald Horne called it in his book *The Lucky Country* written in the mid 1960s (updated several times since). But Australia has always had its share of social ills on the scale of other western countries. An Australian study in 2003 found that among under 16s, the average age of anorexia sufferers had dropped in 18 months from 14 to 12 and the condition had affected girls as young as nine and, in one case, a child of four. One in three cases researched was a boy.

A paediatrician was quoted as saying that children were developing anorexia – which affects one in 250 teenage girls worldwide – as a response to an uncertain social environment. Among migrants the increase had been dramatic. It is now well over 60 years since I was a nurse, but one of the cases that I clearly remember in-volved a just pre-teen girl, the daughter of Greek parents, being given shock treatment for anorexia. It wasn't a common condition then, and certainly not one anybody talked about. The child was admitted to the private wing of the hospital, under the care of a psychiatrist, because she was convinced any food she swallowed was eating her insides. She weighed 5 stone (today's conversion is 31.8 kg).

Naturally it was bewildering for her parents, but for nurses like me – I had come from a relatively sheltered upbringing and wasn't all that much older than this girl – this example of obsessive behaviour was overwhelming. And the treatment itself was extremely disturbing. It was believed that the use of electro convulsive therapy (ECT) would cause a break in the thought patterns; in this young girl's case she would 'forget' her obsessive idea about food. After a number of treatments she would eat normally and would be allowed to go home when she had put on 2 stone (14 kg).

The child who left was much more cheerful than the one who arrived at the hospital, and her physical improvement was amazing, but the prognosis was not good – which I found most disheartening and probably why it is so etched in my memory. The psychiatrist said he was sure she'd be back in four years or so, that the treatment could never be a cure. He had the outside hope that in those years she might recover from the condition by herself, would become more confident and involved with friends and school, and the fixation would not dominate her life.

Fortunately modern research has produced greater understanding of anorexia and other eating disorders, combining cognitive, biological, emotional and somatic processes, involving clinicians and neuroscientists. But it remains a worldwide problem.

Though after two years I left nursing to be married (at that time, only single women could be trainees) and went into journalism, a nurse I met at the Big 4 campsite at Port Augusta made me realise how significant the role can be. It was a balmy evening and we were both drawn out into it, me from the Hiace and she from her caravan, by the close and urgent sounds of sirens and helicopters.

She was sipping a cup of coffee and I asked her if she knew what was happening.

– It's probably a crash on the highway.

– But which highway?

It might seem an odd question but Port Augusta is at the centre of many: the Lincoln Highway heads south to the Eyre Peninsula, the Eyre Highway goes west to Western Australia (where we'd come from) and, as Highway 1, continues south to Adelaide, and the Stuart takes you north through Woomera and Coober Pedy to the Northern Territory.

The nurse, Sue, was familiar with them all and she said all were equally likely to have accidents on them at night, usually because of vehicles hitting ever-problematical wildlife. They are a well known and ever-present hazard on most roads after dark. There's little drivers can do to avoid them.

Sue told me she lived south of Adelaide but was employed by the Royal Flying Doctor Service (RFDS) as a flight nurse. She worked 12-hour shifts over 10 days during which time she lived in the caravan, then went home for a well-earned break.

– I've just finished a shift but I am still on call. I hope I won't be needed.

The crisis on the highway didn't require her presence so, in the pleasantly warm evening air, we were able to talk about her job, a part of which was running maternity clinics for the Aborigines in the outback. These, she felt, were well intended but not always successful.

– We might get those women who are having their first baby but we rarely see them through the whole pregnancy. If we do blood tests for sexually transmitted infections or diabetes they might not even come back for the results. We can give them information about staying healthy and looking after themselves, but they are more likely to listen to their own people and follow their traditional ways. It's very frustrating, but we feel it is important that we try.

The flight nurses and pilots do the travelling from 20 different locations, to 7,500 clinics in isolated communities where there isn't a resident doctor to carry out health checks, and to attend to emergencies. The doctors stay on the ground in telephone or radio contact day and night to answer questions and advise, and take to the air when necessary.

Every day pilots and flight nurses on shift can contend with heat, flies, turbulence, low mist and cloud over an area that covers 7.15 million sq km; in a year the planes fly over 11 million km. To land, a plane needs a length of 1,000 metres and a width of 60 metres and a surface on which a car can be driven comfortably at 60kph. What a job.

For anyone who lives, works or travels in Australia's outback the RFDS is an incredible back up. We were fortunate in not ever having to call on it, but also we never really went off the beaten track. We did put the Hiace to the test to see 80-mile Beach, in northern Western Australia, which was reached by a 2-km stretch of unmade road on which were a couple of cattle grids to add extra piquancy. Some humorist had altered one of the GRID warning signs to GRIN, which helped us see the funny side of driving at 15 kph while 4WD vehicles zoomed by, raising the inevitable red dust which engulfed us.

80-mile Beach has a most attractive palm-fringed campsite and the beach is renowned for both its fishing and its sunsets. (If you're going there, JustinCase no one mentions it, do put on lots of anti-bug stuff. The sandflies were among the most vicious we came across.)

MOST PEOPLE WHO TAKE TO THE ROAD AS WE DID ARE usually more interested in quiet than noise. And when you come across it, particularly in a place that's miles from anywhere, it can be a shock. Certain traditions hold good in the country in all the states: the bachelors' and spinsters' balls are renowned for their all-night-long rowdiness, as are the pre-wedding 'bucks' parties' organised by the best men for the grooms. And it has become younger with the schoolies' parties, 'schoolies' being the Oz-contracted word describing school leavers. In November, the end of the school year, those who've completed their secondary education celebrate – and on the east and west coasts they can be a riot.

Considered a rite of passage in Australia since the 1980s, the celebrations on the Gold Coast, south of Brisbane, are notorious. This has become 'the place' where thousands – 50,000 was one figure I read – of 17 and 18 year olds gather to have fun, dancing on the beach to live bands and drinking in clubs and pubs until the early hours. After several years of bad publicity because of sexual offences (including rapes), assaults, thefts and public disorder offences, the police presence is now most apparent. This is the state where an under 18-year-old caught drinking in a public place will receive a hefty fine. (When I lived in Queensland in the 1960s, the drinking age was 21 – I always carried proof of age to produce on demand.)

'Schoolies' are also just as likely to book up cabins in campsites on the coast, especially at free-and-easy places like Byron Bay in New South Wales. All you can do is hope you're not anywhere near them and that the site security won't let them party all night. You'll be reassured to know that Australian campsites, especially the very large ones, take security seriously and are well alert to the sound of empty bottles being tossed cavalierly into the garbage tin. I found that earplugs help, too.

18

A LAND TO CHERISH AND PROTECT

WHAT I LEARNT ON MY JOURNEY

ON THE MORNING we arrived in Australia, at the start of our gap year, I heard the welcoming sound of the kookaburra and I realised I had heard that call in my head all the time I've lived away and can conjure it up at any time. (The sound I made certainly amused my children as babies!) At first light in the east, this marvellous bird's laughter is quite languid and restrained, and the pace increases as the sun gradually rises until the *oo-oo-aa-waa-oo-oo-aa-waa* sounds run more closely together and become louder.

This gorgeous cackle, plus seven months travelling around the country, has helped me understand how passionately I feel about the land where I was born – even though I discovered most of it for the first time many years after I had left it. It wasn't the cities that made my heart beat faster, but the vast wide-open spaces, the extraordinary topography, the mountains, rivers and forests, birds and other animals that are like nowhere else in the world.

During the trip I heard two stories about the emu and kangaroo on the country's coat of arms. One was that they show what an unusual country Australia is, to proudly display a bird that can't fly and an animal that can't run. The second was that as neither animal is able to walk backwards they are representative of a forward-thinking country, a fine idea for the new Commonwealth way back in 1901. Both hold true, but what's important today is that everyone keeps looking far enough ahead – without losing sight of what needs to be done now to ensure a vital future.

Having seen so many of its treasures for myself (and missed far too many, I suspect), I hope all those people in, or even out of, power give thoughtful consideration to what Australia would be like without them. Neither politicians nor voters can afford to be blasé and getting the priorities right should be a shared endeavour, not motivated by greed but by the realisation of how impossible it would be to replace so much that is unique. They mustn't, whatever their views, allow the marketing catchcry 'when it's gone, it's gone' to be part of the country's philosophy.

I think of our trip as the year of summers. The weather might have been up to putty on occasion, but I basked in the good humour and jokey approach found everywhere, enjoyed the smiles and cheerful greetings of those who served in shops, supermarkets and restaurants and was delighted that, after living away for so long in cooler northern climes, I could stand the heat (mostly) after all. And there's no doubt much has changed since I lived there. Australia has lost its insularity and is on a roll. The talents of its people – writers, artists, musicians, cooks – are recognised all over the world.

It was good having a lot of time available, without any need to hurry, as this allowed the stunningly wonderful land to reveal itself, to wake in me a sense of responsibility for it. Did I, as Germaine Greer wants all Australians to do, discover my Aboriginality? In 2004, she wrote in *The Guardian*: "Aboriginality is not a matter of blood or genes; Aborigines themselves have to learn Aboriginality. They have to master knowledge of their own country, and of their relationships with neighbouring peoples, and the languages appropriate to trade, negotiation and celebration."

Maybe that's what happened to me. Travelling through every state certainly helped me get a perspective of the continent that I would never have found in any other way, and raised my sensitivities to the dangers of complacency, of letting the devil take tomorrow.

I hope that everyone, no matter where you travel in this large country, will keep your ears and eyes open, to experience this joyous feeling. If you follow in our footsteps, tread carefully and take your time so you too will come to appreciate what makes the island of Australia so different from the other continents, why it is so rare and why it has much to cherish and protect.

As I was finishing this book, there was news of a mouse plague in Australia affecting a lot of the eastern side of the country. Caused by optimal weather conditions for breeding after the two-year drought of 2017-19, it is a problem that may take time to resolve. But there was good news too.

I read in *The Guardian* about a mouse, believed to have been extinct for 150 years, found alive and well. Researching the decline of native species since the arrival of Europeans in 1788, scientists compared DNA of eight native rodents and 42 of their living relatives. To their delight, the 'extinct' Gould's mouse was indistinguishable from the Shark Bay mouse living on several small islands off the coast of Western Australia. This large state just added another treasure to its trove.

Then, to my horror, I came across a website that stopped me in my tracks. On BushHeritage.Actionit.com.au it states there are 463 animals and 1336 plants on the threatened species list. The numbers are alarming and horrifying. The group gives native animals and plants a chance to survive and flourish, by buying and managing 11.3million hectares of ecologically important land. They partner with Aboriginal groups and other landowners to help them do the same. It is a very critical time in Australia's history. I will be supporting their endeavours.

ACKNOWLEDGMENTS

I went to a wide range of sources to check my information in the book and where necessary these are referred to in the Subject Index which lists each chapter. I have made every effort to ensure that there are no errors but after a long career in journalism I have had to accept that they can and do happen, and I apologise in advance if any occur.

Australia is not backward in coming forward about itself. The States, cities and towns in Australia all promote themselves very well which is very helpful to travellers. Museum websites also offered facts and figures about areas that we might, or might not, have been to.

The map at the front of the book shows the rough positioning of many of the places mentioned and the route of Highway 1 which you have to go off to find the island's many wonders. We covered a lot of miles and a large area on our seven-month trip through the states in our campervan but we realised we could probably do that several times and not see all its attractions.

My husband Ian not only travelled with me but gave tremendous support during the writing of the book and I'm grateful to friend and talented designer Alan Reinl for his valued work on the production. In deciding to self publish DISCOVERING OZ, I doubt it could have been achieved without Vellum, the thoughtful word processing method that goes hand in hand with Amazon KDP, and the helpdesk that gave advice freely during the creative period.

SUBJECT INDEX

A QUICK REFERENCE

garoo Down, Sport—Pat Rafter—googly—Richie Benaud—Don Bradman—Steve Irwin—*I am Australian*—*Advance Australia Fair*—Paul Hogan—*Crocodile Dundee*—Mel Gibson—Aussie expressions—galahs—The Pinnacles WA—Aussie Rules—*They're a Weird Mob*—John O'-Grady/Nino Culotta—'strine'—convict stock—Warren Halloway—*The Fatal Shore*—Aussie English—Wimbledon—Rachel Perkins—indigenous language—Aboriginal lore—Native Title Tribunals—Tasmania—*Citizen Labilladiere*—La Perouse—Robert Menzies—Doc Evatt—pollies and rorts—ANZACS—mateship—sheela na gigs—Sydney Pride—swearing—Kingsford Smith Airport—customs—food supplements—prescribed medicines—Know Before You Go

Chapter 3: COMFORT IS AN ATTITUDE OF MIND
Toyota Hiace—Winnebago—Lucille Ball—*The Long Long Trailer*—Gillies Highway Qld—Wet Tropics World Heritage area—ute plus trailer—caravan/car combination—single deck bus— tinnie—small space living—humidity—high and low temperatures—Townsville Qld—Tropic of Capricorn—Magnetic Island—adding an annexe—test for compatibility—flying insects—Nullabor—*The Great Australia Gazetteer*—Ceduna SA—shade cloth—moisture and mould—Tasmanian summer—Cradle Mountain—rufous wallabies—Landcruiser

Chapter 4: HELPING OTHERS IS AN AUSSIE TRAIT
Sydney Olympics—senior volunteers—Don and Maureen Halloway—Australia Day—Invasion Day—Paralympic Games—child volunteers—Warren and Maureen

tralian Commonwealth—squattocracy—Britain and its empire—*Elders*—Peter McConchie—Aborigines and Torres Strait Islanders—1967 Referendum—Coranderrk

Chapter 6: PROBABILITY OF CHANCE ENCOUNTERS

Top End/Outback—Falconio incident—Joanne Lees—white van—Stuart Highway—Highway 87—Highway 66 via Camooweal Qld—Red Centre—Radio National—wild camping—Highway 1—cattle stations—road trains—drive on the left—seatbelts—Undara National Park Qld—Georgetown—Karumba—Gulf of Carpentaria—Normanton to Cloncurry—brolgas—The Ghan—road signs—radar and road traps—Frank Moorhouse—fuel stops—NRMA—Douglas Daly Resort NT—*Rough Guide to Australia*—WA quarantine regulations—skin cancer—sunscreens—Clive Hamer—Tasmania—ozone layer—Vitamin D—Cradle Mountain-Lake St Clair National Park—wombat—leeches—dingoes—mosquitoes—Bunbury—Ross River Fever—Dengue Fever—anaphylactic shock—antihistamine syringe—Vegemite—ticks and treatment—Lyme Disease—bindi-eyes—spiders—cockroaches—snakes—salties/crocodiles

Chapter 7: KNOW WHERE THE GOING IS GOOD

Landcruiser—Porta-potty—Portaloo—time differences—Nullabor dingo—waterproof slip-ons—fungal infections—ablution blocks—Croydon Qld—Cradle Mountain Tassie—Cooinda NT—en suite sites—Hi-Way Roadhouse NT—Sheffield Tassie—Banbury WA—en suite sites—Knotts Crossing—broadwalks—Bunbury dolphins—Bremer Bay—moth invasion—Jabiru WA—Halls

—national long weekends—tinnies—fishing—Northern Territory—boat safety regulations—sharks—salties/crocodiles—air-sea rescuers—beach volunteers—warning flags—'buddy' system—tsunami—water temperature—safe swimming—distress signals—Surf Lifesaving Association—resuscitation—snorkelling—scuba diving—*Open Water*—Harold Holt—John Stonehouse MP—Thursday Island—psychological trauma—Town of 1770—*Gregory's Road Atlas*—whales—Lady Musgrave Island—Ningaloo Reef—rogue waves—injuries at sea

Chapter 11: START FROM SCRATCH IN THE NORTH

poste restante—resorts for travellers—CBD—city transport—sandflies—mosquitoes—Chinese market—Asian influences—year-round temperature—crocodiles—jellyfish—marine stingers—deadly sea wasps—anaphylactic shock—stone fish—sandflies—mangroves—Scottish midges—British insects—Charles Darwin—John Lort Stokes—Point Torment—Palmerston—Cyclone Tracy—gold discovery—pearl cultivation—disenfranchisement—Greek divers—White Australia Policy—Families Against Race Restrictions—Harold Holt—Point Samson—*Rough Guide to Australia*—Ross River Fever—Dengue Fever—Murray Valley encephalitis—insect-repelling fabrics

Chapter 12: ECOLOGICAL WONDERS OF THE WEST

Dirk Hartog Island—pewter plate—Malgana people—Wirruwana—fishing—school sharks—blowholes—seabirds—Willem de Vlamingh—William Dampier—Nicolas Baudin—*Géographe*—de Freycinet—*Naturaliste*—

Printed in Great Britain
by Amazon

64304091R00181